# Praise for *Watching for Dra*

T0007755

*Watching for Dragonflies* is an inspirational story of personal growth through adversity that will bring comfort and companionship to other caregivers. An intimate and empowering memoir.

—**Rachel Howard**, author of *The Lost Night* and *The Risk of Us*

In *Watching for Dragonflies*, Suzanne Marriott writes about her journey with her husband through the good times and the moments that challenge their relationship after his diagnosis of MS. It's a story of love, letting go, and working together as a couple to live fully with awareness and growth on their spiritual journey of body and soul. This book is an important testament about the ups and downs of being a caregiver, and useful to anyone facing health challenges with someone they love.

—**Linda Joy Myers**, author *The Forger of Marseille*,
*The Power of Memoir*, and *Song of the Plains*

In *Watching for Dragonflies*, Suzanne Marriott generously shares her deeply spiritual journey as a caregiver to her husband who suffers from multiple sclerosis. In the throes of loss, disappointment, and pain, courage and love keep arising to meet each challenge. This is an honest and inspiring story of how true intimacy can help carry us through seemingly unbearable loss.

—**Jim Cunningham**, physical therapist and marriage
and family therapist specializing in trauma resolution

Suzanne Marriott's caring memoir of her love, marriage, joy, grief, and spiritual seeking, and of the distresses and challenges of her long caregiving is stunningly honest and inspiring.

—**Judith Van Herik**, Professor Emerita of Religious Studies, Penn State University

Services for—and recognition of—family caregivers simply must improve. Honest storytelling like that in *Watching for Dragonflies* will start a revolution.

—**Gretchen Staebler**, author of *Mother Lode: Confessions of a Reluctant Caregiver*

Suzanne's intimate story of living through the diagnosis, long decline, and death of a loved partner helps one imagine the unimaginable in such a human way. By sharing her story, she helps us face our own fears, and to see that such challenges can bring even deeper connection.

—**Kathryn McCamant**, author *Cohousing: A Contemporary Approach to Housing Ourselves* and *Creating Cohousing: Building Sustainable Communities.*

Thank you for sharing your memoir with me. It's a moving and compassionate story.

—**Dr. Arthur Hastings**, Professor Emeritus, Institute of Transpersonal Psychology (now Sophia University)

Suzanne Marriott's touching memoir stays with the reader long after its final present-tense paragraph. This is a book that needs to be read by anyone who wishes to know what it's like to go through the stages of a chronic illness. Along with Michael, who has MS, and Suzanne, his wife and caregiver, we experience joy in their successful activities and disappointment in the ineptness of some of their health care providers. We follow the couple through years of health challenges and learn of the events that bond them together and the mishaps that appear to tear them apart. Aided by the author's journals, which include her dreams, we are treated to realistic descriptions of the couple's day-to-day lives as well as Suzanne's premonitions. A very moving true story.

—**Evelyn Kohl LaTorre**, author of *Love in Any Language: A Memoir of a Cross-Cultural Marriage* and *Between Inca Walls: A Peace Corps Memoir*

Thank you for the moving, beautiful experience.

—**Mike Contino**, educator at California State University East Bay and retired executive secretary of the California Mathematics Council

# WATCHING FOR DRAGONFLIES

# WATCHING FOR DRAGONFLIES

## A CAREGIVER'S
## TRANSFORMATIVE JOURNEY

Suzanne Marriott

SHE WRITES PRESS

Copyright © 2023, Suzanne Marriott

All rights reserved. No part of this publication may be reproduced, distrib-
uted, or transmitted in any form or by any means, including photocopying,
recording, digital scanning, or other electronic or mechanical methods,
without the prior written permission of the publisher, except in the case of
brief quotations embodied in critical reviews and certain other noncommer-
cial uses permitted by copyright law. For permission requests, please address
She Writes Press.

Published 2023
Printed in the United States of America
Print ISBN: 978-1-64742-436-7
E-ISBN: 978-1-64742-437-4
Library of Congress Control Number: 2022916449

For information, address:
She Writes Press
1569 Solano Ave #546
Berkeley, CA 94707

Interior Design by Kiran Spees

She Writes Press is a division of SparkPoint Studio, LLC.

All company and/or product names may be trade names, logos, trademarks,
and/or registered trademarks and are the property of their respective owners.

Names and identifying characteristics have been changed to protect the
privacy of certain individuals.

Dragonfly Vector by Vecteezy

*We must let go of the life we have planned,*
*so as to accept the one that is waiting for us.*
— Joseph Campbell

*Start by doing what's necessary; then do what's possible;*
*and suddenly you are doing the impossible.*
— Francis of Assisi

# Introduction

The dragonfly goes through three stages in its journey of life: egg, larva, and adult. In keeping with these changes, the dragonfly appears as a symbol of transformation in the mythology of many cultures. Throughout my journey as caregiver to my husband who suffered from multiple sclerosis, at times I would turn to the Medicine Cards to find clarification and guidance from Native American wisdom. Of the dragonfly, they noted: "If you feel the need for change, call on Dragonfly to guide you through the mists of illusion to the pathway of transformation." As the dragonfly guided my husband on his journey to wholeness, he guides me still on mine. May the dragonfly guide you, too, as you read this memoir and as you struggle to meet the challenges you face on your own transformative journey.

My story is as factual and true to life as I can possibly make it, and the medical information I include in my story is not pertinent to anyone other than my husband. The specifics of my story, medical or otherwise, are time related and not intended to provide advice or guidance. The names of the medical doctors who treated Michael are fictitious; all other names are real, and the terms I use in reference to persons with a disability are those used at the time of my story. I have included specific reference to Michael's youngest daughter, Zoie, and not to his other two daughters as they prefer not to be included in my memoir. I only allude to them when they are intrinsic to my story and not by name.

I have learned that growth is the act of discovering our inclination and power to evolve—to co-create in the spiral of life—and the rays of awareness are imbedded in the darkness of suffering and chaos. They need only to be seen. I hope my tale will strike a chord in the hearts and minds of others who face a personal or family crisis, including caring for a loved one. I struggled in deciding what to divulge and what to hold back—how much of my vulnerability and how many of my mistakes to include. In the end, I've laid it all out, whitewashing nothing and no one, even though I cringed with sorrow and guilt when I wrote, and rewrote, some of the more upsetting episodes of my journey.

I've learned that to be human means to be vulnerable and to make mistakes, and I am nothing if not human. Above all, I wanted to write a story that was real and spoke to our human condition. We all have crises in our lives, and we all have loved ones—whether spouses, friends, or relatives—who will become ill or leave us behind. As others deal with challenges in their lives, I hope they can be kind to themselves and accept and learn from their inevitable mistakes without too much reproach. This task is not easy for me, yet together, perhaps, we can all move toward acceptance—of ourselves and others—and value the love, successes, and fortitude that see us through.

# Chapter 1
# Crisis

He couldn't get into his truck. This is how it started: Michael couldn't climb into the cab of his eighteen-wheeler because his arms and legs wouldn't work.

It doesn't make sense. This is supposed to be the day when the exhaustion finally lifts; after a year of working nights, he's finally back on the day shift. Now he's telling me he said no to an ambulance (*an ambulance?*) and somehow managed to drive home in our Honda to call me instead.

My hands tighten on the phone as I struggle to take in his words. *Has he had a stroke? A heart attack? Did he fall?*

"Call the clinic and try to get an appointment right away with Dr. Roberts." His voice is strained.

Suddenly I have to be with him, not sitting here making phone calls. "I'm on my way home right now," I tell him. There's a pause. Then he tells me to make the call first. He will lie down and see if that helps.

Somehow my fingers punch the buttons on the phone. Someone answers and switches me to the emergency line.

"How may I help you?" The nurse's voice is cheerful.

"Something has happened to my husband—I don't know what. He's a truck driver, and he couldn't get up into his truck."

"Is he conscious?"

"Yes, he called me."

I quickly give her Michael's medical record number.

"You shouldn't have been put through to this line. It's only for life-and-death situations. Please hold."

My hands are starting to sweat, and I feel as if I'm suffocating. Finally, she returns. "His doctor isn't seeing patients today. Michael's symptoms might indicate a stroke. You should take him directly to the emergency room."

I dash out of the building, and when I unlock my car, the alarm goes off—even though I hadn't set it. I reach in, and, desperate to make the shrieking stop, flip the switch back and forth. A coworker comes out to help but has no idea what to do. We look in the trunk. Nothing. I open the hood and see a horn-shaped object on the left. On impulse I pull a red wire, and the ear-piercing noise stops. I think of the proverbial grandfather's clock that "stopped short, never to go again, when the old man died."

At last I'm on the freeway, but the traffic is crawling; every tail-light in front of me glares red. Tense and impatient, I'm right on the bumper of the car ahead. I eye the carpool lane; I check the clock. It's only twenty minutes into the lane-restriction time.

I pull over, relieved to be getting closer and closer to home. Suddenly I see a California Highway Patrol car ahead on the left shoulder. *Shit!* There's one on the right shoulder too. Fighting back tears, I switch lanes. Almost immediately, one of them appears in my rearview mirror, lights flashing, and I pull over.

When the officer reaches the window on the passenger side of my car, I tell him I'm a teacher and my husband is a truck driver and he has just called me at work to tell me he has collapsed on the job. My mind, trying desperately to forge a connection, figures if he knows

I'm a teacher, he will believe me—and, after all, truckers and CHP officers share the same world.

He asks where my husband is now.

"He's at home, and I'm trying to get to him as soon as I can." I gaze up through my tears, silently pleading for help.

Unmoved, the officer asks to see my driver's license and registration and takes them back to his car. Staring into the rearview mirror in disbelief, I watch him write a ticket. For a second, I had fantasized he would be my knight in shining armor—maybe even an escort home.

"I know you're in a hurry to get home," he tells me as he hands me the ticket. "I wrote you a citation," he adds, as if I don't know what he's handing me. I take it and my license and registration without comment. Following his instructions to merge carefully, I get back on the freeway. Now—insult added to injury—I feel abandoned as well as panicked.

I'm still only halfway home, and the gray concrete of Interstate 880 and its looming sound walls make me feel trapped. Then my exit comes up, and the brighter colors of the barrio let me know I'm only fifteen minutes away. I continue on the main surface road through Hayward and finally reach Castro Valley, the middle-class suburb where we live—and where my husband is waiting.

My anxiety builds as I'm stopped by the last traffic light. I know Michael would never have called me at work unless it was a dire emergency; he's the type of man who rarely asks for help, proud that he can get the job done himself—*meet the bell*, he says.

The light finally turns green, and I turn off the crowded street, bouncing the car too fast over the too-deep depression in the road that always tells me I'm almost home. As I pull into the driveway, the house looks just like it always does—no sign that a crisis is unfolding inside.

I don't know whether I'll find Michael passed out on the floor or miraculously recovered, but I fear the worst as I run up the steps from the garage to the living room. Yet there he is, sitting quietly in his chair; I see he has gotten my father's cane to help him balance. I rush to his side and help him up. I'm desperate to know what happened, but I can see from the grim look on his face that he needs to concentrate just to get out of the chair. This is no time for questions. We move awkwardly down the steps to the garage and get into the car. As we race to the hospital, he tells me how hot it was at work, and that as soon as he put one foot and arm up to climb inside the cab, he knew he wasn't going to make it. No matter how hard he tried, he just couldn't do it.

In the emergency room, the admitting nurse asks Michael when he started using a cane.

"Today."

The nurse pauses to look at him before continuing with his questions. When he's finished, we take our places in the waiting room, where Michael manages to keep his spirits up, joking about inane fantasy creatures on the TV. We exchange a complicit smile, glad for some comic relief.

Soon we're ushered into an exam room, and Michael lies down on the table. It's not long enough for his six-foot, five-inch frame, and his feet stick out over the end. A doctor enters and asks more questions, then tests Michael's reflexes. When a neurologist joins us, the seriousness of the situation starts to hit me. *Something must be very wrong if a specialist is brought into the ER.* Suddenly, I want to protect my husband and, moving closer, I take his hand. Michael looks up at me with concern in his eyes. Meeting his gaze, I feel my heart expand. It's as if our fears are joined, and I can hold them both.

The doctors leave, and we wait. Someone has left a crumpled newspaper in the exam room; I pick it up and begin to read an article aloud to distract him. Instead it seems remote and meaningless. Discarding the paper, I give voice to what I know Michael must be feeling. "It's strange, isn't it?" I ask him. "You're not in control. People tell you how it's going to be."

His response has a chilling effect on me. "I'll take whatever they dish out," he says, his face hardening as his body tenses to receive whatever blow is about to be dealt. Suddenly he's ready for the worst. *But am I? What in God's name is going to happen?*

The first doctor comes back in and says he has arranged for us to see our primary care physician, Dr. Roberts, the following afternoon. He tells us the situation is serious. I think he wants to frighten us so we will be sure to keep the appointment.

"This is definitely a neurological problem," he adds. "At least you haven't hurt yourself yet."

In the days to come, we will hear this phrase or another—"At least you haven't fallen down yet"—many times, and we'll come to understand just how much Michael's balance is becoming impaired. But right now, we wonder why he's telling us this. We want to know exactly what he means, but we don't risk asking; instead, we just nod. More bad news can wait; we've had all we can handle today.

I bring the car around, and Michael slowly gets in. We're quiet on the drive back. Both of us are tired and, I think, more than a little in shock. I make some tea when we get home, and we sit in the living room and try to make sense of what has just happened.

As we talk, it becomes clear we are facing a problem that isn't really new; it's been coming on for years. Several summers ago, we vacationed in the Northwest. On one of the islands off the coast of Washington, we went for a hike, during which Michael found the perfect branch to use for a walking stick. During the next week, he collected shells and bought rawhide and beads to decorate it. On Victoria Island, he commissioned a woman at the Native American Crafts Fair to make a deerskin cap for the top of the stick, and she attached the shells and beads on rawhide strings. We thought of it as a crafts project, but that concealed the stick's real purpose, one we weren't willing to admit: Michael was losing his ability to walk and to keep his balance.

There were other signs we ignored or greeted with denial. Michael had always been the one in the lead on our hikes, often turning around to urge me on or retracing his steps to help me over rocks on the trail. Now, rather than Michael, it was I who began taking the lead. I remember feeling increasing concern as I noticed his left leg beginning to drag shortly into a walk. I noticed, too, he began to turn his left foot out to compensate for its growing weakness.

"You're getting stronger," he would say as he lagged behind, attributing the change to me and not himself.

He also began to do less strenuous work around the house. The last time we gardened together, I found myself getting annoyed. I was doing all the work while he sat in a chair and watched, only doing a little raking for a few minutes. This was the same man who, bare-chested and glistening with sweat, would work for hours without a break, digging garden plots or laying winding stone paths.

He made excuses such as, "I'm tired because I work nights," or "My leg drags because of the way I sit in the truck." And that was that. Michael was never one to go to doctors; he decided what was so—about himself or anyone else—and his opinions could not be changed by me, by others, or even, sometimes, by the facts. His pronouncements became a protective blanket under which he hid from the realities he'd rather not face.

This time, however, is different. Now there are doctors involved. We are finally up against it. Our uncharted journey has begun.

# Chapter 2
# End of a Dream?

We see Dr. Roberts the following day, May 29, 1996. He doesn't alleviate our worries. Along with other possible causes for Michael's condition, he tells us, it could be multiple sclerosis. In any case, however, we need to see a neurologist.

Michael seems distant; he doesn't say much, and we both try not to speculate. It will all become clearer tomorrow.

Yet—in just two days—my whole world seems off course. I think of our plans to retire in the next few years, sell the house, and buy a big RV—travel the country. We'll be free—free to discover new places and have all kinds of marvelous adventures. Michael will be able to drive for fun, not for a job, and we'll go wherever our fancy takes us. I don't talk about this to Michael, but I wonder, *Is this going to destroy our plans? Must we give up our dreams?*

The next day, Dr. Nichols, the neurologist, examines Michael and delivers his diagnosis. It is, indeed, MS: Michael's own T cells are attacking the myelin sheaths that protect his neural axons, causing multiple scarring—multiple sclerosis.

"He knew it all the time!" Michael says later, referring to Dr. Roberts. Michael feels manipulated and angry. He thinks people aren't being straight with him—he has never trusted doctors, and this just proves it for him.

Even so, we listen to Dr. Nichols because he's all we have. According to his calculations, this is Michael's second "exacerbation." We learn this unfamiliar word refers to the sudden appearance of a new, debilitating symptom. His first exacerbation, the doctor tells us, was an undiagnosed case of optic neuritis when Michael had vision problems in his left eye several years earlier. It had soon cleared up, and we forgot all about it.

This second exacerbation is characterized by increased weakness and lack of coordination in his left leg. Heat is the enemy of people with MS, we learn. Since it's summer now, and the temperature was hot on the day Michael returned to the day shift, the heat caused him to become so weak—and his left leg so incapacitated—he was literally unable to climb up into his truck's cab.

Michael and I lock eyes, and I reach for his hand. Both of us are feeling numb, but we aren't defeated. At least we have a name for what is wrong with Michael, and this name offers us some small degree of leverage, some power to help us cope. We learn Michael's immediate symptoms can be treated. Dr. Nichols books an appointment for the next day at the infusion clinic in Walnut Creek. Here, we're told, Michael will receive intravenous medication to help him regain his strength. We're relieved there's something that can be done, and we hold on tightly to the treatment's promise.

On the morning Michael is scheduled to be at the infusion clinic, we get up early, hoping the medical system can save us. As we get ready to leave home, Michael grabs hold of the cane and walks slowly and carefully to the car. We're both a bit frightened but believe somehow the procedure Michael is about to undergo will return our lives to normal.

Once we arrive at the clinic, we're ushered into a room filled with people sitting in recliner chairs equipped with TV sets. Needles stuck into their veins deliver medication from IV bags hung on poles above them. It looks like a scene out of a science fiction movie, but over the next few days, it will become familiar. The treatment consists of infusions of Solu-Medrol, a cortisol solution that helps counteract the effects of an exacerbation. The nurse tells us Michael will undergo three consecutive days of infusion therapy, and the treatment should reduce the swelling associated with the nerve problems in his brain and reduce his symptoms of weakness.

"I've seen patients arrive in wheelchairs and leave walking," she tells us brightly.

Michael and I exchange hopeful glances, and I smile at him encouragingly. His spirits are up as he sits watching CNN on his personal TV. He covers his anxiety with jokes and surprises me with his next comment.

"I might look into volunteering," he says. "Think of all the people who have to go through something like this and have no one to help them through it."

I look around and see there are several people here who appear to be alone. Others have a spouse or friend at their side. As he smiles up at me, I feel grateful that I'm able to be here with him—that he isn't one of those people who must face a medical crisis alone.

As I sit next to Michael, my mind wanders back to our first week living together. It was twenty years ago, in June, and I was on vacation from my job teaching remedial reading to middle school children in the San Francisco Bay Area. Michael was working at his truck driving job, doing local runs. One day he arranged to come home for lunch, and I decided to make it a special occasion: fresh cracked Dungeness crab, French bread, and chilled Pouilly Fuissé served outside on the picnic table under the flowering vines. When he saw the table decked out for lunch, his face lit up with surprise and pleasure.

"Is it okay to have a drink of wine at lunch?" I asked hesitantly, concerned I'd blown it by choosing to serve wine in the middle of his shift.

"Oh, that's not a problem at all," he assured me. I was still too much in love to question anything he told me.

Years later, Michael said if he had had any doubts about being in love with me, that lunch took care of them.

As we step outside again after Michael's first infusion, a blast of hot air hits us. I suggest he wait in front while I get the car from the garage so he won't have to walk. I look carefully at the traffic patterns and note that cars are exiting the garage right in front of the building where Michael will be waiting.

Confident that my plan is a good one, I'm dismayed when I leave the garage to discover I'm not where I thought I'd be. I panic and retrace my route, thinking I've missed the right exit, but I come out again in the same place. I don't know where I am, and I'm getting worried about Michael. Impulsively, I take the next exit I come to and turn onto the street ahead. Now I can see the building, but I can only pull over to the red curb some distance from where Michael stands waiting for me. He sees me and starts to walk the ten yards or so to the car. As he gets closer, I notice he's having difficulty walking, and I can hear him swearing.

When he gets in the car, he says, "Why did you do this to me?"

I start to tear up; I feel awful.

"I'm worse off now than I was yesterday. And I have to pee!"

Suddenly, I feel defeated and incompetent. I'm not used to being the one in charge, the one doing the driving.

"Drive up the hill," he orders.

I do as he says without comment.

"Stop the car!" He struggles to get out of the car and pees on some bushes.

*This is ridiculous,* I think, *stumbling off into the bushes on a cane to pee.*

We drive home in silence, but once there, we talk. He tells me he's sorry he snapped at me, and I say I'm sorry he had to stand in the heat.

"I know that was the last thing you intended," he soothes me.

As I fall into his arms, I'm relieved that this day is finally over—but I know new challenges and mistakes lie ahead. Resting my head on his shoulder, I can feel his strength, and I take it on as my own. For better or worse, we're in this together.

Michael and I have two more days of infusion therapy ahead of us, and it doesn't look like the weather will get any cooler. At least now we know more about what to expect. We realize we need to get a handicapped placard to hang on the rearview mirror as soon as we can, but since we don't have one yet, we develop a smarter plan for parking, drop-off, and pickup.

I know my best intentions won't always be enough. Inevitably, there will be times when I will screw up and feel guilty and inadequate, and Michael will feel angry and neglected. I guess we'll just have to learn from our mistakes and keep on truckin'.

# Chapter 3
# Change

It's now the beginning of June. After three days of hour-long infusions, Michael's strength is beginning to return and he can walk again without a cane. It seems a miracle, yet we remind ourselves that this is only a temporary reprieve; Michael has been diagnosed with relapsing-remitting MS, a form of the disease that promises to put him through repeated cycles of getting worse and getting better.

Michael's legs jerk wildly at night, and on many occasions, I have to ask him to get up from our bed ("the marriage bed," as he likes to call it) and move down the hall into one of the spare bedrooms so I can get enough sleep to be able to work the next day. I always hate to do this and feel guilty, as if I'm sending him away for being bad. He doesn't hold it against me; in fact, he often goes of his own accord before I have to ask—yet neither of us likes it.

Sleeping together has always been important to me; I feel connected and content lying next to him at night. When I was little, I used to fall asleep imagining scenarios in which I'd meet my one true love. Lying next to Michael, I no longer need fantasies to fall asleep; I finally have what I've always wanted. We usually cuddle spoon fashion, and when we move apart during sleep, he stretches out an arm and pulls me toward him, "like a bear reaching for his mate," he likes to say. Now, too often, I'm sending him away and remaining alone in the bed, tossing and turning. I hate it. I hate the way this illness has come between us.

By late June, almost one month after his infusions, the benefits of the Solu-Medrol have worn off, and Michael is again dependent on a cane and struggling to walk. It's a lazy and hot Sunday, and Michael is sleeping downstairs where it's cooler. This large room, off the garage on the lower level of our split-level house, was intended as a family room, but when we moved in several years ago, we turned it into our bedroom. We put a large Chinese rug on the floor and a hammock suspended above it. Our bed was in the far corner with a view of the lower garden. We created quite a romantic hideaway. After several years, we bought a new bed and moved into a bedroom upstairs, using the downstairs room as a TV room, though it still contained a bed.

Alone in the living room, once again my mind drifts back to that special lunch we had twenty years ago when our relationship was new, and, again, I'm struck by how much our life has changed. Tears begin to form, and my eyes start to burn as I remember how I watched him trying to walk earlier today, trying to make his legs do what his brain was telling them to do—so different from the confident, jaunty way he used to walk. In my imagination, I see his brain firing off the right messages and the scarring from MS stopping them: impotent waves of neurons missing their mark.

He's being so brave, and I'm amazed by how he can keep his spirits up as much as he does. Despite his fear of falling down, for instance, he continues to go alone on excursions to Berkeley to walk slowly down College Avenue and take in the sights or indulge in a treat and

a latte. He likes us to go back to places we enjoyed before his diagnosis, such as the Oakland Rose Garden—where we were married—or
the garden at Levi Plaza in San Francisco. He tries walking the paths
and steps that he once maneuvered so effortlessly, and when he can
still manage them with his cane, he's encouraged and savors the
sense of accomplishment. He's determined to not be beaten down
by this disease. Yet often his legs feel tired and heavy after one of
these forays, and he's fatigued and slow moving at night. At times like
these, he feels trapped and frightened. Recently, he awoke at three in
the morning, unable to breathe—and in the darkness, he felt like he
was being buried alive.

When Michael is despairing and depressed, often he will open up
to me and share his feelings. He's drawing closer to me now, yet he
also worries I'll come to resent him.

"If I get irritated and snappish with you, don't just excuse it
because of my condition," he tells me. Since this is an ongoing habit
of his, I think, *I probably won't*—but decide to keep that thought to
myself.

I am grateful I can be here for him and that he's not alone. But
sometimes, it's true, I do feel resentment creeping in; the spotlight
is on him now, and I've been relegated to a shadowy, supportive role.

As doubts assail me, I wonder if I'm truly capable of meeting all
the challenges of caregiving that may lie ahead. I wonder if I will be
able to give him all the support he'll need if this disease progresses,
as I fear it will. *What will I be called upon to do? What will he expect
of me? Am I condemned to live in the shadow of MS? Is he? Where will
the light come from?*

The next day, we talk about how we still don't have all the facts.
It could be MS, but maybe—just maybe—it's something else. Maybe
he can get better. I have a friend who knows someone who gets along

just fine with MS. We grasp at straws; we tell each other we don't really know yet. But it has only been a matter of weeks since his infusions, and already I see him beginning to deteriorate. The day before, he couldn't move his legs after he had struggled into bed for a nap; I moved them for him so he could get settled. They seem thinner and heavier now. I can remember when they were strong and muscular.

There was a time, not so long ago at all, when we'd hike the East Bay trails near our home, Michael's body agile and his energy seemingly unlimited. I was in good shape too; I had to work twice as hard he just to keep up. He had fine legs then, long, strong, and dependable. Oh, how we took things for granted!

My mind retreats to memories of the early days of our relationship. How different it was then; how far away it seems now.

I was thirty-four and fresh out of a four-year relationship. Since true love had proven to be merely a fairy tale, I vowed to stop looking for it; henceforth, I would look for a man with money. That, at least, would compensate for my dashed dreams of romance.

A few days after I reached this decision, Michael appeared at my door. I was living communally in Oakland with two men and a woman, and the woman was about to move out. Michael answered an ad for our room to rent, attracted by the calligraphy on the index card we had posted on the bulletin board of the Berkeley Coop grocery store.

"What's so is," he announced when I opened the door. "I'm here to look at the room." His "What's so is" statement identified him as a fellow graduate of est, or Erhard Seminar Training for personal growth—but this wasn't the only factor in his favor.

I quickly judged him to be an attractive potential housemate, close to my age: He was tall, slim, and well-dressed in slacks and the kind of form-fitting shirt typical of the 1970s. He had a long, youthful face with smooth, tanned cheeks and engaging clear, blue eyes. His hair was brown and full, with just a hint of silver at the temples. His expression was both friendly and serious as he held out a half gallon of Los Hermanos and told me his name was Michael. I took the wine and invited him in.

"You're here to join us for dinner and to look at the room, right?" I asked.

"No," he replied. "Not for dinner; just to meet everyone."

*Funny*, I thought. *I was sure we had invited him to dinner.* As it turned out, he did stay, although he ate very little. I found out later he had recently lost a hundred pounds on a self-prescribed diet of hard-boiled eggs and white wine, and he was determined to keep the weight off.

We all liked Michael, but I was especially drawn to him—and he to me. We talked into the night, long after my housemates had wandered off to bed. I learned he loved being in nature, as did I. He especially enjoyed hiking and backpacking along the Stanislaus River in the Sierra Nevada. He looked very fit and healthy, which I attributed to his outdoor adventures. I was drawn to his height—six foot five, he said. I, too, was tall at almost five foot ten. He was a Teamster and drove a truck for a living. I liked that he had a blue-collar job. My father was a farmer, and, as a child, I loved going with him into the men's world: the hardware store, the lumberyard, and that special evening time we shared when my dog and I would ride with him in his pickup to check the irrigation water. Like Michael, I was a union member. As a teacher, I belonged to my local chapter of the California Federation of Teachers. I was drawn to his seriousness as we talked of museums we'd gone to and books we'd read. Although I had college degrees and he didn't, I was attracted to his intelligence and intellectual curiosity. As the evening went on, I felt an ineffable, almost visceral connection with Michael. Our energies were aligned. It was as if, in some way, we'd known each other for a very long time; yet, the newness of it intrigued me. Before he left, he placed a tender, brief kiss on my lips.

*How nice,* I thought. *No fast moves, no pressure. I like that.*

The next morning, he phoned and invited me to go swimming in the pool at his bachelor apartment complex. Later he told me he hadn't been able to sleep all night because he couldn't stop thinking about me.

It was June 23, 1976, and I was on summer vacation. Michael had decided to take the day off work, something he did as often as possible that summer. We had fun that day, and I discovered his sexy, playful side as we competed in water volleyball with some of his friends. He wore mirrored sunglasses and always seemed to be looking across the net in my direction. I couldn't tell exactly where he was looking, but since I was in a bikini, it wasn't hard to figure out. It was soon obvious to both of us that this was much more than a passing flirtation.

"I didn't plan on this," he told me later, feigning regret. "I never expected to fall in love. I was having a great time playing the field."

And, indeed he was. As an est volunteer, he made follow-up phone calls to people who had missed their post-est training seminars or in other ways "failed to keep their agreements." When there was a woman on the other end of the line whom Michael found interesting, he was often successful in arranging a date. He presented himself as "Mr. est," which gave him an aura of self-confidence and astuteness that I, and others, found appealing.

The est program was conceived and offered by Werner Erhard

or one of his trainees as an intensive two-weekend-long program in which we learned to live our lives in a more authentic, less programmed manner. We were challenged to be ourselves, free from our past. As I later learned, after the training, both Michael and his wife became so freed from their past that their marriage no longer suited either of them. So, when I met Michael, he was newly single and open to new experiences.

In the course of the following week, Michael moved into our house—but not into the vacant room. He wasn't the man with money I had vowed to find; he was the love of my life, the one I had despaired of ever finding. Feeling elated by his ardor, yet still insecure, I wrote the following in my journal:

> *What I have is the most fantastic and beautiful and joyful experience of my life. What I have gained is a new sense of myself, my worth. I want this to work. I love you, Michael, and I experience your love for me. Communication is key to its all working. That was there from the start. I'm only afraid you might leave because I really don't know if I truly deserve you. I need to work through these feelings.*

Two years and a day after we met, Michael and I were married in the Oakland Rose Garden, and his young daughters were our bridesmaids.

When I first met Michael, I was only vaguely aware that he had children. He'd mentioned them, but they were visiting their maternal grandparents in another state, and they didn't seem quite real to me. (At that time, Michael and his first wife were in the final stages of divorce, which took a full year in California.) But as our relationship grew and we moved in together, they stayed with us often.

Just two weeks after we were married, Michael's children came to live with us full-time. Their mother had moved to Oregon to live in a spiritual community. Michael had told me early on that he was determined to have his children live with him someday, so he readily agreed to take them when his ex-wife asked him to. His only stipulation was he be awarded joint physical custody. So the papers were drawn up and signed, and—seemingly overnight—we became a family of five.

Soon our small apartment became too confining, and I convinced Michael that we needed to buy a house. I continued having automatic withdrawals from my paycheck, and, within a year, we were able to move.

As a father, Michael was focused on logistics. He brought home the paycheck every week and made sure his children had a roof over their heads, food on the table, and clothes on their backs. He prided himself on being a better father than his father, who, although a responsible provider, had been distant, punitive, and shaming. Unlike his father, Michael was close to his children. He liked to read to them, take them places—such as the Oakland Zoo—and lend a compassionate ear when they needed one. Because I was a teacher, he insisted I take charge of their education, and this I gladly did, going to parent-teacher meetings and monitoring their progress.

In junior high, Zoie, the youngest, went to live with her mother, who had reentered her life and was living in another state. This was not an easy change. I really didn't want her to leave, but I believed that, if she had the full attention of her mother, she would be happier than she was with me. There had been times when I had taken her with me on trips connected with my job as a teacher—one was learning about technology for educators and the other was related to my role in my teachers' union—and she had been happy, her rebelliousness absent and her outlook cheery. We had had fun together. I thought she would thrive living with her mother who, I believed, would give her more of that one-on-one attention than I could. Besides, it was what both of them wanted.

As Michael and I enter this uncharted phase of our lives, the girls are grown and living on their own. Zoie, now married and still living out of state, is able to visit us from time to time.

Now, so many years later, we have a new challenge. Will our love carry us through whatever storms may lie ahead? I believe that it will. After each setback in the many years of our marriage, we always came back together—with renewed commitment, laughter, lusty sex, and growing love. I will never give up on us, and neither will he. We can face and survive this new challenge and be stronger for it. I know we can.

# Chapter 4

# Uncertainty

I'm sitting in our living room, alone, taking stock of my life and how it's changed. Michael's big leather chair feels empty as I let my weight sink into its cushion, stretching my long legs on top of the matching beige ottoman. We used to fill up this chair together, me sitting on Michael's lap, resting my head on his shoulder, snuggling my forehead into that warm space against his neck.

As the light coming through the window behind me fades and shadows lengthen, I let my thoughts drift. It's just days since we received his diagnosis, and I'm aware of how nervous I am much of the time. I'm trying to deal with so much uncertainty. A million questions crowd my mind: *Can he go back to work? If not, who will take care of him in the fall when I have to go back? How can we learn more about this disease? What will he need now to help him get better, or at least not get worse? What is my role now? How will our life together change?* The questions go on and on. I know both of us are adrift on this sea of uncertainty, unsure of what to do next.

There's a saying that when faced with two road signs, one that says "Heaven" and the other "Read about Heaven," some follow the second sign. I'm one of them—but in this case, it isn't heaven I'm trying to figure out. Now, believing that with knowledge comes power, I determine to learn as much as I can about multiple sclerosis.

In addition to our clinic's online database and a medical library in San Francisco, our major source of information is the local chapter of the National Multiple Sclerosis Society. We learn MS is a chronic, progressive illness that affects the nerves in the brain, spinal cord, and other parts of the central nervous system. According to the latest theory, it's an autoimmune disease, which means that Michael's body is attacking itself. Even before he knew this, more than once he had said, "I feel like my body has betrayed me."

We learn that about 400,000 people in the United States have MS, and 2.5 million worldwide. It occurs two to three times more often in women than in men. There are four forms of the disease: relapsing-remitting, primary progressive, secondary progressive, and progressive-relapsing. The neurologist says Michael has the first kind, which is true for about 80 percent of MS patients. He can expect to have periodic attacks, or exacerbations, when a new symptom will appear, and he will become extremely weak. This will be followed by a period of recovery—though probably not complete recovery—and then the pattern will repeat.

Secondary progressive acts more like the relapsing-remitting form in its early stages, but then a more continuous loss of physical and cognitive functions develops, and remissions become less common. Fifty percent of people with relapsing-remitting MS will develop secondary progressive MS within ten years of their initial diagnosis.

The primary progressive form, which affects about 10 percent of MS patients, causes a gradual loss of physical and cognitive functions and does not include periods of remission. The rarest form, progressive-relapsing, is similar, except the person's steady decline is accompanied by sudden, and acute, exacerbations. It only affects about 5 percent of patients. Finally, we learn one's diagnosis can change; it can get worse.

At his neurologist's suggestion, Michael and I attend a workshop for the newly diagnosed presented by the Oakland chapter of the MS Society. The daylong event takes place in a windowless room in which a dozen people are seated around a long conference table. As we join the group, I notice everyone seems to be uneasy and hyperalert, as if scanning each person who walks in for answers to fearful questions: *Am I better off than she is? Is someone going to arrive in a wheelchair and scare the shit out of me?* We're like a classroom of elementary school kids waiting for the new teacher and hoping she's nice. Most of the people here are younger than Michael and I are, in their twenties or thirties, and most are women. I see little evidence of disability at first glance, but when I look more closely, I see a cane or two propped against the table. Everyone is in the same boat, and everyone is frightened but hopeful. Like us, they have come to learn about their disease: what to expect, what to do next, and how to make it better.

We learn from experts. A doctor who specializes in MS talks about medical management, a psychologist discusses coping skills and tells us depression is often a companion to people with MS, and a lawyer informs us about the rights of the handicapped in the workplace and the complicated processes of obtaining disability status. All this and lunch—what a bargain! We gain a lot of helpful information, but we also leave with the knowledge that we have been ushered into a new world—the world of disability.

After the workshop, we go to a little coffee shop nearby. It's close to where we used to live in the early days of our relationship, before we were married. We find a small table overlooking Grand Avenue and sit quietly for a while, watching people walking past on the sidewalk, some coming to or from Lake Merritt in jogging attire.

"We used to jog," Michael reminisces.

"Well, you did, anyway. I was usually way behind you, trying to keep up." Still, I enjoyed our jogging times together, and I loved feeling in shape, as did Michael.

Michael looks down at his coffee, and I can see the worry lines cross his brow.

"I guess all that's over now," he says, stirring some sugar into his cup.

I cover his free hand with my own, and he looks up and smiles.

"I'm not going to give up," he says. "I'll beat this thing, one way or another."

"We'll do it together," I say. "And we've learned there's help out there. We're not alone."

As much as we're committed to fighting this disease together and even though we haven't had a real argument since Michael was stricken, I worry that if we argue now, it will weaken him and make him even more vulnerable. Our pattern is long established: he criticizes, and I defend; he withdraws, and I pursue. We both struggle to assert our power over the other, each in our own contentious way.

For the most part, our arguments are over minor occurrences, but they are frequent, and they build up. One of my journals gives a window on our power struggles.

*It was our day to work in the garden. He started to water, then proclaimed that I hadn't been watering enough and the plants were practically dying. I told him they obviously weren't dying, and I didn't want to be put down. I started to cry and accuse him of being unreasonable. I went into the house, leaving the watering and the rest of the chores to him. I was crushed, having looked forward to working outside together. Later, when he came in, I accused him of always criticizing me and not appreciating all I did. He left without a word and went into the back of the house. Impulsively, I followed him, unable to let the matter drop. In tears, I implored him to see my side of things. "I can't let you define me by these negative judgments anymore!" I yelled. He just left and went to another part of the house. I collapsed in tears. Hours later we made up, no apologies, but it felt good to be back in his arms and feel that he loved me again.*

My behavior wasn't new; it went back to my early childhood. Due to his many medical problems, my father, usually loving and over-protective, would fly off the handle without warning. "You're spoiled and ungrateful!" he would yell at me. Yet, just minutes earlier, I was his loveable princess. My anger would meet his in kind, and a shouting match would ensue. "I hate you! I didn't spoil myself!" I would shout. After each confrontation, I would run to my room in tears and slam the door, feeling emotionally abandoned. It was a life-and-death struggle for me at that age. Shortly afterward, he would come in to comfort me, and we would both apologize. Then everything would be all right . . . until the next time.

My mother was always a passive observer in these confrontations, and I didn't see this accomplishing anything. She always implored me to "just keep quiet" whenever my father became angry. But I could never keep quiet. When I was growing up, I saw only two ways of approaching conflict: that of my father—the strong, aggressive model I associated with the masculine—and that of my mother—the weak, passive model I associated with the feminine. I would fall back on this masculine model whenever Michael and I argued. He never accepted that from me; he would withdraw, angering me even more.

Other entries taken from both of our journals show our early, negative dynamics. From mine:

> *It's so weird. When we first fell in love, I could do no wrong. All I had to do was just be me. I was amazed that I didn't have to do anything—just be. Now it seems I can do no right. I'm either a goddess or a witch in this relationship, and a witch more and more. Where did it all go? Who am I? I can't let him define me. I won't!*

Looking back on this now, I realize that my self-worth was all tied up with how the men in my life—my father and Michael—saw me. I felt good about myself if that reflection was positive; I felt bad about myself if that reflection was negative. In the case of the latter, I fought tooth and nail to counter the negative reflection, to make them see how wrong they were. Even if the criticism were warranted, I just couldn't take it in. I only felt loved when I had the approval of the man in my life.

In one of Michael's journals from 1986, he writes of experiencing a seesaw of agreeable and contentious times. This was the year all three girls were in their teens and I was going through menopause. What follows is a compilation of some of his entries from this time.

> *Suzanne is so unhappy with her life. Blames all of us for her unhappiness. Argument ends with her screams and door-slamming.*
>
> . . .
>
> *I'm just often irritated, and Suzanne just stumbles into range.*

. . .

*Been enjoying vacation. Suzanne and I had a nice time doing nothing much, but doing it together was nice.*

. . .

*Am looking forward to ocean. Seems like years since we've last been there. Am tired today more than most Saturday mornings. Been hiding out under the covers much too long and getting outside is a must do thing this weekend.*

. . .

*We go to the beach for the day. Sunshine and sand—great day.*

. . .

*She always attacks me when I'm down.*

I know so much of our struggles came from a lack of communication, the one thing that was so strong in our early years. In retrospect, I see that often when Michael was distant or irritated with me, he was in pain or depressed. But he didn't tell me how he felt, and I took his actions to be deliberately unloving and hostile. I would pursue him aggressively, demanding an explanation and apology. I think that he didn't know how to express himself in the face of my verbal assaults. Feeling overwhelmed—and unable or unwilling to acknowledge his vulnerability—he just shut down. In one journal entry, one that he didn't share with me at the time and that now I find heart-wrenching, he wrote about his feelings:

*Feel at a loss, but will remove the tension that wraps itself around my heart and tightens and tightens with each contact with her. Her unhappiness will no longer bleed over onto me!*

Yes, I was unhappy when I felt I had lost Michael's love, whether he criticized me or withdrew from me. And I pushed back and pursued him relentlessly until I felt his love again, not realizing that my pursuit pushed him further away. Perhaps Michael and I were fated to engage in our power struggle. Perhaps now is our chance to create a more compassionate and positive relationship. I so hope that it is.

I'm resolved to react less angrily when Michael and I have differences. I realize this is doubly important now, and I think I've already made some progress. I'm pleased I didn't try to defend myself or argue with Michael when he reproached me for leaving him standing out in the heat that day of his first infusion. I clearly saw how exhausted he was; I could feel his despair, his frustration at not being in control of his situation. I know I have to keep working on putting him first and believing in my own self-worth, independent of his perceptions.

I think back to a two-day retreat with Sogyal Rinpoche, the founder of a Tibetan Buddhist group called Rigpa, that I had attended earlier this year, and see this as a harbinger of positive change. Before he became ill, both Michael and I had studied meditation at a Rigpa sangha, or spiritual community, in Berkeley. At the retreat, Rinpoche addressed many issues, but the most important for me was his message that karmic patterns can end. With support, he told us, one can struggle to overcome negative patterns established lifetimes ago and emerge a different person.

Maybe our power struggles went back further than my relationship with my father. Maybe it *was* karmic; maybe both of us had been working on this issue for lifetimes. If this were so, I would have chosen my family before this incarnation to create the situation needed to further this work.

Hearing Rinpoche's message at the retreat, I felt a shift in perception. In that instant, I became aware of how often I operate unconsciously in a reactive mode and realized I had other options. Suddenly I felt lighter, as if a heavy coat had been lifted from my shoulders. As time goes on, I hope to get better at responding to what is actually happening in the moment, rather than reacting out of negative past habits—habits that helped me survive when I was a child and maybe in other lifetimes but are now no longer needed or appropriate.

About this time, my new awareness allowed us to avoid an angry confrontation. We had plans to go to San Francisco, and I had made reservations for lunch at one of our favorite restaurants. Then, when I was dressed and ready to go, Michael said he had changed his mind. This took me by surprise; I thought we had both been looking forward to getting out of the house.

"I decided to stay in bed," he announced. "You always come up with some way to ruin the day."

With that, I felt hurt and anger welling up inside me. I was ready to explode with righteous indignation and give forth with a litany of reasons why he was wrong. But this time, instead of giving in to these feelings, I was able to consider the situation and respond to it consciously instead of blindly reacting. It was as if someone had hit the pause button on a tape recorder.

"I understand that you need to rest," I said evenly. "Maybe we can just spend a quiet day at home." Then I left the room for a while and spent some time alone, observing my feelings and thoughts. As it turned out, we did spend a quiet day at home, reading and watching TV—and that evening, we made love.

As time moves on, I notice that more often, instead of blaming Michael when things aren't working out as I had hoped or planned, I'm able to respond appropriately. I can step back and assess the situation, as if I were a witness to my own process. In this way, I can choose what to say or do rather than allow myself to run on automatic and have old, negative habits take the lead. The long-standing issues are still there, but I'm developing a new relationship with them.

In a way, it all comes down to learning how to take care of myself. I've come to realize that I need to be proactive in doing this; Michael can't meet all of my needs all of the time, especially now. Sometimes I just need to go for a walk or take in a movie with a friend. When I feel the need to have an honest discussion with him, I find it's best to wait until he's in a good space to do that rather than push to resolve things immediately. I'm beginning to feel more self-confident as my ability to recognize and meet my own, as well as Michael's, needs increases; I realize I'm powerless to change Michael's patterns—but I *can* begin to change my own.

# Chapter 5

# Symptoms

On June 27, we see Dr. Nichols and get the results of Michael's MRI: three white spots in his brain that are indicative of MS. This, along with a vision test, confirms the diagnosis. We learn Michael exhibits 90 percent of MS symptoms; an especially telling one is his extreme intolerance to heat. Others include early temporary vision loss, fatigue, urinary problems, difficulty concentrating, short-term memory loss, loss of balance, and decreased large-and fine-motor coordination. The only good news is that Dr. Nichols doesn't think a spinal tap is necessary, so at least Michael escapes that one.

It's his intolerance for heat that presents the most immediate problem. For my part, I have always thrived in hot weather, and I find Michael's new aversion to heat particularly unsettling. I was raised a farmer's daughter, at home in the hot, Mediterranean climate of Brentwood, a small agricultural town of two thousand people about fifty-five miles east of San Francisco. I loved feeling the sun's heat on my body as I wandered through my father's orchards, accompanied by my dog or my friend Jeanie. I loved to go down to the creek that ran along our property, explore the fort some local boys had made, and swing out over the shallow water on the knotted rope that hung from an ancient oak. I have fond memories of picnics with my family at nearby Curry Creek on scorching summer days: the smell of the dry, brown grass on the hills and the old, green metal cooler that carried dry ice to chill my mother's deviled eggs and macaroni salad.

After I met Michael, summers were magical for us. I had ten weeks off every year, and he would take as many vacation days as he could manage. We went hiking, mountain biking, camping, and swimming together, sometimes stopping to simply lie in the sun.

Some of my most vivid memories are of two glorious weeks in a rustic cabin at Lake Tahoe, right near the water's edge. Most days we took off on our mountain bikes for a new adventure, relishing the challenge of high mountain climbs and fast, exhilarating descents. Michael always preceded me on the uphill climb and followed me coming down so he could come to my aid if I fell, which I rarely did. I can still see his tanned, muscular calves moving in flexing arcs ahead of me or straining to climb as he stood on the pedals. We always started the day off with a hearty breakfast and were fond of stopping our bikes along the route for an energy bar to keep us going. We named one favorite stopping place Fibar Meadow—Fibars were one of the few energy snacks available then, and we came to relish them. Our day usually finished with a shower in the evening and dinner at a nearby Mexican restaurant. Then we'd go back to our cabin and make love.

We took up mountain biking early, before it became a popular sport. With directions from a local bike shop, we discovered the beauty and challenge of the Flume Trail high above Lake Tahoe long before it became crowded. Its name came from a box flume that the narrow path had once boasted; it carried water from Marlette Lake down to Tunnel Creek Station during the gold and silver mining booms of the 1800s. I especially remember one hot summer day when we interrupted our biking to skinny-dip in the ice-cold waters of Marlette Lake, its seclusion being another advantage of early discovery.

Now, as the demands of MS settle around us, we know our mountain biking days are over. Still, we find some hope for dealing with the debilitating aspects of the summer's heat. The nurse calls with a recommendation from the doctor that Michael take cold showers during the day to help with the fatigue caused by the spike in his body temperature. I come up with the idea of putting ice packs on his neck and spine as he lies on the bed; he says when the ice is in place, it's as if a switch has been thrown and he can feel his legs "come on." He also feels suddenly conscious then. He's been zoning out a lot in the heat, and the cold revives him. We even discover a way to fix an ice pack to his neck so it will stay on when he gets up to read the paper in the living room. With the fan on and a glass of ice water, it's amazing how he becomes his old, cheerful self again. Bandannas that have been moistened, frozen, and tied around his forehead also afford some relief when he's out and about.

Because it's so hot this summer, we often lie naked on the bed with the fan blowing cooling air over us. This is an opportunity for us to be together, free for a while from the onslaught of so many changes. It's nice just to lie there, to comfort Michael, and to receive comfort in return. He especially likes it when I stroke his back and legs, which carry so much strain and spasticity. We create ever new ways of enjoying each other physically, taking our time and being in the moment, accepting and never judging.

When we first met, we couldn't keep our hands off each other. Sex was exciting, fulfilling, carnal, spiritual, all-encompassing, passionate, and ubiquitous. We were totally in love and, Michael liked to add, *in lust*. As time went on, the frequency may have lessened, but never the joy of coming together in a profound intimacy that enriched our everyday lives. We knew at a very deep level that we were meant to be together.

Michael had three dreams weeks before his diagnosis that, I worry, might be precognitive. In one, he saw little dough people, shaped by cookie cutters, being spit out by a big machine. Dressed in medieval attire, some on horseback, they went about a myriad of activities, completely unaware that they were nearing the end of the conveyor belt and would soon abruptly fall off. He saw the whole progression at once, from one end of the belt to the other; new cookies were being spit out at one end as old cookies dropped off at the other.

Another time, not realizing he was asleep, I woke him from a nap.

"I was dreaming," he told me. "I was with some dead guys. I was talking, laughing it up and enjoying myself with some of the guys, all of them dead." I thought back to a month earlier, when he had dreamed of his mother in her grave. She was all bones—a skeleton— clad in an evening dress.

As curious and foreboding as these seemed at the time, remembering them now I feel pessimistic and frightened: *Is this to be the last phase of his life? Do dreams show his life in a truer perspective, from beginning to end, with an emphasis on the end? Where are we headed? What happens next?*

# Chapter 6

# Loss

More than once, in these summer months after his collapse, Michael asks, "What is happening to me?" It's more a bewildered lament than a question.

As his legs stubbornly refuse to respond to his will, he begins to feel that his body has betrayed him. He can no longer control it; he is no longer himself, and his image of his old self is inexorably slipping away. His worst fear is ending up in a wheelchair. "I'd kill myself first," he says.

Our growing anxiety continues to be echoed in our dreams. In a recent one of Michael's, he's driving a big truck down the highway when suddenly he loses control and panics; the truck veers sharply out of its lane. He is terrified.

In one of my own, I witness a showdown. We are somewhere in the Wild West. Michael appears youthful, in jeans and a plaid cotton shirt. We want to go through a gate in a fence, but a huge, intimidating animal bars our path. It looks like a kangaroo with a seal's head, and, as Michael attempts to pass, it continues to threaten him. He's afraid, but he confronts this unnatural animal, refusing to flee. I can see his body begin to shake, and he finally decides to turn back. I, in turn, am left to wonder whether I have the strength and courage to face down this beast by myself.

When I fell in love with Michael, I knew very little about him. But as we grew closer and shared our stories, I became fascinated with his history. It told me so much about him: who he is and who he was.

Michael spent his childhood in south Seattle. He liked to roam the back woods behind his house, most often to places where his father forbade him to go. If he wasn't supposed to go there, he reasoned, it must be worth investigating.

Sometimes he would join other boys in trying to outwit a neighbor's especially ornery horse. The horse became irate whenever anyone trespassed on his property—and so, naturally, dashing across the pasture became the boys' great challenge. When the horse was grazing a good distance away, the game was to see who could make it across the field without getting bitten by the horse, who furiously pursued them with bared teeth. At times one or more of them ended up trapped in a tree, at least until the horse got bored and moved a safe distance away.

Some of Michael's most treasured memories were of accompanying his maternal step-grandfather, Granite Ward, to Native American villages, where he saw salmon drying on wooden racks and could mingle with the people who lived there. He learned many skills during his time with Granite, including how to hunt and fish and be a caring man.

When Michael was a teenager, his family moved to Illinois, near Chicago. But he remained nostalgic for the Pacific Northwest, with its cool weather, overcast skies, and pungent smell of the sea. It's no wonder Michael felt at home in this area—the Marriotts, originally from England, had lived in Seattle since the early 1900s. This side of his family had strong ties to trucking; his paternal grandfather, Frank Marriott, had been one of the early teamsters who drove horse-drawn wagons laden with goods across the country. The Teamsters Union—whose logo still features the proud heads of two such horses—was the union of Michael's grandfather and represented the rough-and-tumble life his family honored. I once saw a black-and-white photograph of Michael's grandfather as a young man and immediately recognized my husband in his grandfather's lithe body, his elongated, handsome face, and his intense, almost defiant, gaze.

Michael's father, John, also started off as a Teamster, working in trucking (the days of horse-drawn wagons were long over). He chose to go into management, becoming a vice-president of a major trucking line and a contract negotiator. His own father had died when John was young, leaving his mother to raise him and his older brother alone. I always imagined those difficult times were what had hardened the man who would become my father-in-law—and I don't think his mother softened his life with much nurturing. Michael's memory of his grandmother, Alice, was of a stern, stingy woman who would only allow him one cookie with his milk; in contrast, his maternal grandmother, Josephine Ward, always offered him unlimited quantities of freshly baked cookies.

Alice was born Alice Madeline McNulty, and her parents emigrated from Ireland in 1888. They had both been Catholics from Belfast. Alice had six siblings, three of whom died of the plague in 1890. Life must have been hard for the McNultys, and that, and the Depression, could explain her stinginess. Few came from Ireland untouched by hardship, and things were rarely easy once they arrived in America. Michael inherited a strong dose of Irish culture and good looks and, as a young man, was known to spontaneously break into a jig when he'd been to an Irish pub and had too much to drink.

Not surprisingly, Michael and his younger brother, Steve, grew up in a household where work and frugality were the paramount values. Michael remembers his father saying it was time to "tighten our belts" and cautioning the boys to always "pay yourself first"—squirrel away some money in savings or investments before paying any bills. According to Michael, Steve became a saver who planned for a tomorrow that seemed never to come, and he, Michael, became a spender who seldom planned ahead. For example, when we first met, I had put away $5,000 for future travel. Michael didn't even have a savings account. He lived from paycheck to paycheck, confident he would always work and have an income.

Michael's father shaped Michael's personality in other ways. Often John would tantalize young Michael with plans to take him somewhere exciting, such as the zoo or a ball game. Mostly, these plans failed to materialize, and Michael was left confused and disappointed. Afraid to show his emotions for fear of his father's ridicule, he learned to hide behind an expressionless mask, one he continued to wear often as an adult. His feelings were rarely evident, even when he was happy or pleased. This hard, protective exterior hid a soft and vulnerable interior, an aspect of Michael I recognized and valued.

From an early age, trucks had fascinated Michael. I have an old photo of him at about thirteen, leaning casually against the door of a truck's cab and looking shyly pleased, with the hint of a swaggering smile playing about his lips. While still in high school, he joined the Teamsters Union and worked at the Chicago docks, earning an astounding amount of money for a kid that age.

At that time, Michael and his family lived in one of Chicago's upscale suburbs. In high school, he played tackle on the football team, until he was kicked off for driving his car across the football field as a finale to a reckless night of drinking. As it turned out, this was an unexpected blessing. His strength and height had made his participation in football a given, but his heart was never in it.

Because of his height and growing ability to adopt that impenetrable mask and stare down anyone who questioned him, he passed for twenty-one when he was sixteen and often spent evenings at jazz clubs in Chicago. In one of them, he ran into one of his teachers who challenged his fledgling self-confidence by coming on to him. One of his lifelong regrets was that he didn't have the nerve to meet her halfway.

He was popular, had plenty of spending money, and never seriously thought of doing any type of work other than trucking. He had no incentive from his parents to attend college, and he chose to follow his growing intellectual interests on his own terms. In school he slid by, putting effort only into those classes that interested him and not taking others very seriously. When some of his friends entered college, he liked to browse through the college bookstore, buying those texts that caught his fancy and reading them on his own. He especially liked art, literature, philosophy, and political science. This was the source of his rather amusing habit of mispronouncing words, having been deprived of scholarly discussions. Once, after I had corrected his pronunciation of hyperbole, he exclaimed, "You mean it's not *hyper-bowl*? I've been saying that all my life!"

"Didn't anyone ever correct you?" I asked.

"No—everyone I know just assumes I know what I'm talking about."

I wasn't surprised; undoubtedly, he had most of his fellow workers snowed. Michael was always a master of the bluff, his expression betraying no chink in his armor, and he presented his assertions and opinions with a conviction that left little room for dissent. Yet, if caught in a fabrication or somehow outsmarted, he would break out in a guilty, self-conscious smile that always proved disarming, at least to me.

In junior high school, several days after taking an IQ test with the rest of his class, he was summoned to the principal's office. Not sure why he was there, but—as he was often in trouble—considering several plausible reasons, he was surprised when the principal began scolding him because he had scored 140 on the IQ test. Rather than congratulating him, the principal berated Michael for wasting his life and not applying himself to his studies. Not surprisingly, this conference did nothing to change his behavior.

By choosing trucking as his vocation, Michael followed in his father's footsteps and entered a macho and confrontational world. Here was a boy who, in sixth grade, broke into tears when his teacher played an opera record for the class—but also a boy who liked to harass his younger brother and get into fistfights at school. It was this aggressive part, at the expense of his more sensitive nature, that saw him through his career as a truck driver and union steward. But his intelligence served him well, allowing him to do his job on his own terms, just as he had conducted himself in high school.

He often managed to have an inordinate amount of free time for reading or exploring, in or out of his truck. During the 1960s, for instance, he had a San Francisco run and managed to spend ample time browsing the books in City Lights Bookstore and making friends with the merchants in Chinatown. One day, he had been shown the subterranean tunnels that snake though that part of the city, where bare light bulbs dangle from the musty ceilings and secret doors lead to underground entrances. He learned these tunnels had been used by the hundreds of thousands of Chinese emigrants who had fled famine in China in the 1800s. Draconian immigration policies forbidding men to bring their families over resulted in the illegal importation of Chinese girls and women as slaves, who were smuggled from the port through the tunnels. Tunnels had also been used to rid the city of Chinese victims of epidemics that the city's power brokers were determined to keep secret. Thousands of bodies were clandestinely dumped into sewer tunnels, to be swept into the bay and eventually carried out to sea on the tides.

Michael enjoyed talking and joking with the people to whom he delivered, and he did his job with pride and a sense of humor that made him many friends along the way. His employer often lost accounts when a company for which Michael picked up or delivered was switched to another driver.

He always remained a union worker—even though, after reviewing his application test scores, early bosses had offered him the choice of working either labor or management. He chose labor because he didn't want to be like his father and because he believed in it. He never regretted his choice. For twenty-six years, he worked for a trucking line in the San Francisco East Bay Area. When it went out of business, he worked several other jobs in trucking until, that morning in May of 1996, he could no longer get into his truck.

# Chapter 7

# Lessons

Now, in late July, almost two months since his diagnosis, Michael is using two hiking poles to maintain balance instead of one cane. More and more, he's using cruise control on our Honda Accord, even when driving in town, relying on the ACCEL and DECEL buttons instead of the accelerator and brake. As one who can shift a truck without using the clutch and expertly anticipate traffic changes, gearing down instead of braking, he is less disturbed by this behavior than I am.

It frightens me to watch his body deteriorate, his legs refusing to work and his muscles beginning to atrophy. I wish with all my heart I had the power to stop—to reverse—these changes. But I can't, and I wonder just how much I *will* be able to do. *Am I really up to this challenge? Will I find the strength to face this new and uncertain future?*

Yesterday we were in the kitchen together, making sandwiches for lunch. Suddenly he stopped spreading mayonnaise on a piece of bread. "I'm frightened," he said.

I put my arms around him and told him I was frightened too.

As we held each other, an image flashed in my mind of a picture I had once seen of two sea otters hugging each other in an instinctual act of comfort as a hunter prepared to bring a club down on their heads.

We grow so close in the initial weeks of shock and adjustment that Michael almost seems to be clinging to me at times. Being a person who rarely goes to doctors, he needs guidance through our HMO system. I can do such things as make appointments for him, be his second set of ears when we see the doctor, and keep a list of the questions we need to ask. But he also needs emotional support and an anchor, as do I. We find ourselves developing a whole new type of intimacy and interdependence. He's more open to sharing his feelings and symptoms with me, and my empathy for him and sense of responsibility for his wellbeing are growing. More and more, we are working together. Once again feeling hope, I vow to myself that I will be here for him, now and forever, whatever the future may hold.

One July Sunday, we decide to go to San Francisco for a concert at Stern Grove, a lovely outdoor amphitheater where a free performing-arts series is held every year. The San Francisco Symphony is scheduled to play. Characteristically, we do not research what physical obstacles this venture may entail; we still have a habit of doing things on the spur of the moment.

Michael wants to drive to the city. He's usually the one to drive, and we don't anticipate his need to conserve energy for the day ahead. He reasons that morning is his best time to be active, before the heat of the day sets in. It has been a warm summer this year, even in San Francisco. When we stop at the local ATM, he's already stressed by the hometown traffic. By the time we hit the freeway, he's spewing invectives at other drivers and is clearly upset. Suddenly, he asks whether I brought the restaurant guide from last Sunday's newspaper. I have not.

"In a week, neither one of us could get it in the car?" he exclaims, his frustration clearly on the rise.

I try to placate him by recalling some of the restaurants named on the list. The first one I mention, however, is the one he swore he'd never go back to. My second suggestion is met with stony silence. This is nothing new. Traffic always produces stress in Michael, and he often becomes angry with me as well. His anger is usually expressed as accusations or silent withdrawal. By this time, I know that MS makes people unable to deal with multiple stimuli and that attempting to do so results in frustration and stress; stress, in turn, worsens the symptoms. Despite this knowledge and my resolve not to let Michael push my buttons, my feelings are hurt, and I react with tears I try to hide.

By the time we get on the San Francisco Bay Bridge, traffic has thinned, and he has calmed down. Feigning ignorance, he asks me what's wrong. I tell him evenly that I'm having a hard time dealing with his irritation and impatience. There was a time in our lives when, at this point, he would have turned the car around and headed for home. I would have accused him of acting unreasonably and ruining our day, and he would have responded with counteraccusations or more brooding silence. Instead, none of this happens.

"I realize what's going on," he tells me. "I'm just stressed over traffic."

Relief washes over me.

After we talk for a bit, he's over it, and things are back to normal. His growing ability to be more conscious of his reactions and to express his insights takes resolve and hard work. This will increase over time, and it will assist me in becoming more conscious of my own process. As long as we can communicate what's going on inside, we can stay ahead of the game. We aren't always able to do this—but, thankfully, this time we are.

We make a brief stop to pick up lattes and muffins at our favorite bakery, Il Fornaio, just off the Embarcadero and then head toward the ocean side of San Francisco. We find a place to park about two blocks from where people are entering the grove carrying baskets, chairs, and other picnic paraphernalia. Unfortunately, we haven't planned ahead and have none of these accoutrements. Nevertheless, we park and set off, Michael walking ahead with the aid of his two hiking poles.

The asphalt path down to the bowl-shaped grove proves to be steep, winding, and long. Michael proceeds slowly and carefully, becoming more and more silent. I become increasingly concerned, wondering what we have gotten ourselves into. *How will he possibly get back up? Why go all the way down if we probably won't be able to get back up? Not only haven't we brought food, I also haven't researched the site, and we are completely unprepared for the terrain.* As crowds of people pass us on the way down, I express my concerns to Michael, but he ignores me and plods on unsteadily, saying very little, which increases my anxiety. Upon reaching the bottom, we find a log to the back and side of the large area that fronts the stage. Michael sits down on the log and is very still and quiet. I don't know what's going on with him, and fear begins to well up inside me. I don't know what to do! I sit down beside him, and at that moment, I notice a road near the path. I offer to go back and pick him up with the car. Looking at the road, I notice a bus bringing seniors and disabled people down from the street level. If we had only known about that before starting down the path! At least we will be able to take the bus back up.

"No," he finally replies to my offer to bring down the car. "We're here, and we'll stay."

Yet the fact that he keeps closing his eyes and then staring ahead without expression contradicts his resolve.

*Should I get the car anyway?* I have no idea what is going on with him or how to take care of him at this moment, and my anxiety increases. *If he collapses, what should I do?*

Finally, he begins to talk to me. "I couldn't have moved even if I had wanted to," he tells me. "All I needed was to rest awhile, and sitting on this log is just fine."

"So, when something like this happens," I say, "I should just wait it out?"

"Yes," he says, his head still drooping. He adds that he's fine; we're in the shade, and the log doesn't press on the wrong parts of his legs, like most chairs do.

I begin to relax, realizing that sometimes he'll get so tired from exertion that he'll just have to rest on the spot. Fatigue, from exertion or for no apparent reason, will become a constant companion in his life. It's a symptom all people with MS and those near to them must learn to expect and accommodate. In the days to come, we also discover that eating will often cause Michael to become fatigued. Apparently, the body spends so much energy digesting the food it has little left for anything else. Fortunately, he didn't eat much before we began the long walk down, but still, the food is probably having its effects.

He mentions that because of the stress of driving he already felt tired before he began the walk down. But he was determined to make it and had to focus all of his attention on not falling because he knew he wouldn't be able to get up.

After he assures me he's all right, I feel much better. Our position on the log turns out to be just fine; we have excellent seats to hear the symphony, but we can't see a thing. I am only grateful we didn't pick a day when the ballet was performing.

After the concert, we take the shuttle bus up the hill and return to the car somewhat rested. I drive home. Michael only experiences stress one more time, when traffic is disrupted due to the Gay Pride Parade. Not expecting this either, we make the mistake of driving through downtown.

Lessons learned: Research, plan ahead, be prepared, stay mindful, keep communication open, and keep on truckin'.

Michael is becoming a different person as a result of experiences like the one at Stern Grove. He slowly begins the long process of seeing himself differently. The first time he had to revise his self-image was when the company for which he'd worked for twenty-six years went out of business, and he'd remained unemployed for many months. His role as a truck driver had long been the basis of his identity. He filled his time by riding his bicycle along the country roads near our house, but he had time on his hands and was uncomfortable not working. When he did go back to work for other companies, he put all his energy into his new jobs, viewing his increasing fatigue and weakness on the job with rationalizations and denial. He insisted that just a good night's sleep and more exercise would surely put him back at the top of his game. Or it was the seat in his truck that screwed up his legs. Or he just hadn't adjusted to working nights. Or it was drinking too much coffee that made his legs jump. The time for rationalization and denial is over. His working life is finished and done.

At this point, he's even more unsure of who he is. Once a person who commanded attention for his good looks, height, and take-charge manner, he's suddenly attracting attention for entirely differ-ent reasons. People seem annoyed by his slowness, such as when he holds up the line at the supermarket, fumbling in his wallet for the right cards. Yet often the type of attention he attracts includes generosity and compassion from people who hold doors open for him or offer assistance in a myriad of other ways. In the past, he was never one to accept help. He could function on his own, and he saw himself as always in control. Acknowledging his need for assistance is hard at first and accepting it even harder, but gradually he comes to appreciate help—and, much later, to rely on it. Learning to appreciate the kindness of others also increases his own generosity and compassion. Gradually, he becomes a more caring person and comes to acknowledge this change in himself as one for the better.

My own father had neurological problems similar to Michael's. He had difficulty walking and, when Michael and I got married, was using a cane. While we were visiting my parents at their house one day, my father came back from the grocery store and, embarrassed and discouraged, told us he had fallen down in the aisle. Michael had seen my father maneuver around his own house very well, and later Michael confided in me that he didn't believe my father had fallen in the store. Now, years later and dependent on his hiking poles, Michael recalls this time and tells me he knows there's a big difference between getting around familiar surroundings and trying to maneuver in public places.

"I wish I had gotten to know Bob better," he says, referring to my father. "I understand what he was going through." By now, Michael has fallen down many times and is afraid he might seriously hurt himself.

As Michael learns how to operate within the limits of his disability, he comes to value the things he can still do. Often, he says to me, "I'm going to do what I can today because I don't know what I'll be able to do tomorrow."

More and more, he comes to concentrate on those things that are doable: With two hiking poles, for instance, he can still walk at Lake Chabot, our local recreation area, and we can still go out to dinner, to museums and concerts, and even on vacation. He is constantly testing himself to see whether his limits have changed, to find new limits, and to excel within these newfound boundaries. As his world opens up, so does mine, and once again I have hope for our future.

# Chapter 8
# How, Not If

July sees Michael determined to turn his diagnosis into a wake-up call rather than a death sentence. He will discover new information, make judgments, and take action. For example, MS has already affected his short-term memory, and he can remember only part of what the doctor tells him during appointments. Accordingly, he has asked me to be his memory backup.

After a recent visit to Dr. Nichols, the neurologist, I went over his explanation of MS. Multiple sclerosis, we learned, is thought to be an autoimmune disease in which T cells attack the myelin sheaths around the nerves, mistaking them for foreign invaders. After getting this down, Michael began spending time "talking to" his T cells to put them back on the right track. I have always been impressed by his ability to visualize, and I'm glad he's using it to promote his own healing; I know of studies in which imaging has affected autonomic functioning in a positive manner.

Because he finds he is forgetting more and more lately, Michael forms a new habit of making lists, carrying a day planner with him wherever he goes, and making notations of things he wants to remember or do.

Because he can still walk up the hills at Lake Chabot with the assistance of his two hiking poles, he feels things are not so bad after all. He sees the benefit in no longer having to work and his good fortune in being able to enjoy the outdoors, despite his physical limitations: "Early retirement with a twist," he calls it. He experiences a wonderful sense of accomplishment when he's first able to crest a particularly steep hill on the outskirts of the park. One day he returns from a walk up that hill and tells me of a special meeting he had with a calf. (Ranchers use parts of the Chabot Regional Park for grazing land, and it's now calving season.)

"I stood watching some cows and their calves on the other side of that wood-and-wire fence at the top of the hill," he tells me. "One adventurous little guy was really curious, and he came right up to me. I just stood there without moving, and he came right up and put his soft little calf nose on my leg."

I sensed this had been a special moment for both of them. For some reason, Michael has always felt a mysterious connection with cows.

"I used to worry about inconsequential things," he tells me. "Now I don't worry about anything anymore except myself, and I think I'm doing the right thing for myself right now. MS has really put things in perspective for me."

As Michael comes to terms with the changes in his body and the limitations to his mobility, at times he rejects being comforted, feeling he has to remain strong and tough it out. He usually prefers to do routine activities of daily living without my assistance, even though he might struggle or they might take him an inordinate amount of time. "What if you weren't here?" he reasons. "I have to do as much as I can by myself."

It's not easy; I want to jump in and help, but I resolve to let Michael do as much as he can for himself. I want to bolster his sense of control and self-esteem; I want him to be as independent as possible.

Michael is not one to accept much sympathy, either, even from me. "I don't want consoling," he insists. "I just want understanding and acceptance." I try to give him those things, even though so often I just want to comfort him and tell him everything will be all right. "Don't *ever* feel sorry for me," he says.

He likes to recall the words of Sogyal Rinpoche from *The Tibetan Book of Living and Dying*: "If you're wearing the eyeglasses of suffering, you see everything as suffering." We are beginning to realize that attitude shapes experience.

I am so inspired by Michael's courage and determination and his refusal to give into self-pity or to accept anyone else's pity. Even though I'm afraid of what the future may bring and I grieve our loss of the future we had planned, I try hard to maintain a hopeful and positive approach to the challenges our new life presents. I research the disease, try new diets for him, fill out disability forms, discuss alternative approaches to healing, and do the million other things that have to be done. But mostly I see Michael as Michael, not as a disabled person. Our marriage hasn't changed, just our situation. He's still my husband, but he's coping with new problems and finding new solutions, and I'm right here with him every step of the way. We're definitely in this together.

Michael has always been one to push himself to the limit and beyond, as in his struggles to climb the hills at Lake Chabot. When we first met, I knew nothing about hiking, backpacking, or camping; it was Michael who introduced me to the wonderful world of outdoor adventure. This fit perfectly with my own love of nature and being outdoors. My father grew nectarines, cherries, apricots, walnuts, corn, and tomatoes. When I was a child, my bedroom window looked out on the nectarine trees, and I came to know and love the seasonal changes: the cyclical rhythm of dormancy, blossoming, and the bearing of fruit. I spent many hours in the orchards, alone with my dog and my imagination, reluctantly returning to the house only when I heard my mother ring the dinner bell. I loved to explore the wonders that grew from the soil and to sit against a tree and feel the hot sun wash over me as I watched birds wing in and out of view, disappearing and reappearing among the green leaves and brown branches.

So I took to camping and hiking naturally. Michael always walked ahead, always wanted to push on to the limit of his endurance, and often insistently pushed me beyond where I thought I could go.

"We're almost there," he would encourage me when I began to complain. Or, "It's all downhill after this one." (*Yeah, right.*) Or, "Look sharp, now, there are people up ahead on the trail."

I loved feeling my legs growing stronger, finding out what was just around the bend, or easing naked into the cold, clear waters of the Stanislaus River, stretching out in a natural granite pool after a hot and challenging hike.

During our first, shimmering summer, when we were so newly in love, Michael took me to the Stanislaus River for the first time. I remember the excitement of being together, the high of being in love, the pungent smell of the pines, and the wonder of the rushing river that cut through the rugged granite boulders. We would make love in the shade under a tree or inside our tent or, once, against the rocks beneath the trail—where we were momentarily discovered and, fortunately, ignored. We cooked over campfires or the Bluet stove and slept intertwined under the shooting stars. We never doubted for a moment that we would always come back to our river, roam its trails, and sink thankfully into its refreshing waters. And we did go back—often—but all too soon, we could return only in our memories and in our dreams.

Another place Michael and I loved to visit was Half Moon Bay on the California coast south of San Francisco and north of Santa Cruz. Before MS, Michael and I had spent many happy hours wandering its beaches, biking its nearby mountain trails, following its creeks, and exploring the shops and restaurants of the cozy seaside town. Michael was not one to give up on these adventures, but how we managed them was destined to change.

We haven't gone to Half Moon Bay since Michael was diagnosed with MS, so today we decide to give it a try. We get up early and share a fruit and yogurt drink and bagels for breakfast. When we arrive after less than an hour on the road, we are met with one of those extraordinarily clear and gorgeous days at the coast. Driving along Highway 1, we marvel at the profusion of wildflowers that have spilled their colors across the countryside. The ocean and sky seem to merge in a clear and endless blue.

Eating well is an integral part of going to Half Moon Bay. First, we stop in town for lattes at McCoffee's, which we pair with some fruit bars from the bakery next door and enjoy on a nearby sidewalk bench. Then we head to the San Benito House to pick up a couple of sandwiches. The San Benito House is a historic hotel in the center of town known for its delicious, overflowing sandwiches made on home-baked whole wheat bread. But these are for later; now we are off to the ocean.

South of Half Moon Bay, Pebble Beach is one of our favorite destinations. It's a small beach, strewn with millions of pebbles of various shapes and hues. The endless ocean waves have pockmarked a section of rough, flat rock near the water's edge. Pebbles glisten inside these holes, their colors intensified by a veneer of saltwater. Occasionally, sea lions bob and bark near the shore, and the air smells of brine and seaweed. It feels good just to be here, to walk down the gentle steps carved out of the rugged cliffs that enclose the beach. It's a magical place that we're always excited to visit and explore.

But this time, the steps down to the beach look too formidable, and we decide to walk along the trail to the south that runs just above the water. Michael is using his hiking poles, and we're moving slowly. The path is flat but full of ruts that are treacherous for him to maneuver, due to his faltering sense of balance. His left foot begins to drag more and more as we proceed; nevertheless, he continues for about a third of a mile before turning back.

We eat our sandwiches quietly in the car, looking out to sea and watching the seals. With the windows down, the car is cooled by a soft sea breeze, and we're happy just to be here and to be together. After eating, Michael feels tired and decides to nap for a while. I, meanwhile—always searching for answers—read Andrew Weil's book *Spontaneous Healing*. (Later, after reading it himself, Michael will credit portions of the book for helping him to regain a sense of control.)

After his nap, Michael is up for more adventure. We decide to drive up Higgins Road to a redwood park in the coastal range where we used to mountain bike. We choose to walk the broader fire road next to the creek instead of the trail. I've never seen it so lovely here. There are a multitude of flowers and ferns growing along the gently moving creek that meanders along one side of our path. From time to time, we see miniature waterfalls percolating up from hillside springs and trickling down into the creek. At one point, we stop at an especially lovely place, where fallen redwood logs offer us a seat. While Michael rests, I take off by myself for a short exercise walk. The dirt road is smooth, and I feel comfortable leaving him alone by the creek. I take Michael's watch with me so I won't be gone for more than twenty minutes.

On my way back, I'm surprised to meet him walking toward me. He says it's nice to just walk alone at his own pace and adds that sometimes when we hiked—before we knew what was wrong—I would look back at him with impatience and disapproval. I know that's true; I hadn't understood why he was walking so slowly, when usually he was the one to wait for me. He often attributed it to having gotten out of shape, and I didn't understand why he was letting himself go since exercising had always been a priority for him.

At least now we know what's really going on, and we can be easier on each other and on ourselves. We vow that as each new limitation arises, we'll find a way to accommodate it so we can continue to be active and adventurous. Life becomes a question of how—not if—we can do what we've always loved to do.

# Chapter 9

# Perspective

As we move toward summer's end, the normal tasks of daily living steadily become harder for Michael, and my time seems to overflow with paperwork and worry.

Applying for state disability compensation, for instance, is especially stressful. We go through a long process, lasting many months, of navigating the system and filling out endless forms for Michael to receive benefits. Throughout, more and more of the planning, scheduling, and work falls to me; Michael is just not able to handle it by himself. Because of his short-term memory loss and confusion, he is unable to plan ahead, and he becomes overloaded when presented with more than one task at a time.

One evening at dinner, I mention that one of us should call Dr. Nichols to get the state disability payments extended. I want to stay on top of this so we will continue to get his weekly checks. He becomes agitated and insists he doesn't want an extension until after he sees the doctor again; he worries it might look as if he's "trying to con" the doctor. Then he reasons that, since we haven't even gotten our first check yet, we shouldn't be concerned about an extension. The atmosphere in the room becomes strained, and I can feel the tension in my stomach as I give up on eating. To smooth things over, I say we will do whatever he wants, and if we do miss a week, it will be no big deal. He just sits there at the table for a while, and I know he's controlling himself, trying not to criticize me. Then he says he's tired and goes to lie down, leaving me with the half-eaten dinner I had taken special care to prepare.

I'm left with many feelings: anger because he didn't finish his dinner (and, therefore, appears not to appreciate my work and time spent preparing it), frustration that he won't help me deal with the doctors and state bureaucracy in a timely manner, hurt that he's angry with me, and frightened because he isn't making sense. I feel alone, realizing I might have to make most of the major decisions from now on and be responsible for getting everything done. In the future, there will indeed be times I will feel the weight of his growing dependence on me and the increasing responsibilities—for him, for earning and managing our money, and for seeing that a myriad of things get done.

It's August, over two and a half months since his diagnosis, and I'm concerned that Michael still doesn't seem to realize how ill he is. He insists on taking things step by step. I remind myself that even before we knew he had MS, he would become upset if anyone wanted him to deal with B before A. For him, it's always one thing at a time; even an abrupt change of topics during a conversation can throw him off. Perhaps that was MS all along (*How long had he had it?*) or perhaps just a masculine need to be linear. As frustrating as this is, however, more upsetting is Michael's idea that he might be seen as "conning" his way into disability payments. No one would ever accuse him of that; it's all too obvious that he would be a danger on the highway if he ever got behind the wheel of a truck again. But he can't see himself that way. Not yet. At times like these, he slips into denial, and it blinds him to the reality of his situation.

Knowing that I'll be going back to work at the end of summer *and* taking care of all the burdens that await us suddenly seems too much to bear. Yet, upon further reflection, I realize that, above all, I'm glad I'm here to help him through this. He would never be able to do it alone, and we can talk about all this again when he isn't tired out from a long, hot day. It's all about perspective and timing, I remind myself.

"It all happened so fast," he says the next day, referring to his physical decline. I notice then he's developed a new facial expression, which I identify as "sad determination"—his version of keeping a stiff upper lip.

The next morning, he goes for a walk at Lake Chabot, leaving early, before it gets too hot. When he comes home, after lunch and a brief rest, he says I should call Dr. Nichols about the disability extension. "I don't want to miss a payment," he says.

Michael manages to remain positive much of the time, but he has his moments of depression. I can see it in his artwork. Michael keeps an art journal in which he draws with ink and colors with pastels. His art comes directly from his unconscious; it's his way of expression, his way of letting out his feelings. Lately, his journal has been filled with jagged lines, dark colors, and maze-like structures that remind me of Escher's paintings: dimensions confused, no exit possible. He does these without comment, uninterested in analyzing them. Sometimes I tell him what I see, but he's already moved on.

I remind him that he can see this period of not working as a positive thing, even though there is so much bad in it. This appeals to him, and he begins to make plans to find ways to exercise and lose weight.

These are days of tiny triumphs and heartbreaking wins. Today is an especially hot day, and we spend most of it in bed watching a rented video. When it's over, Michael gets up to put on his clothes. "I'm going to take the video back now," he tells me.

Because he's unable to balance on one foot, he sits on the bed to dress. I watch him struggle to raise his legs as he tries to put on his shorts. I check my impulse to help him. He's told me he wants to do things on his own, without my help, as much as he can. After he manages to get his clothes on, he comments dryly, "The biggest accomplishment of my day: putting on my shorts."

All of a sudden, my breath catches and my eyes fill with tears. I feel so sorry for him; it saddens me so much that he has been reduced to this. I put my arms around him and ask him to hold me. I have been covering up this type of sorrow by trying to show him a positive, hopeful attitude—letting him do what he can on his own. Yet sometimes it just kills me to see him like this. Often, he'll reject my sympathy and attempts to comfort him, but at other times—like today—he ends up comforting me.

Suddenly, money becomes a worry; we'd always relied on our paychecks alone for living expenses, and we have only $600 in savings. Now I'm the principal breadwinner, the only one with a job.

More worries flood my mind, as if they are ganging up on me. I am still six years from retirement, but now the idea that I might have to work longer looms in my mind. I worry about leaving Michael alone when I'm at work. He's still driving our family car, and I worry he might become too tired to get home safely if he goes very far. I worry that he won't call me when I'm at work if he has a problem for fear of bothering or worrying me. He's always been self-reliant, and he doesn't like to be interfered with or told what to do. I worry that he won't eat correctly, that he'll fall and not be able to get up or even reach the phone, that he'll slip in the shower, and on and on. And I wonder what would happen to Michael if something happened to me.

# Chapter 10

# Accommodation

It is August 7, a short three months after Michael's collapse on the job. I was out for the afternoon, and when I get home, I'm relieved to find him in a really happy mood. With a flush of exuberance, he begins telling me what he's accomplished today.

Almost tripping over his words, he says, "I went to the video store and picked up some movies, bought some bottled water at the grocery store, drove to Montclair to have a latte and bagel for lunch, and then went to the health food store on my way home. I did all this and stopped at the DMV." Slowing down a bit, he adds, "I only had to use my hiking poles at the DMV."

He is very proud of himself; he believes he's getting better.

By five o'clock that evening his mood has done a 180-degree turn. We are both hungry, so I fix a simple dinner. After eating only half his meal, he becomes annoyed and irritated with me, glaring at the table and avoiding eye contact. Hoping to find a neutral topic, I offer to pick up some underwear for him tomorrow, and I ask him what size to buy; I don't know his size because he's only recently started wearing underwear. He prefers their unrestrictive absence, but urinary urgency is changing that.

He mumbles, "Forty-two, forty-four." I don't know exactly what this means and ask for clarification. He becomes very exasperated and snaps, "Forty-two *to* forty-four."

I can't believe this sudden anger, and I feel like I've been punched in the stomach. It seems only minutes ago that he was euphoric and bubbling over with enthusiasm.

"I feel like you're attacking me," I tell him.

"I didn't mean to hurt your feelings," he says, calming down.

Then he suddenly gets up and goes downstairs, leaving his unfinished dinner on the table. I eat the rest of mine, and then I eat the rest of his.

Later that night, he comes upstairs where I'm reading and says he wants to read, too, because he isn't interested in watching the videos he brought home. After a while, he gets up and heats some canned soup. He eats it, and then puts his head down on the table. He suddenly looks so dejected that I become concerned. I walk over and ask what's going on.

"I'm upset because you threw away my food," he tells me.

"I didn't throw it away," I reply. "I ate it."

He turns away and goes back downstairs. I feel rejected, thinking he obviously prefers to sleep alone rather than upstairs with me. In a little while, I venture down.

"I'm just tired. I'm not trying to get back at you," he tells me.

I'm grateful he isn't blaming me and making me wrong. "How about if I just lie down with you for a while and hold you?" I offer.

But he doesn't want that. My feelings are hurt, but I resist the urge to force a closer connection. I can see how tired he is. I kiss him goodnight and tell him to come upstairs if he changes his mind, no matter what time it is. No response. I crawl into bed alone.

As time goes on, I discover that mood swings are an inescapable part of life for people with MS and their caregivers. The symptoms include uncontrollable laughter and tears, angry outbursts, and sudden episodes of euphoria. It's difficult to know just what causes this emotional roller coaster. It could be the result of lesions in the brain in the areas that control emotions, or the biochemical abnormalities such lesions can cause. Or it might be the awful reality of the situation that dawns on him and throws him into despair. Michael has always had mood swings, but they seem to occur more frequently now and often hinge on his level of physical functioning. When he's at his best, he's riding high; when he's at his worst, he crashes emotionally as well as physically. His moods can change in the blink of an eye, and sometimes it seems to come out of nowhere. One minute he's up, and the next he's down. One day he functions well, and the next he has to stay in bed. I find that I, too, experience mood swings more often now, and my moods are usually tied to his. This is nothing new, but now it's more pronounced.

Mood swings are just one unpredictable aspect of living with MS. There are others, such as the sudden onset of fatigue. The last time we went out for dinner, Michael pigged out, eating his way through two appetizers, the main course, and on to his favorite dessert, crème brûlée. It was all he could do that night to make it home, get undressed—with my help—and get into bed.

If we are on the go all day without a break, this will also cause Michael to crash. It's particularly hard for him to take rest periods, as he's used to pushing himself to the limit. I remember when we were both in great shape and used to go mountain biking or hiking. He was always urging me to go just a little farther, up the next steep trail or around the next bend. He was always testing his limits, and, of course, mine too. Now fatigue can so overwhelm him that he has no choice but to stop. His goal becomes to rest well before he reaches the point where he crashes, but he often misses the mark. Since I'm his caregiver, it falls to me to remind him when it's time to take that break. Slowly, we learn what works and what doesn't.

As far as food is concerned, he decides to do some experimenting. He develops a pattern of eating three light meals a day, sometimes with small snacks in between. Eventually, he gives up meat all together; digesting rich food and red meat uses up all his energy. I, too, find being a vegetarian a natural transition.

Michael's Achilles' heel is the impulsive consumption of Cheetos and sweets. My role becomes that of nutritional consultant and impulse controller, which he simultaneously appreciates and resents. The year before his diagnosis, Michael had been working nights. There were few places to find food on the road, and he constantly fought weakness and fatigue. During this time, his eating habits were atrocious. He went for long periods fueled only by large amounts of coffee and chocolate-covered espresso beans, filled up on hamburgers and fries when he did find food, and rewarded himself with doughnuts and coffee in the early morning hours at the end of his shift. Needless to say, these eating habits only made him feel worse, and he gained weight. My offers to make him sandwiches for the road were usually rejected, and it wasn't until years later that I learned about the doughnuts.

My adjustment to all of these changes doesn't come easily. Slowly, I come to realize impermanence is real, whether it relates to physical functioning, moods, or what we choose to put in our mouths. How things go one day does not necessarily have anything to do with how things will go the next.

Not surprisingly, part of me rebels against taking on all the responsibilities inherent in meeting Michael's growing needs, on top of shouldering all the chores of daily life. Sometimes I even resent that all he has to do is deal with his MS and I have to do everything else—on top of dealing with his MS. I find myself afraid MS is going to dictate our whole lives, and I worry I won't be able to handle it. Maybe, too, I'm afraid he'll no longer be able to give me what I need from him.

Realistically, I can't expect the degree of emotional support from Michael I crave and I realize he has new needs and worries that frighten him. I'm sure he wonders how he's going to survive, let alone deal with my needs. His expectations of me are changing, as are my own for myself; I am now his caregiver, in addition to being his wife, lover, friend, and confidante.

Sometimes we both get so involved in our own dramas that we can't see the other person clearly. I always feel guilty when this happens because, after all, I'm not the one with the chronic illness. It's not my physical, mental, and emotional abilities that are compromised. I'm the one who's supposed to make things better; I'm supposed to be the fully functioning one.

This isn't really true. We're both in over our heads, and at times we each lash out at the other. Around this time—early August—Michael and I have one of those crazy arguments over nothing, and I tell him he's being unreasonable.

"There you go again, making me wrong," he shoots back. "Just leave me alone."

"You better be careful—you better not alienate me for your own good, you know."

"What are you talking about?" he demands.

"You might need me to take care of you sometime," I reply.

Suddenly my stomach clenches. *What did I just say?* The tension hangs between us; I'm ashamed of making this threat, even as I'm making it. I want him to really hear me, to take care of me instead of turning away—and here I am, threatening to do that very thing to him. He stares straight ahead, his face an impenetrable mask. I feel dismissed, as if physically pushed away. It won't be until much later that I will apologize and he will let that in.

As practical and emotional challenges increase, I become aware I could use some outside help. I don't have the resources within myself to meet all the challenges MS is throwing my way. I begin going to a psychologist for weekly visits. My therapist's approach is based on the psychology developed by Carl Jung. It's an approach that fits me well and one that will continue to benefit me. I believe my official diagnosis is "adjustment disorder," and it's true—I have a lot of adjustments to make, and I'm not shy about asking for help. Along with her ongoing guidance, my therapist teaches me two things: don't always take everything Michael does or says personally, and remember Michael is now operating from a basic level of need. He is coming from survival.

Shortly thereafter, both Michael and I join MS support groups and gain a great deal of emotional and practical assistance from others in similar situations. Michael's is a peer-led group that gathers once a month and is offered through the Oakland MS Society. Later, he will join a second support group that meets in Pleasanton, about the same distance from us, but in the opposite direction. My group is for caregivers and is called "Friends, Family, and Loved Ones of People with MS."

Support groups put us in touch with people who can relate to and understand our situation. The most important thing it offers Michael is emotional support as he goes through the inevitable and endless adjustments required in dealing with a progressive, chronic illness. Frequently, those who are further down the road than he is offer him glimpses of the future. At other times, he learns what it's like to live with symptoms he doesn't—and, hopefully, will never—have, such as blindness. It also gives him a chance to help others as he shares his own thoughts, symptoms, and insights.

Others' stories and knowledge provide a wealth of information, and the sharing that goes on in a support group is invaluable on both practical and emotional levels. For example, it was not through our neurologist that we learned about our HMO's highly regarded rehabilitation hospital; it was from someone in my MS caregivers' support group. Later, Michael will go to this facility on three separate occasions, and he will gain access to the equipment he needs and learn how to maximize his physical mobility and strength.

For my part, I learn that both patient and caregiver play interdependent roles, and together they establish a unique relationship. To make the relationship work, each person has to establish boundaries and feel empathy toward and receive support from the other. The best foundation for all of this, of course, is love.

# Chapter 11

# Time Out

It's mid-August, and we decide to go on a vacation to Lake Tahoe. We have fond memories of our early mountain biking adventures in the Sierras above the lake, picnics on the boulders at the lake's edge, and refreshing plunges into its ice-cold waters. We realize this time will be different—we can no longer do what we used to—but our longing to be by those sparkling blue shores pulls us on.

This is a chance for me to finally have my summer before I go back to work. I know I need a vacation. I need to wind down from the crazy medical ride we've been on, unwind from work, and get ready to go back again at the end of the month. All summer my focus has been on Michael, and our five days at Lake Tahoe will be a way to bring balance back into my life. I hope Michael understands how important this is for me.

I am really feeling overwhelmed. Our fairly egalitarian marriage has tipped, and too often I seem to be doing all the giving and Michael all the taking. Even worse, sometimes I feel emotionally abandoned by him.

A few days before we decided to go to Lake Tahoe, for instance, I was complaining about how all the housework seemed to be falling on my shoulders. "You can't even take out the garbage anymore," I said, immediately feeling guilty for saying this.

"I'm sorry," he replied sarcastically, quickly going downstairs and closing the door behind him. I followed him and started to apologize, but he cut me off with a hard look and an abrupt "Fine."

A couple of hours later, he seemed to have forgotten the whole incident.

The day before we leave, Michael is irritated again and withdraws without telling me why. Later that day, we're sitting on the bed, and he finally breaks his silence.

"Lie down with me," he says.

Relieved, I cuddle up to him, spoon fashion.

"Are you angry with me?"

I assure him I'm not.

"As we were planning to go out of the house, you said, 'Hurry up, Snookums.'"

Snookums is my pet name for Michael. I knew I had made this remark lightly, but I let him go on.

"That really pushed me over the edge. I was in the bathroom and having a really hard time peeing. When you said that, I just became overwhelmed. Everything I do takes so damn long, and it's so damn frustrating. Like telling my legs to move, and they won't. I feel like there are three Michaels inside me—one who just wants to go to bed and who can't deal with things, one who keeps urging me to get up and get going, and the physical body that won't work. Do you every feel this way—fragmented?"

"Yes, I do," I said. "One time, before we met, I had no energy, and I went to the doctor. He found out I had anemia. I remember being torn between wanting to give up and lie down and wanting to get up and get things done. I was struggling just to keep my head above water."

He gives me a gentle hug. We lie together quietly for a little while longer. Then he gets up, looking refreshed, and begins packing for our trip.

I stay on the bed for a few minutes, thinking about our recent arguments. When I criticize him, it just pushes him farther over the edge. I realize I need to be more patient and understanding, and I hope he can be too.

On August 18, despite everything, we embark on our vacation with renewed hope. Michael insists on driving the whole five hours from the Bay Area to Lake Tahoe. When he feels good, he wants to keep going, and today he's feeling good. When we finally arrive at the lake, we're both hungry so we drive to the West Shore Café, a place we'd been to before, but one I'd forgotten about until this moment. It's a lovely restaurant right on the lake, with a soothing water view. We ask for a table outside, but the only one they have is in partial sunlight. Exposed to the heat of the sun, Michael becomes fatigued and agitated. We ask the waitress to move us, and she assures us she will, but instead she disappears. We give up and disappear too, beaten, tired, and hungry.

Despite our earlier mistake, the bed and breakfast, the Chaney House, turns out to be a charming stone home on the West Shore of Lake Tahoe. I've read about this home, built in the 1920s by an

Italian stonemason, and I can hardly wait to see the interior. Michael pulls into the drive, and I get out to inquire within. As I approach the rounded stone portico, I see a note tacked to the thick wooden door that lets me know the owner is at the dock across the street.

When I return to the car with the news, Michael announces that he has to go pee—urgently. I wonder whether I should search inside for a bathroom or go out to the dock and ask our hostess to rush us to our room. As I stand there, trying to decide what to do, Michael takes off in the car.

"I can't wait," he calls out the window.

*Oh, shit.* I imagine a worst-case scenario in which his foot gets stuck on the accelerator and the car runs off the road and into the lake.

Surrendering to forces beyond my control, I find the owner and check us in. In a little while, a calm and dry Michael reappears, apparently unscathed by his ordeal.

As I'm wondering if we were ever meant to travel again, the owner, a cheerful lady in her mid-seventies, guides us past the living room with its massive stone fireplace reaching to the top of a Gothic cathedral ceiling, and shows us to a lovely large bedroom. I persuade Michael to lie down and take a nap.

As he sleeps, I enjoy having some time for myself. I explore the grounds, which are filled with pine trees, and play ball with the resident dog. At a small market close by, I buy some potato salad and bananas to take up and share with Michael. I'm sure he must still be as hungry as I am.

As Michael peels a banana and smiles at me before digging into the potato salad, I know I've done the right thing. True to his Irish heritage, Michael relishes potatoes—baked, fried, or *en salade.*

Refreshed from his nap and snack, Michael is reenergized. He gives me that sly grin I know so well, and we tumble back into bed. After making love, we lie holding each other. Life feels good again. A little later, we go out for dinner, stopping to partake of a glass of wine and some cheese in the charming downstairs parlor.

We go back to the West Shore Café. The food turns out to be too rich and too expensive, but the view and the ambiance make up for it.

Back at the B&B, we sleep comfortably in our king-size bed. The only problem is that Michael's legs are restless and jerk frequently, waking us both up several times during the night.

The next day, unlike the first, turns out to be a winner in the food department. Our hostess serves us chile rellenos, fruit, muffins, coffee, and orange juice on the garden patio. Breakfast is delicious and graciously presented. Afterward, Michael sits in the living room reading the *San Francisco Chronicle*, and I go for a walk on the bike path along the lake. Then we change into swimsuits and spend the early afternoon on the B&B's private dock. While I swim, Michael relaxes in one of two large chaises, cooled by a welcome breeze off the lake. After a while, he decides to try the water. Its chill allows him to walk in the shallows and even attempt some swimming, but his legs refuse to kick. By the time I get out of the water, Michael has warmed up again on the chaise. But the wind has picked up, and I'm feeling chilled. Under my towel, I change into shorts and a tee. I lie down on top of Michael, pull up my shirt, and warm my breasts on his warm, hairy chest. *How wonderful it is to be here,* I think, *to be together, and to be in love.*

Later, back in our room, Michael surprises me by suggesting we go exploring. It seems the cold water, as always, was restorative. I've read about the Rubicon Trail in Bliss State Park, so I suggest we explore there. Back in the car, we follow the scenic road to the entrance of the park. The trail is easily accessible from the parking lot, and it turns out to be a well-packed dirt trail that climbs gently through the pine forest and granite rocks that border the sparkling blue lake. About fifteen minutes into our walk, however, it becomes too difficult for Michael to follow, even with his hiking poles. Rather than becoming discouraged, Michael is glad just to be here, surrounded by nature.

"I thought I would never get to be in this type of terrain again," he muses.

I know how much he wanted to go back to the Flume Trail, where we used to mountain bike, but he knows he can never do that again. Yet here we are—not as high as the Flume Trail, but above the lake among the boulders and trees. He seems content as he looks out over the water, resting on a granite seat, holding his poles. At this moment, I feel so much love for him that it hurts.

We spend a couple more blissful days at our B&B before settling into other accommodations closer to old haunts where we used to mountain bike. We are a little wistful at times, but mostly we are curious and ready for new experiences.

After an exploration of Tahoe City and a visit to see the giant trout that swim under Fanny Bridge (so called, I believe, because of all the people who lean over the side to watch the fish), where Lake Tahoe spills into the Truckee River, I look forward to relaxing in the big soaking tub in our room. As I soak in the hot water, Michael keeps me company. I know he misses being able to join me, but, because of MS, the hot water would wipe him out. I can't begin to count the hours we shared in hot tubs and natural hot springs during our years together. I can tell he's enjoying my soak, and he's happy that I'm happy.

Finally, we embark on our journey home, this time with me at the wheel. We will miss the fresh, pine-scented air, the clear skies, and the crystal-blue lake, but our memories of this time stack up well against the others.

# Chapter 12
# Serpent

It's fall of '96 and I'm back at work. My days of teaching remedial reading are long over, due to changes in funding priorities. For some time now, I've had a split assignment: teaching psychology at the high school in the morning and writing grant proposals for my school district in the afternoon. I have a space at the district office for the latter, complete with my own computer and phone. Meanwhile, Michael sets up several tasks to gauge whether he's holding his own or getting worse. One of these is attempting a long walk leading to one of our favorite beaches in Half Moon Bay.

It's late on a Sunday afternoon, and he has just come home. As soon as I see him coming into the house, I know things did not go well. He seems tired, and he's holding his head down, walking carefully, and using his hiking poles for balance. "I was really feeling good, and knew I could do this," he tells me. "But it was hotter than I thought it was going to be. I got down the steps to the beach all right, and I was having a good time, but everything turned to shit on the way back. My feet began to drag, and it was all I could do just to make them move at all. I fell down twice, once on the sand and once on the steps."

He lies down on the bed, and I begin to rub his legs. His muscles involuntarily tighten and release, tighten and release, over and over, with a spasticity that jolts him with pain. I think this must drive him crazy, and I wish with all my heart I could relieve him of his disappointment and suffering.

A few weeks later, we have an appointment with the doctor who will determine Michael's eligibility for Social Security disability benefits. I look at Michael incredulously as he tells me of his plans to present himself at his worst so he will be sure to qualify. I realize he still doesn't see himself as truly disabled—despite his recent setback, he just doesn't understand that he's as bad off as he is.

As we discuss his answers for the long Social Security form I'm filling out for him, he begins to feel more and more discouraged. Soon his answers make it evident, even to him, that he's truly unable to work.

The next day Michael goes through the physical exam. The result is quite conclusive: Michael is qualified to receive disability pay. The hardest part for me to watch is the memory test. At the beginning of the exam, the doctor gives Michael three items to remember. At the end of the exam, Michael can remember only two. I squirm inside as I watch him grope for the answer and, finally, realize that he just can't remember.

A few days later, we learn that the government office claims not to have received our application, but a second submission is successful. (I learn the importance of keeping copies.) Soon Michael also qualifies for an early, but small, Teamster pension, and later, for Medicare.

Michael's primary care doctor has prescribed some medications that seem to ease his fatigue, but it isn't until October that he is prescribed baclofen. This medication handles his spasticity quite well, although it always starts up again before it's time for more pills. As his MS progresses, he will need higher and higher doses. Some people with MS require the installation of a baclofen pump that delivers continual doses of the drug—along with morphine—to the spine. Michael is able to tolerate high oral doses and take Vicodin for pain, so he never has to undergo surgery for the pump. There are some drawbacks, however, as there always are with medication, and Michael finds that the baclofen makes him weaker. Because it's a muscle relaxant, it's important to take enough—but not too much. Instead of following directions, however, Michael starts to take it "as needed" and increases the dosage accordingly. This worries me, but it turns out to be a habit Michael will follow with most of his drugs. It seems to work for him, though, and he always reviews his dosages with his neurologist when he goes in for his appointments.

Before starting baclofen, Michael has a particularly vivid dream in which he fixes the engine of an airplane that can't fly. At first, he's frustrated that the engine doesn't run, and he doesn't know how it works. Suddenly the dream changes, he's able to fix the engine, and the plane can fly again. After that Michael seems to feel more positive—and with baclofen giving him some measure of relief, his dream seems to be coming true.

Around this time, Michael asks me if I would like to take a workshop with him about sex and chronic illness. Sex has always been an exciting part of our relationship, a powerful way to express our love through physical intimacy. I sign us up immediately, eager to learn ways to cope with what we both know will be new and inevitable challenges. Much to our disappointment, however, although the workshop offers reminders about good communication skills, it's sorely lacking in practical information. The presenter seems painfully uncomfortable with the topic and mainly just encourages us to find alternative ways of expressing love. That's great—unless, of course, you want to have sex. If we wanted to, I'm sure we could present a *much* more useful workshop ourselves.

As it turns out, we do pretty well on our own, and for me all the stresses of being a caregiver wash away when we come together in body and spirit. There's a wonderful store for sex toys in San Francisco and Berkeley called Good Vibrations. We shopped there before MS, and it continues to offer us creative resources.

I remember one time when we were shopping there, Michael found some sexy lingerie he wanted me to buy. He held it up, moving the outfit back and forth on its hanger to get my attention, an inquisitive expression on his face and a gleam in his eye. He was being playful and completely unselfconscious, which quickly dispelled any embarrassment on my part.

Now that I'm back at work, Michael seems to be getting more independent and takes pride in doing things on his own. He spends time reading *The Tibetan Book of Living and Dying*, highlighting meaningful passages and using these teachings as jumping-off points for inner exploration. In the mornings, he often tells me his dreams, and we explore their meaning. One Sunday, after sleeping alone because his legs have been jerking all night, he comes upstairs and snuggles in bed with me. After we cuddle and go over our dreams, he takes a shower and goes out for a short time. When he returns, he has the paper and a caffe latte for me. We spend a good part of that day in bed; I prepare for my classes, and he reads the paper. It's a fine Sunday, and all is calm.

I'm aware of how often my emotional state mirrors Michael's, so

I'm relieved that, despite his setbacks, Michael's attitude is improving, and he seems positive most of the time. He's becoming more in charge of—and less discouraged by—his MS. He recently started physical therapy, and he's learning how to strengthen his muscles and increase his balance. On his own, he's begun a rigorous physical-fitness program that includes walking with his hiking poles at Lake Chabot. He's getting stronger and developing more stamina.

Michael's take-charge attitude extends to looking forward to his future. Whenever he can, he insists on doing things for himself. Sometimes I still rush in to help him when he struggles to put on a sweater, wash his clothes, or make his bed, but he usually stops me. "What would I do if you weren't here?" he often asks. He doesn't want to become any more dependent on me than he has to; he wants to take care of himself for as long as he can. I admire him for that.

Michael seems to be turning inward more often. He meditates now on the Voyager tarot cards (contemporary cards composed of collage images from various spiritual traditions), draws in his sketchbook, and does some writing. He continues to take a more active role in his treatment and has sought the advice of a urologist for his urgency problems. He even makes a dental appointment, which is a breakthrough, as he has a long-standing fear of dentists. As a child, he raised such a fuss at the dentist's office that the dentist filled several of his teeth without drilling out the cavities. This, of course, led to more dental trauma. Now he's prone to anxiety attacks whenever he sits in a dentist's chair. The only time he remembers enjoying a visit to the dentist was when, years ago, a buxom dental assistant found it necessary to lean over him frequently in the course of her work.

On October 27, Michael and I attend a workshop given by a Jungian process-oriented therapist, Arny Mindell. The notation in my journal reads, "Best day ever!" Michael does some fantastic inner work. Using his imagination, he confronts his hypercritical father and realizes how his sense of self-worth was severely damaged in his early childhood.

Michael was a kid who loved to take things apart, trying to figure out how they worked; he liked to disassemble anything he found in the garage, from lawnmowers to screwdrivers, in his quest to discover and understand. He'd also strip trees of their bark to run his fingers over the smooth, wet wonders underneath. This behavior outraged his father, who chastised Michael and called him evil and destructive. Once, when Michael was about five years old, his father drove him far out into the countryside and threatened to kick him out of the car and abandon him because he was such a bad little boy.

Bringing these memories to consciousness helps Michael's psyche become more integrated. By being aware of how his boyhood self-image and fear of abandonment are still active in his unconscious, he is able to lessen their influence.

The Sanskrit term kundalini refers to a primal energy that resides at the base of the spine, coiled like a sleeping serpent. When awakened, this energy uncoils and moves up the central channel of the body to the top of the head. Often it feels like an electric current charging up the length of the spine. Although he has never delved into the Hindu religion or considered its practices, the night after the workshop, Michael has a strong kundalini experience. During sexual foreplay, he begins panting as a rush of energy uncoils from the base of his spine and surges up through his body. I realize what is happening, and I tell him to let the energy release through the top of his head. "Wow, it felt like a freight train traveling through my body," he says when he can finally speak. We hold each other as his breathing gradually returns to normal, feeling exquisitely close and connected. A lot of healing has taken place this day.

# Chapter 13

# New Year

As we enter November and approach the end of 1996, the weather cools, and I'm surprised that Michael is frequently irritated and angry, most often with me. With the break from the heat, I expected him to function better and have a more positive outlook. He's sometimes so angry that I'm afraid he'll turn against me—and not just verbally, but physically as well. I struggle to distinguish between what is acceptable and what is abusive. Because Michael has MS, am I supposed to take his verbal attacks in stride? People are always telling me to take care of myself or else I won't be able to take care of Michael. Does "taking care of myself" mean drawing clearer boundaries and letting him know what actions I will not accept? What does "will not accept" mean? Would I ever leave him? How do I draw boundaries, and how do I enforce them?

Sometimes I feel exploited and unappreciated. I wonder just what he expects me to do and what I should expect from him in return. Other times, I reproach myself for not loving unconditionally. I feel that I need to be there for him no matter what and that I'm supposed to do this selflessly. I often feel I'm at war with myself.

Being Michael's caregiver is new for me, and being someone who needs care is new for Michael. I guess it's going to take some time for us both to adjust to these new roles. Michael will need to give up some control—of his situation and of me—in order to let me do things for him that he can no longer do. I know this will be hard for him, but we will need to learn to work together if we are to meet the challenges of this disease. I hope that we can.

As the year comes to a close, we manage to get through the holidays on a cheerful note, connecting with family and learning to be patient with each other. Michael stands by with minimal criticism as I put the lights and decorations on the Christmas tree. Never one to relish Christmas, he is nevertheless agreeable and, at times, even festive. We have fun at a holiday party with friends from my teachers' union; Michael is always in good spirits among friends, and I enjoy watching how he interacts, joking and having a good time with others. We are not very social, so when we do get together with other people, it's a treat.

On Christmas, we have a quiet day. We connect with Zoie by phone. Everyone is excited about the birth of Zoie's baby, Michael's first grandchild—a boy. He was born just a few days before Christmas.

We look forward to the New Year with hope in our hearts.

On New Year's Day, 1997, I take out the Medicine Cards and deal a "Pathway Spread." These cards and the accompanying book are based on Native American spirituality and animal lore. Each card in the deck pictures an animal, and the qualities and lessons of each are described in the book. Since we're starting our first full year with MS as our companion, we do this practice to receive spiritual guidance for the year ahead. As a method of tapping into the unconscious and tuning into higher levels of perception, the Medicine Cards have often proved quite powerful for us.

I lay out the first spread for myself, hoping it will answer some of my nagging questions and offer some guidance.

The card that I deal to the east position is the deer—but upside down, or "in contrary." This speaks to me of a need to develop love, compassion, and gentleness rather than fear. I see this as related to my reactions to MS and to Michael's unpredictable emotional states. I feel I'm being offered an opportunity to align with the gentleness of the fawn and the heart space of a great spirit. It tells me to stop pushing others to change and to love them the way they are.

The south card shows I need to trust myself and nurture my growing process: to teach the child within. It is the ant, and it represents patience and tells me to trust that what is needed will be provided.

In the west, the place of internal solutions to present life challenges, is the eagle. The eagle represents spirit—a soaring to higher mind, wisdom, and compassion. This card foreshadows a shared spiritual journey that will reveal itself more fully in the years to come. For now, it reminds me to aspire to a higher level of relationship.

The north card is the elk. It teaches stamina—going the distance. The elk reminds me to pace myself, to not overburden myself, and to rely on friendship for strength. I relate this to maintaining balance: diet, exercise, and supportive friendships with other women. I will also have to go the distance with the disease, wherever that leads.

The present is represented by the "sacred mountain card," which is the snake. The snake is a powerful symbol of transformation, its presence offering me a transcendent view of living and coping with a chronic disease. We are most definitely beginning a process of transformation in our lives now, and its outcome remains unknown.

The next card reveals the forces working for me at this time. It is the raven—magic. Magic brings courage to enter the void, a change in consciousness, and healing guides who offer wellness. The raven is the courier of healing energy via smoke. I am reminded that healing and being cured are not the same thing; healing is wholeness at a deep, inner level.

The last card speaks of the energy working against me: coyote, the trickster and master of self-sabotage. Coyote also takes itself too seriously and sometimes cannot see the obvious. Hmmm . . . there's an uncanny resemblance to my own process here that's too relevant for me to miss.

This spread of the Medicine Cards holds wisdom and insight for us both. I feel supported and inspired after completing the process, at the dawn of this New Year. After I do my card spread, Michael shuffles the deck and lays them all out in an oval, face down. Then he picks one card at random. It is the deer, in contrary—the same as my first card.

A few days after reading the cards, Michael comes home with a small figurine of a fawn as a reminder for us to develop more gentleness with each other.

As the month goes on, we seem to be on a spiritual roll.

On the evening of January 20, a Sunday, Michael shares a new psychedelic CD by Trance Mission that he's just purchased. He lights candles, and our bedroom takes on a soft, warm glow as shadows lick the walls.

I undress first, then help Michael. We lie down on the bed and begin to stroke and caress each other. Placing our hands on each other's heart, we create a surprisingly vibrant connection. Gazing into each other's eyes, we feel a profound movement of energy surging between and within us.

Michael talks for a while about having been armored and closed off in his heart much of his life. His mother was distant, and he never heard his father say, "I love you."

A glimmer of sunlight drapes a warm glow over our bed as we talk, and our bodies mirror the tints of the setting sun.

"I love you so much," he murmurs, his mouth pressed to my ear. Then, slowly at first, we begin to make love, moving in time with the music.

I have been studying Tibetan Buddhism under the guidance of Sogyal Rinpoche for some time now. This January, with the advent of the New Year, Michael and I begin going together for lessons and meditation every Monday night. Michael is opening up to exploring and doing more; he realizes he has the time now to follow his true interests. He is realizing, too, that he has to live his life right now; he can no longer put things off.

To conserve his energy, he begins to rest each day, lying down from four to five in the afternoon while listening to a CD. Music has always been a passion for Michael, and he allows it to transport him to a safe and happy place. He begins to draw and paint more often, using colored pencils, pastels, and watercolors, and to write in his journal. Here is where he records his thoughts and feelings—and his suffering. It's a powerful coping strategy for him. He also buys and reads books with great zeal, following his interests in politics, spirituality, philosophy, and humor. Two of his current books are *Thoughts Without a Thinker* by Mark Epstein and *Meeting the Shadow: The Hidden Power of the Dark Side of Human Nature*, a compilation of essays on the Jungian archetype of the shadow, the unconscious part of the human psyche that we deny in ourselves and project onto others. We go to all sorts of movies or watch them together on TV. Michael has always loved films, and he delights in analyzing and deconstructing them. He seems to be coming into his own now, pursuing his interests with a passion that has been constrained for much of his life.

New medications are also helping Michael to cope. Hytrin, prescribed by his urologist, is working to regulate his urinary system. Baclofen continues to help alleviate his spasticity, and amantadine (Symmetrel) helps him fight fatigue.

At the end of the month, Michael's health seems to be holding steady. We go for a walk in the redwoods and kiss beneath my umbrella in the rain. It's the dawning of a new year, and things seem good. Michael is taking charge of his life again; he's taking the initiative, doing the things he loves, and following his diverse interests. Just a few months earlier, I had been feeling exploited and unappreciated. Now, at this moment, I feel more aligned with Michael than ever before.

# Chapter 14

# Curves

In late March, I have the following dream:

*I'm riding in a car as a passenger, and Michael is driving. We are going much too fast on a curving mountain road, speeding uphill in the outside lane. Thousands of feet below, I can see a beautiful valley, full of blooming yellow mustard, reminiscent of the Napa Valley in springtime. Then I see the edge of the cliff very clearly—and suddenly realize it's beginning to crumble. We are falling. We didn't make the turn, and the road is falling away beneath us. As we plummet downward, I say to Michael, "You are killing us!" I am shocked and frightened, and I know we will hit bottom soon. I stare at him. He has a strange, almost evil, smile on his lips. He shows no fear.*

Reflecting on this dream, I am aware that my world—my solid ground—is beginning to crumble under the weight of MS, and sometimes I feel as if I am out of control, falling into the unknown. Perhaps the demonic force that is MS has taken possession of Michael. Perhaps we are both hurtling toward destruction.

As we move toward summer, a new element is added to our lives in the form of a powerful medication. Michael starts weekly self-injections of Avonex, a drug that treats MS itself, not just its symptoms. Avonex is not a cure for MS, but clinical trials have shown it can decrease the number of exacerbations and slow the progress of the disease. It isn't the weekly injections that prove to be difficult, but rather the accompanying side effects. Michael's neurologist warns us that flu-like symptoms such as headache, fatigue, fever, chills, and muscle and joint aches may occur. This proves to be an understatement, and the recommended doses of Tylenol do little to help. Michael becomes, for all practical purposes, unable to function for two to three days out of every seven. During these times, he is often unable to sleep and wakes up at two, three, or four in the morning with hallucinations and suicidal thoughts. Usually he spends these nights in his downstairs bed, restless, depressed, and confused.

One night, he tells me he felt as if he were six years old again, sleeping in his childhood basement bedroom. Though still awake, he imagined his beloved granny coming downstairs to comfort him. He finds times like this disorienting and often draws in his journal afterward. A recurring image is of a black fish with red eyes and teeth that eat into his brain. This is the demyelination process, the stripping of the sheath that protects the nerves. Another image is a demonic face. Thick black lines funnel downward from the top of the paper tracing the upward arc of two empty ovals, blind eyes glaring menacingly above a mocking smile. The left eye is covered in a red wash. This is MS itself—Satanic and evil. Drawing from his lessons in Tibetan Buddhism, he meditates on these images, trying to obtain some degree of detachment and insight.

Despite the suffering, he tries to carry on and be active. On days he feels better, he continues walking at Lake Chabot, using both of his hiking poles and choosing easier trails. Usually he is active in the morning and rests in the afternoon, though he often pushes himself too far and for too long. He's dedicated himself to making our dinners and doing the shopping on his own whenever he can. In the grocery stores, he maintains his balance by leaning his weight on the shopping cart.

The "Avonex days" prove to be difficult for me too. On the third day after one of his weekly injections, Michael is withdrawn, uncommunicative, and walking with extreme difficulty.

"How are you doing, Snookums?" I ask.

He replies in a monotone, with no affect, "I'm fine." It's obvious to me that he's not fine. When he tells me he's going out to run an errand, I begin to protest.

"Why don't I come with you, and I can drive?"

Ignoring me and fumbling around for his keys, he leaves the house without another word. I feel conflicted: I don't want to let him drive, and yet, I don't want to go with him as his passenger. His current condition reminds me of my nightmare in which he nearly plunged us over a cliff. I remember times when I've gone along as his passenger and ended up fearing for my life. Lately, he tends to make poor judgments and to take unnecessary risks.

Fortunately, he isn't gone long, but when he returns he's exhausted. He lets me persuade him to lie down and take a nap.

Increasingly, I find myself arguing with him in situations like this. I really want to help, but he just won't let me. When he becomes annoyed with me or withdrawn, my feelings are hurt, even though I know he is struggling to find his way and to live his life on his own terms, as much as he can.

More and more I find myself asking him questions such as: Do you want me to open the door? Fix dinner tonight? Water the garden for you? What video do you want? Do you want me to drive? Do you want me to get that for you? Do that for you? Go with you? More often than not, I get a gruff or rude answer in reply. He becomes annoyed with my eternal questions, my hovering. Yet, on those occasions when I don't intuit what he wants, he becomes angry and accusative: "Couldn't you see I was having trouble with that? Why did you do that?"

I don't know which is harder for him, asking for help or accepting it. I think both put a spotlight on his needs, needs he doesn't want to acknowledge. Meanwhile, I continue to worry and feel inept, often lamenting to him, "You're not helping me to help you."

As he continues to suffer from the side effects of Avonex, I try to stay by his side when he leaves the house, and, at times, I am able to convince him to let me drive. At other times, he goes off on his own, and somehow everything turns out okay. But I shudder to think what would have happened if he had been alone one evening this past August in San Francisco.

We have come to the city to see the play *Three Tall Women* by Edward Albee at the Herbst Theater in Civic Center, taking BART—Bay Area Rapid Transit—from our home station in Castro Valley. It's approximately a four-block walk from the station to the theater, a walk Michael thinks he can manage. He almost can't.

As his progress becomes more difficult, he focuses more and more on the process of walking, looking down at the sidewalk and blocking out all other stimuli, including my voice. He walks right through a homeless encampment in front of City Hall, paying no attention to me when I tell him to follow me to the right to get back on the sidewalk. The sun is in his eyes, and he is only aware of walking and of the sun. I, of course, stay by his side.

Our outing started off poorly—so, I think, this is perfectly in tune. Both elevators at the Civic Center BART station, the one to the upper level and the one to the street, are filthy and reek of urine.

When we finally get near the theater, I realize Michael isn't thinking clearly at all and he needs to sit down. I suggest he go across the street to Stars Café and rest there; I'll pick up the tickets and meet him in a few minutes. Fortunately, he takes my advice. He's exhausted, and the play won't start for another forty-five minutes, anyway. When I return with the tickets, I join him and get to relax with a glass of wine before the performance.

Somewhat revived, we enter the theater, where I know he can rest and stretch out his legs, as I have reserved an aisle seat for him. Much to my consternation, his seat is not on the aisle at all. We are seated, instead, in the middle of a balcony row shoved up against the wall. Michael remains passive, saying in a monotone that it's "okay." Well, it isn't. I realize I'll have to do something, and I tell the usher we've been assured an aisle seat by the ticketing agency, and my husband obviously needs the leg room—because of his six-foot, five-inch frame, his knees are shoved toward his body in an untenable position. The kind usher goes to check with the manager and comes back to tell me I should check with the box office for an available aisle seat. Over Michael's weak protestations, I do this. With difficulty, Michael gets up, and we descend the theater's levels via a clean elevator. This time, one of the seats is on the aisle. We get seated just before the curtain rises.

After all this, we find the performance to be dreadful and boring.

Leaving the theater afterward, we try for a taxi to BART, but to no avail. So we walk. Back down the urine-soaked elevator we go.

Now—not at the theater, but now—Michael has to go the bathroom. The station agent informs us the bathroom is a block away in the opposite direction from the second elevator that will take us to the platform. Michael decides to tough it out, but I know this isn't going to work.

When we reach the second elevator, I notice an employees' bathroom. Interestingly, the only clean area in BART seems to be this employees' area. I notice a custodian nearby. On impulse, I ask him to let Michael use the employees' bathroom. I explain that it's an emergency and my husband is disabled. Graciously, he helps us out and unlocks the bathroom door.

After thanking this person profusely, we suffer the elevator ride down to the platform. We sit and wait—and wait and wait. I begin to wonder whether our train is running at all. Michael seems uninterested and continues to sit, passively waiting. I get up and try to contact the station agent on the BART phone, but it's dead. A few minutes later, someone asks us a question about the system and, in trying to help this person, I discover the time schedule. Our train was supposed to have come at 11:06 and it is now 11:15. The next, and second to last, train is supposed to arrive at 11:26. I'm worried, but Michael is oblivious. Just then, I notice a uniformed BART policeman complete with canine. At first, I hesitate to ask him for information because he looks so formidable. Nevertheless, summoning my courage, I approach him, and he turns out to be a pussycat. I learn that, due to track work, there will be *no* more trains out of this station that will take us home to Castro Valley. We need to get on the next train that comes and transfer on the other side of the bay. I've heard no announcements about this, but then we couldn't have heard them anyway because the station's PA system is unintelligible tonight. The electronic message boards do not divulge this information to us, either.

We finally make it home. I help Michael get undressed, and we collapse into bed. As I lie there, it hits me that, even though there will be times when Michael will be fine on his own, there are going to be more times like this when I will need to be the one in charge.

One thing is becoming clear: these are not just minor matters involving one of us getting our way and one of us not—these are survival issues.

Right now, I'm just grateful to be home. I know that, somehow, we'll muddle through, and things will work out. Snuggling up to Michael, feeling his warmth along the length of my body, I surrender to sleep, feeling reassured as my breath begins to match the rhythm of his breathing.

# Chapter 15

# Freedom

It's the summer of 1997, and I'm on vacation from work. Amid Michael's Avonex ups and downs, we make a major purchase: a used RV. It's a cute little setup—a Winnebago LeSharo. It's tall and small—able to fit into a normal parking space—and extremely compact. It has a little stove, and the middle and rear seats make up into two comfortable beds. It has a large driver's seat that works well for Michael and even a toilet. We had always planned to travel the country in an RV when we both retired and figure if we want to come close to that dream, we'd better do it now.

Although Michael doesn't trust the French Renault engine and swears, after we purchase it, that he wasn't thinking clearly because of Avonex, I trust the RV completely. It will, in fact, serve us faithfully. We will never be stranded in some remote outpost, as Michael sometimes fears, waiting for parts from France that never arrive. Instead, it turns out to be a purchase that brings adventure and fun back into our lives.

On our first trip together, we venture up the coast to Point Reyes in Marin County. This is a beautiful natural area where cows graze in green pastures and small towns dot the landscape along Tomalas Bay. The Point Reyes National Seashore is rugged and sparsely populated, but replete with wild elk and deer and home to the occasional dairy or oyster farm. We have come here many times in the past to hike and explore, staying in a secluded cabin or a treetop room in a B&B, but this time we have our lodging with us. A new world of freedom is opening up, one that allows us to become spontaneous again, able to stay overnight wherever and whenever we want—sometimes because we just feel like it and sometimes because Michael is too tired to make the trip home. We were so fortunate to find a neighbor who was selling this RV at a price we could afford. This, coupled with our plans to stay at state campgrounds, will make our travel almost as inexpensive as staying home, gas being pretty cheap now.

Most of the time, Michael chooses to drive. Sitting up high, as he once did in his truck, he feels more comfortable than he does driving a car. His legs are in a better position, and he is able to get in and out of the RV fairly easily. I have fun furnishing the LeSharo with all the necessary accoutrements: pots and pans and plates and such. The cabinets are ample, and we learn quickly to make sure they are securely shut before we start off. As it turns out, we never use the refrigerator, which only works when the RV is perfectly level. Since we seldom stay on a concrete pad in an RV park, perfectly level doesn't exist for us. Nevertheless, we are fine with an ice chest, canned food, and selections from local grocery stores and restaurants. I have never felt as prepared and self-contained as when we are traveling in our RV.

In early August, we set off for Monterey, traveling south on Highway 1 past Half Moon Bay. It's a gorgeous, clear day with blue skies and white, billowy clouds forming an endless ceiling above the sea on our right and the carefully tilled green fields on our left. We stop at our beloved Pebble Beach, where sea gulls, pelicans, sea lions, and a multitude of marine life abound. We pick up handfuls of pebbles and gently scatter them around, feeling our souls connecting anew to each other and to the beautiful seascape surrounding us.

Returning to the RV, I unwrap sandwiches and brew coffee for Michael and tea for myself on our little stove. Content, we settle down to enjoy the view out our large back window. Later, I go for a hike along the cliff above the ocean and Michael rests.

Coming into Santa Cruz, we head downtown to Pacific Avenue. For me, Santa Cruz is a second home; I've been coming here all my life to visit my father's family, Dutch relatives who settled here and in nearby Aptos and Rio Del Mar. The white-and-gray Victorian houses I remember from my childhood are now decked out in a myriad of colors, and the rather drab downtown has come alive with bricks and trees—and, above all, a montage of colorful, strolling pedestrians. For me and for millions of others, Santa Cruz Beach means the boardwalk, with its merry-go-round and roller coaster and the thrill of swimming and bodysurfing in the cold ocean waves. There's nothing like the taste of saltwater in my mouth and the sting of salt in my nose to make me feel six years old again. But, for now, we explore the treasures of the marketplace, buying books on RV-ing and the McDougall diet at Bookshop Santa Cruz, scoring more lattes, and getting information on a play being presented that night on the UC Santa Cruz campus.

The play, *As You Like It*, is to be performed in the glen under redwood trees. While Michael rests on campus in the RV, I get the tickets and am pleased and relieved to learn disabled seating is available. With the assistance of some helpful people associated with the production, we are given excellent seats and are shown the perfect place to park on the road above the glen, just a few feet from our seating area. This turns out to be an ideal setup, as Michael is able to walk back to the RV at intermission to nap, and I'm able to stay and enjoy the rest of the play. Having traveling beds proves to be one of the most rewarding aspects of the RV.

We aren't sure it's allowed, but we spend the night in our parking spot, warding off all intervention—we hope—by displaying Michael's handicapped placard. We leave early, heading for the facilities on West Cliff Drive just north of the boardwalk and overlooking the ocean. We will become quite knowledgeable about where toilets are located over the course of owning our RV. Although we have our own toilet on wheels, we prefer to use it as little as possible.

After that we head for Monterey, where I get some food for dinner at a grocery store while Michael rests again. We find a nice public parking spot in a lot overlooking the bay, eat fruit and cheese for dinner, and decide to spend the night in the parking lot. I worry we'll be discovered and told to move, but Michael is optimistic. As it turns out, we're not bothered at all.

There are public toilets in the parking lot, but no showers, and in the morning I awake with a desperate craving for a shower. I spy a nearby public phone and call around. I have the idea that one of the many resort hotels in Monterey might allow day-use of their pool (and, hopefully, the accompanying shower rooms). Though I don't find such a place, the concierge at the Marriott Hotel tells me of a place that turns out to be a real find—the Monterey Sports Center, which is owned by the city. For $5.50 a day and fifty cents for a towel, we have everything we need: toilets, showers, swimming pool, and an easily accessible therapy pool. I do seventeen laps in the large lap pool while Michael spends his time in the spacious, warm-but-not-too-warm therapy pool. He loves it, and so do I. We play together in the therapy pool after I swim, making use of the many water-aerobics toys available. We are ready to move to Monterey just to use this facility; it's a real treasure to discover a place both Michael and I can enjoy and one that meets his needs.

We return home happy and renewed, our trip having confirmed the wisdom of our RV purchase, and we embark on the McDougall diet. This low-fat, vegetarian approach will prove beneficial for Michael and will give him more energy. It also proves to be easy for me to cook meals like these, as we have been moving in this direction for some time.

After several more trips down the coast, Labor Day marks the end of our RV summer. We spend a quiet day parked at the San Francisco Marina, looking out at the blue waters of San Francisco Bay. Here we eat lunch and drink tea and hot chocolate. I walk to the Golden Gate Bridge and back along the marina pathway while Michael rests. After watching a beautiful sunset, we drive home across the Bay Bridge to Castro Valley—a fitting ending to another lovely day.

During these times of adventure, we don't argue, and I never have to work on suppressing my negative patterns. Life is good and I'm happy; the future looks promising, despite our uninvited passenger: MS.

We will remember this year as our year of the RV, a time when the quality of our life together improves. We will go more places, have a safe place of refuge when things take a downturn, and discover a new sense of freedom. Michael and I have always been adventurous and active. For a while, we find a way to still be these things.

# Chapter 16

# Drugs

Fall and winter prove to be times of change and flux. Despite our stimulating travels in the RV, Michael's condition continues to deteriorate. Improvement comes in the form of medication, increased mindfulness, and exercise. As Michael struggles to control his life and maintain his functioning, inevitably he makes both good and bad choices—but he always keeps on truckin'. As for me, I find myself dealing with the combined stresses of work, Michael's condition, and even my own health issues. It's difficult to stay on top of things at times, to remain mindful, and to consider all the consequences before acting.

We're both amazed at how many drugs Michael is taking. As I review them, I realize almost all of them target symptoms. Baclofen helps control the painful spasticity, cramping, and convulsions in his legs. Prozac helps him through depression. Amantadine—although actually a drug for Parkinson's disease symptoms and an antiviral—helps counteract the fatigue caused by MS and by some of his other drugs, notably baclofen. Hytrin helps him with his urinary functioning. He takes Vicodin for pain, and Restoril helps him sleep. Only Avonex, which can slow the progression of the disease, treats the MS directly.

I'm excited to see that Michael is channeling his energy into creative expression as a way of dealing with MS and the debilitating effects of the Avonex. He has always had an artistic bent, and now he has the time to follow his inclinations and explore this part of himself. When he started receiving Avonex injections, he began keeping a new journal for his writings and drawings. Much of what he puts into that journal has been prompted by insomnia and hallucinations following the injections. This is when he does some of his most intense drawings, such as the demonic face with a red left eye that represents his disease.

Now he decides to purchase another journal just for recording positive entries, such as whimsical watercolor paintings.

"Why a separate journal?" I ask him.

"I realized most of what I've been writing is negative, 'poor me' stuff," he explains, looking for my approval to spend money on something he already has.

"I think this is a really cool thing for you to do," I tell him, and I give him an encouraging smile.

I'm happy he's being introspective and taking action in a positive direction. He seems to be gaining distance and perspective on his situation now, giving weight and expression to the positive elements in his life. Just the act of buying this journal and setting his intention is helping him focus more on the positive. He's becoming more aware of his emotional states and the nature of his thoughts. More and more, I realize how tied my emotions are to his. Because he's feeling more positive, so am I. It's as if a cloud has lifted, allowing me to be more of a wife and companion and less of a caregiver.

In early October, he shows me a journal entry he wrote about his attitude and his delight at seeing recent pictures of his first grandchild:

*Am going to be more positive. Force myself to go through this spasticity and muscle tightness. As long as I can move, I'm going to have to push myself. Keep a positive attitude in everything I do—and lighten up [on] myself in all I do. I did that today—stayed loose, made jokes with those I came into contact with, and had a good time today. Can't shut my system down tonight. Probably a killer cup of coffee at 5 PM—when will I learn? Bob Marley and the Wailers on the headphones. Reggae becoming my favorite for late-night listening. Love the bass line and simple rhythm. Conga drum easy to listen to. Card and photos of my grandson arrived today. Little guy looks just like I do, or I like to think so, anyway. He's awful cute—as he should be. Hope to see him for Christmas this year. He's not staying little much longer.*

About this time, I'm encouraged to find that Michael has decided to stop caffeine. While he was working, he relied on coffee to keep going. He used coffee, usually triple lattes or double espressos, and even chocolate-covered espresso beans, to keep his energy high enough to get through the workday. This behavior didn't end on the weekends. I remember many times when we would be out for the day—a trip to Point Reyes or a day in the city—and it seemed that all we did was go from one coffee shop to another. At the time, I didn't understand why he needed to keep doing this, and, feeling dragged around, I'd accuse him of being addicted to caffeine. Irritable from the coffee and in denial about his need for it, he would often snap at me and tell me to get off his back. Invariably, we would end up arguing.

Now that he no longer needs to push himself to the limit just to make it through work and the drugs help stabilize his energy, he can quit. His irritability level immediately drops. We also notice that he no longer has to make so many mad dashes to the toilet. The caffeine highs and crashes are finally over.

Michael is on a roll, and he's attempting to live a healthier life-style. He switches from regular tap water to purified water and cuts way back on sugar and fat. He even decides to give acupuncture and herbal medicine a try. I research therapists and clinics for him, and he selects a doctor in Berkeley who practices Chinese medicine and is on the list from the Portland MS Center. The doctor starts him on a program of detoxification with Chinese herbs and acupuncture, but, unfortunately, Michael soon becomes disillusioned and abandons this idea.

"He's just putting me through some kind of generic stuff," he complains. "He's not even considering me as a person." Whether or not this is true, I don't argue with him. When Michael's mind is made up, it's made up.

Beginning and suddenly ending treatments becomes a pattern for Michael. In the future, we will try many alternative approaches, but Michael will choose to forgo most of them. One that he does try, abandon, and then return to for good is going vegetarian and cutting down on fat. He finds his energy increases with a vegetarian diet, and eating red meat and animal fat causes immediate and extreme fatigue. The less his body has to work to digest his food, he finds, the more energy he has for doing other things.

Throughout his illness, besides seeking out and suggesting various alternative and complementary approaches to dealing with MS, I will do extensive online research on the disease, print out reams of paper, fill file folders with information, and hang on to the hope that we will find answers. Possible treatments range widely: bee-sting therapy, removal of mercury dental fillings, hypnosis, guided imagery, an MS clinic in Colorado, the Swank MS Diet[1], and Andrew Weil's suggestions for food and supplements. The last two we incorporate into our lives for a while. At one point, I spend hours compiling vitamin recommendations from various health books and write up a supplement program targeting MS symptoms and recommendations for Michael to follow. For a few months he does, and it appears to be helping.

Then one day I notice the list has disappeared, and I ask him where it is. "I threw it away," he says offhandedly. "I know what to take; I don't need it."

Soon after that, I notice most of the bottles have disappeared. When I ask him to get back on his supplements, he tells me he's forgotten what he was taking, and most of the bottles are gone, anyway.

So I learn the hard way that if I ever do something like this again, I'd better keep a record for myself. It's obvious we can't rely on his memory, and his cavalier attitude frustrates me. Why search for things to make him feel better if he just sabotages my efforts?

When I was in my twenties, sometimes I would consult the I Ching, the ancient Chinese book of divination. It always seemed to come up with the message, "Perseverance furthers." I was never satisfied with this; I would have preferred to receive a more mystical message. The dictionary told me "perseverance" means "continued, patient effort." That seemed tedious, at best. Yet, thirty years later, perseverance

---

1   Dr. Roy Swank discovered that a low-fat diet, very low in saturated fats and polyunsaturated oils, helps MS patients live healthy and productive lives. It is also low in red and other fatty meats, and high in grains, fruits, and vegetables.

turns out to serve us well throughout Michael's illness. In many of my life battles and in much of the mundane, perseverance has saved the day for me.

I now find perseverance to be indispensable. At times, I'm called on to let Michael take the lead, and at other times I must lead. In either case, I learn I need to hang in there with "continued, patient effort" and strive to keep my awareness sharp and my intentions pure. We're both learning by trial and error what is required of us, and we need to learn to tolerate mistakes as well. I know Michael needs the space to test his new limitations and to find his areas of strength. He must try things at his own pace, and we both, in truth, have to persevere.

Michael takes to heart the message a physical therapist gives him: if a muscle works, it can be strengthened. When I go back to work after summer vacation, he decides to apply this information to an activity called water walking. We join the YMCA in Berkeley, a thirty-minute car trip from home. Two or three times a week for about thirty minutes, he walks up and down the two specially reserved water-walking lanes at the Berkeley Y indoor swimming pool. The buoyancy of the water helps him keep his balance, and the resistance helps strengthen his muscles. Whenever I can, on weekends or if he goes after my workday, I swim laps in the same pool while he walks. When I'm finished, I dive under the rope separating the lap lanes from the water-walking lanes and come up dripping and grinning beside him. If he isn't ready to quit, I join him in walking for a while. Then we go to our separate locker rooms, shower and dress, and meet to go home. If I go in with him, I usually do the driving on the trip home. If he goes by himself in the morning or early afternoon, he has to rest before he sets off for home.

Water walking keeps Michael active, on his feet, and moving, and it gives him a great sense of accomplishment. As his strength and stamina improve, his ability to walk on land, as well as in water, also improves. When I go to the Y with Michael, I feel happy. It's a stress-free way for us to share good times and to keep fit, and I love to swim. I hope these good times last.

At the end of October, just as things seem to be stabilizing, Michael decides he's doing so well with his water walking that he'll stop all of his oral medications. This is one of his spur-of-the-moment, impulsive decisions that I dread. He stops Prozac, amantadine, baclofen, Hytrin, and even Vicodin. When I plead with him not to stop all of them at once because they're such strong medications, he refuses to listen to me and becomes hostile. To his way of thinking, he should get them out of his system as soon as possible, precisely because they *are* so strong. Michael has always hated the idea of taking medications, especially a lot of them, and he suddenly goes into complete denial of his need for them. When I beg him to talk to his doctor first, he refuses, and we again end up in an argument.

I find myself feeling worried and frustrated after this last struggle. But after he cools off, he's suddenly in high spirits again, and I find it hard not to share his good mood. We laugh, hug, kiss, and lie together in bed listening to John Denver, reliving the early days of our relationship.

Yet the next night, unable to sleep, he's distant and defensive. "It feels like I have electrical charges in my legs," he tells me. The next day, he calls me at work to tell me he has started drooling.

I'm experiencing a lot of stress at work right now; a grant is due in a few days, and it requires all my attention. I dread going home to deal with his mood swings and increasing MS symptoms. I'm angry that he's made this decision to stop his drugs without listening to me and that he's not considered at all how his decision will affect *my* life—yet he expects me to support him and take care of him, no matter what he does. (I completely ignore the fact that I did something similar by stopping my hormone replacement therapy not long ago, only to start it up again when my mood swings got out of hand.) Now his mood swings are increasing in both frequency and intensity, and I'm feeling hurt and frightened.

Two days after he stops his pills, he goes back on them. He acknowledges that he's becoming too weak to function.

It amazes me how drastically he has been affected in just this short time. He's still withdrawn and, I know, horribly disappointed. He had hoped, somehow, he could be okay again. I feel so sorry it didn't work out for him, and I wish so much that he'd listened to me in the first place. But I keep those thoughts to myself. "It was nice not to take the pills, even if just for a short time," he tells me.

As soon as he can, he goes back to water walking, but his mood is so down he isn't enjoying it as much. When his daughters or his younger brother, Steve, who lives out of state, call, he tells them nothing of what he has done or how he feels; instead he sounds cheerful on the phone and assures them he's fine. Typically, he puts on a good act for others and likes to appear upbeat and in control. He's especially jovial with Steve, who shares his sense of humor. I'm annoyed by this, and my mood descends as his appears to elevate; I feel as if I'm all alone and carrying the burden of his condition and its accompanying depression. Part of me wants to spread it around a little. He never thinks of it that way, though—it's as if, by putting forth a bright facade, he too can believe it for a little while.

Though Michael's MS is the big health issue in our lives, I, too, am not immune to illness. Going back to work amid the onslaught of colds and flu that infest the public education arena always results in my getting sick at least once, usually in the fall or early winter. This fall, I come down with a respiratory flu virus and spend a whole week at home. Lying in bed, I have time to think about the direction my life is taking.

I find myself slipping into self-pity, wishing I could be the one being taken care of, not the one who has to do all the caregiving. As I begin to cry, Michael overhears me and comes into the bedroom. I pour out my feelings to him, and he really listens to me. As he comforts me, I feel my strength and resolve returning. I remind myself that Michael is contributing all he can, that he loves me, and that he hates the inequity now plaguing our lives.

Feeling loved and heard, I get up and take a shower, but I'm still lethargic. I decide to meditate on Padmasambhava's[2] picture, as this always centers me and calms my mind. Afterward, I have renewed focus and feel encouraged. Finally, I feel healthier, more in control, and more positive. As I begin to feel better, I spend most of my recovery time meditating, reading inspirational works, and just resting and gazing at the trees outside my bedroom window.

I remind myself that caregiving isn't new to me. Perhaps, in the beginning, it was motivated by my sense that I had failed my father. He had many ailments, and, as a child, I believed that if I could be a "good girl" all the time—if I just loved him enough—he'd be well and happy. More than once he told me, in apparent jest, "All I want is a good little girl." In college, I was the one who looked after my girlfriends and drove them safely home when we'd all had too much to drink. (Still, it never occurred to me to drink less when I drove;

2   Padmasambhava was an early master of Tibetan Buddhism.

drinking was an indispensable part of our college culture.) From high school on, friends would confide in me, sharing their secrets, hopes, and fears. I was a good listener—interested and nonjudgmental. As an adult, I chose teaching as a career, and I committed to raising Michael's children as my own, equally sharing all the parenting and financial obligations. And now I'm an "official" caregiver, wholeheartedly committed to caring for Michael. It's not the future we planned, but it's the one I chose.

After a week, I'm ready to go back to work—finally feeling healthy again—and we make plans for more weekend adventures in our RV. We go to Santa Cruz, Carmel, and Monterey, not the least reason being to use the Monterey Sports Center facilities again. This time we park overnight on a street in Carmel, right in front of an inn where we once stayed. The parking police do not challenge us, probably because our RV is small enough to fit into a regular parking space, and we could easily be curled up in a nearby B&B. In Santa Cruz, we luxuriate in a hot tub in town. It's delicious, slipping into the embrace of that warm water—but heat always makes Michael weak, and this time is no exception. Fortunately, all he has to do is get back to the RV after our soak. Needless to say, once again we spend the night in a parking lot.

Christmas is fast approaching. On December 3, Zoie and her one-year-old son come out to visit. It's so good to see them both. Michael delights in the presence of his grandson, and he loves to read him pop-up books about dragons. I, too, am enchanted with the boy; I have fun playing with him using a hand puppet of a green dragon and encouraging him to engage in a conversation with the dragon.

At one point, he tells the dragon, "You're not real!"

"Yes, I am!" the dragon says playfully. With that, my step-grandson looks puzzled, not really sure what to think.

When spring comes, we decide to travel to see Zoie, her husband, and son again. It turns out to be a great trip, despite Michael's struggle after injecting Avonex. It warms our hearts to see what a good mother his daughter has become; she seems to thrive in that role. She attends to her son with love and care, administering to his every need. I'm not surprised, as she was always a caring, loving child (albeit rebellious and self-willed). It's good to see her again—and to travel again, this being the first time we've been so far from home since Michael's diagnosis.

In August, Michael quits Avonex. He has no alternative; it's just too hard on him. His doctor starts him on Copaxone, another injectable. With this new drug, he injects daily rather than weekly. Fortunately, he has no side effects from it, and, like Avonex, it's supposed to delay the progression of the disease. We can only hope that it will.

As we continue on this uncharted journey that is MS, forms of medication and exercise will change, and Michael's ability to function will fluctuate. The one constant we will strive to maintain is mindfulness—the ability to see clearly what's happening, what's working and what isn't, and what's going on inside ourselves that limits, inspires, sabotages, or supports. This will remain the key to our ability to persevere and to survive.

# Chapter 17

# Adventure

On December 27, 1997, a little over a year and a half since Michael's diagnosis, we head out to Death Valley in our camper. This is our first big RV adventure, and we're excited.

Once we hit the desert, we decide to overnight in Tecopa, just off Highway 127. Tecopa is a strange sight to behold. It seems to appear out of nowhere in the middle of nowhere, emerging like a funky mirage in the desert. We discover it's a county-owned park with RV spaces and hot springs. Venturing into the office, I'm greeted by a friendly lady who, because Michael is disabled, offers us the use of the "invalid pool" and hands me a key. I'm a bit taken aback by the name, but am eager to find out what kind of pool this will be.

After we park, we take some towels and follow the woman's directions to the "invalid pool." It turns out to be a large, private soaking pool behind a padlocked door between the men's and women's pools. It's cemented, painted blue, rectangular, and very clean, and we have it all to ourselves. As I step down onto the long concrete platform that stretches the length of the pool, the warm water caresses my feet, ankles, and calves. Slipping up to my neck below the surface, I allow a long *Ahhhhh* to escape. I smile up at Michael, who is still undressing. He gets into the water carefully, and we sprawl out, letting the liquid warmth soothe our bodies.

It's a good thing I'm here with Michael because, after about thirty minutes, he can hardly walk and has difficulty getting out of the pool and getting dressed. The heat has made him extremely weak, as we knew it would. Nevertheless, he feels relaxed and is able to make it back to the RV, which we have parked close to the bathhouse.

In the morning, we take time to check out our surroundings more fully. There are lots of RVs around that seem to be long-term fixtures. I notice some rustic cabins advertising "Kitchens and Springs." Upon arrival, I wondered how people even knew about this place; it seems such a remote and bleak destination. But after soaking in the natural spring waters, I know why they're here. To our disappointment, the baths are closed for cleaning this morning, but it's just as well. Our destination is close by, and we're ready to move on.

We spend our first night in Death Valley at Furnace Creek Ranch, which offers RV parking. In the morning, we discover breakfast is served in their restaurant. We both allow ourselves to indulge in eggs, bacon, soggy hash browns, and buttered toast, and we both drink tea, as Michael is still off coffee and doing well.

After a day of sightseeing, we continue traveling north on Highway 190. Our first stop is Salt Creek. Michael, with the help of his two hiking poles, is able to make the half-mile trek on the boardwalk that stretches over the wetland area. It's really lovely. The creek is all that's left of a big, fresh-water lake. Over many years, it has dried up and become a very salty creek. Only the hardy pupfish were able to make the transition. Unfortunately, although we look hard, we don't see any pupfish. (In my mind, they're little puppies with fins.) At the far end of the boardwalk, we take off into "the hills." These are sand mounds crusted over with salt. We follow a dry streambed created by rainwater runoff and see gorgeous rocks of varying colors. Some are lava at the base, transitioning beautifully to quartz of rose and white hues.

Michael rests back at the RV, feeling pleased with his accomplishment and inspired by the beauty of the desert. I eat an apple and feed some to a raven (or maybe it's a crow) that seems to be hanging out with us. Life is good.

New Year's Eve 1997 is perhaps our best day. We rise early and enjoy fresh grapefruit, muffins, and oolong tea for breakfast in the RV. We're camped at a place called Stovepipe.

Our destination for the day is Mosaic Canyon, which is up a gravel road just east of the campground. We take water with us and head out on foot into the canyon, leaving the RV at the end of the road. We follow a wide dirt path, awed by the gorgeous strata of marble and the multicolored stones embedded in the canyon walls that tower above us on both sides. Because it's a canyon, it's shady and cool inside. Michael has on his good hiking boots, a back belt for support, and his dark blue Filson hat, and he uses his hiking poles with the sharp points exposed to help him maneuver. Parts of the hike are very hard for him, as when the path narrows to a foot trail, or when there are rocks to climb over. He does fall once, and he has to climb some places on his hands and knees, but he keeps at it. We're both stunned by the beauty of this place, the canyon's richly colored walls of corrugated orange, red, gold, and purple stretching high to touch the endless blue sky. The air we breathe is rich and dry, and the whole experience of the place makes us feel as if we've been dropped into another world.

There is one slippery marble area on the trail that slopes down to form a slide several feet long. We stop to watch some children and their parents repeatedly slide down and climb back up. We try it, too, but only I go back up to repeat the process; Michael is satisfied with a one-way trip. At this point, his struggle to get back up will keep for later. We continue to hike until the canyon opens to sunlight.

Michael decides to stop here, and I agree. I think we've seen the best part, and the sunny area ahead is much too warm.

We make it back to the RV with no mishaps, and I heat up some canned clam chowder for lunch. It tastes good. It turns out we've been hiking for over two hours. We both take a nap; I, too, am tired.

Back in Stovepipe, we stop at the general store and gift shop. My eye is caught by a small pewter eagle with widespread wings, perched atop a piece of rugged amethyst. Remembering the eagle from the Medicine Card spread and its message of wisdom and compassion, I buy the pewter eagle, welcoming its reappearance in my life in this magical place called Death Valley.

In the evening, we witness a romantic golden sunset. We have a 360-degree view of sand dunes and far-off mountains, all bathed in colors of ever-changing hue and intensity. The whole sky is awash in shades of gold, red, orange, pink, and blue that vary as we turn full circle. The mountains to the east have taken on the blue and violet hues, and the sandy dunes subtly reflect the warmer colors of the sunset. I walk a little way out onto the dunes. Michael watches from the RV and then walks out to meet me on my return. As we hold each other close in the falling darkness, we're once again young and newly in love.

Even though it's New Year's Eve, we go to bed early, awaking only briefly at midnight when we hear whoops and hollers coming from the nearby saloon. We are content. It has been one of the best days ever, and tomorrow is the beginning of the New Year—1998.

We seem to have gotten into the rhythm of nature in Death Valley, going to bed soon after the sunset and waking up with the sunrise. The stars at night are fantastically bright in the clear desert air, which feels so fresh and pure. We feel connected with the earth here and sense that it's revealing its secrets and wonders to us.

The day we visit the Harmony Borax Works, Michael is too tired to take the interpretive walk, so while he rests, I follow the trail out onto the salt flats where the Chinese workers mined for borax. It's so still and beautiful, looking out over the glistening salt and desert expanses beyond. I'm alone, with no other tourists in sight.

The sky is vivid blue above the bright salt white of the playa. Magnificent gray and cotton-white clouds move north in the wind, creating a Rorschach of form and pattern. As I watch, I see a giant eagle in cloud relief against the blue of the sky. With wings spread wide, it swoops down toward me, yet the wind moves it slowly backward. I watch transfixed until the vision fades.

Wondrous things can appear if we stop to see as well as to look, I muse. When I return to the RV, I share my experience with Michael.

"I wish I had been with you to see that," he says with a sleepy smile.

On the third day of the New Year, we start our trip home. We know we will miss Death Valley—the fresh air, lack of crowds, gorgeous sunsets, open spaces, constantly changing colors, and astounding views. Michael has felt renewed and invigorated here, and I, too, have felt reenergized.

On the way home, it starts to rain, and my back begins to ache. All the time I was in Death Valley's dry climate I was free of the arthritic back pain that sometimes hinders my movements. Until this moment, in fact, I had forgotten all about it. Things are getting back to normal, I guess. Much to my disappointment, Michael starts drinking coffee again when we stop in Visalia at Apple Annie's for a compensatory breakfast pig-out. After that, it seems we're home again in no time at all.

# Chapter 18

# Dragonflies

On July 7, 1998, we take a two-week RV trip up the North Coast to the border of California and Oregon. This trip turns out to be a little different from the others—longer, and a mix of both good and bad times.

Michael has reservations about taking this trip. Although his ongoing depression lifted for a while after our trip to Death Valley, it has returned and persisted. Taking Prozac does keep him from plummeting to the depths of despair—or, at least, it allows him to return when he does. Most often, his depression is tied to his physical functioning. When spasticity and pain render him immobile, he becomes more and more silent and withdrawn as his mood darkens; when he can be out and about, his spirits lift, and we can talk and kid around. Now, as we plan for our trip, he worries the weather will be too hot and he'll become physically and mentally incapacitated.

The day before we plan to leave, still vacillating between trepidation and excitement, Michael washes the RV at our local do-it-yourself carwash, purges the holding tanks, and fuels her up.

"She's ready to go," he tells me, but he doesn't sound all that enthusiastic. "I wish I were as ready as the RV is," he admits. "I'm looking at this as a disaster. I see myself falling apart in the heat."

As he says this, I begin to have second thoughts myself. Still, I hold on to the memory of the fun we had on our last adventure, and I decide to take a wait-and-see attitude. If things go wrong, we'll deal with them when the time comes.

It does turn out to be exceptionally hot the day we are to leave. Michael's body shuts down, and his mind right along with it. Defeated, he takes to his bed and sleeps through most of the day. Reluctantly, we decide to put off our departure.

On the following day, by waiting for the cool of the night, we manage to hit the road. Michael likes to drive at night. He drove nights many times in the truck and enjoys the dearth of traffic. Nevertheless, we encounter plenty while getting out of the Bay Area, hitting Highway 80 at eight o'clock after stopping for dinner in Oakland. He becomes irritable as the traffic increases, but once it lightens up, so does he. Finally, we're ready for an adventure. I've packed sufficient food for the first part of the trip, and we plan to stay in state parks along the coast and make our way north at a leisurely pace.

As it turns out, we do stay in several state parks, delighted at the half-price fees we're charged thanks to Michael's disability status. We become expert at locating the handicapped camp sites, always near the necessary facilities, and at remembering to stock up on quarters for the coin-operated showers. We have never appreciated the American for Disabilities Act more. Without it, we couldn't have made this trip.

But that first night, we're too tired to find a campground. At one in the morning, we finally pull off the road in a turnout near Fort Bragg. Both of us bed down immediately, but I'm the only one to get a good night's sleep. Logging trucks barrel continually down the road. They don't keep me awake because I became accustomed to such noises as the daughter of a farmer; my father often hired the early morning "duster" plane to spray the orchard just beyond my bedroom windows. To my ears, the truck sounds are similar to the sounds of farm equipment and duster planes. But Michael spends the night listening intently to the trucks, aware of when drivers have their Jake Brakes on and who's in the right or wrong gear.

Nevertheless, we get up at six in the morning and stop at a restaurant for breakfast. On this trip, we're to be equally split between having breakfast at a local place and making our own in the RV. Whichever we do, we will eat well.

As we drive on, we find camping spaces near the ocean. From the fog-shrouded cliffs, we can look down to the sea below and watch the whitecaps hurling themselves against gray boulders and golden sand. The scenery is wild and desolate and beautiful, earning its name—the Lost Coast. There are few other travelers, even though it's summer, so we're spared the inquisitive glances of strangers. As we let the mystery and drama of the northern Pacific Coast seep deep into our bones, we're renewed and reenergized. We begin to realize that we can slow down, relax, and have a good time.

The lure of the open road has dispelled Michael's depression. He marvels at the beauty of the scenery, compares it to the places of his youth in Seattle—where he lived until he moved near Chicago at fifteen—and wonders what lies ahead, just beyond the next bend. At home he worried about losing his mobility and being confined to the downstairs bedroom when he didn't have the energy to venture out. Now possibilities have returned, and his horizons have broadened.

We don't need to be anywhere at any particular time, so nothing is stopping us from following our inclinations. Around lunchtime one day, we stop on a long bluff overlooking the sea and park the RV not far from the cliff. I open a can of chili for lunch, and we eat it outside with some olives and a juicy grapefruit. I set up a folding table, cover it with a blue-and-white-checked tablecloth, and set it between our two folding chairs. We spend most of the day there, just relaxing and looking out at the ocean. I take some of that time to write in my journal.

About three thirty, Michael decides to take a nap back in the RV. He has just taken all of his pills and is tired. He has a hard time getting up out of the chair and finds my attempts to help him annoying. I decide to leave him alone and go to the RV to get a book to read, but I watch him over my shoulder to ensure that he gets up all right. When I see him standing by his chair, I go inside the RV and find my book, come out, and start back to our little table to read.

When I look up, I expect to see Michael walking toward me, but he isn't; I don't see him anywhere. I notice one of his hiking poles is propped up against a post behind his chair. Fear grips me. I run to the cliff and look down, expecting to see him sprawled on the beach below. Thank God, he *isn't* sprawled on the beach. I call him, feeling icy tentacles clutching my chest in a cold band of fear. No answer. I go running back to the RV and gasp as I round the back corner. There he stands, peeing next to the side door. Slowly, I realize we had each walked past the other—but on opposite sides of the RV. He finds this hilarious and can't stop laughing. I'm not amused, and my bound-up stress releases in tears. He comforts me, still laughing, until I can laugh at the whole thing too.

"I was afraid you had fallen over the cliff, Snookums," I blubber between tears and laughter.

"Everything's all right, baby," he says, enveloping me in his arms until I relax.

The next day, back on the road, we find ourselves traveling on an especially scenic part of Highway 1. The wooded and green landscape around us is draped in fog. At one point, we're stopped by a flagman directing traffic around Caltrans workers who are repairing the road after the destruction caused by El Niño. In many places, due to highway work already completed, we drive on brand-new road. On some sections, they're still painting the white fog line or putting down center reflectors.

Michael never misses an opportunity to talk to people, and he always brings away interesting information—in this case, where to eat. At one point, stopped by the roadwork, Michael rolls down the window and yells to the flagman, "Hey, guy, where's a good place for breakfast?"

Thanks to the worker's recommendation, we have a great breakfast in Garberville, at a small café in the middle of town that serves delicious buckwheat pancakes. Michael opts for the "Really Hungry Special." But the memorable thing about this stop turns out to be watching a guy at the counter who keeps cracking up laughing. He has a deep, thundering belly laugh that rings out continually as he talks with a friend. We soon put two and two together after noticing he looks very much like the picture of Falstaff on the SHAKESPEARE AT BENBOW poster we saw entering town. We decide this must be the actor, practicing his laugh. We feel fortunate to have been at the right place at the right time, as we wouldn't be staying in the area long enough to see the play. At least we see Falstaff, and I'm sure he will be as great in the play as he is in the restaurant.

Our next stop is at a state campground on the Eel River. After we do some scouting around for trails, we try one that proves too difficult for Michael, so we turn around. Back at the RV, we're ready for showers. I take mine first while Michael rests, then prepare to heat up some soup for dinner while Michael goes to take his shower. After I get things ready and the picnic table set with our blue-and-white-checked tablecloth, I have an urge to check on Michael—I'm worried because he was very weak and fatigued from our walk. Fortunately, the handicapped showers are large, roll-in showers that have a pull-down bench for him to sit on. I call to him from outside but get no response. I try the door, but it's locked. I wait until I hear the water go off, thinking he can't hear me over the sound of the shower, and call again. This time he hears me and unlocks the door. It turns out he does need help, and he's relieved to see me. He's pretty much immobile. The shower was too hot, and he couldn't adjust it cooler. I had used this shower earlier and had not been able to adjust it correctly, either, but I thought it was just me. Now I blame myself because I hadn't gone into the shower with him to be sure everything was okay.

"I got really confused and wasn't thinking right," Michael explains. "I'm really glad you came to check up on me, baby."

I can see my being here now is helping him to reorient, and relief begins to replace his anxiety.

"I was thinking it would be a good idea to just lie down on the shower floor for a while," he states flatly as I help him dry off and get dressed.

We're both thankful I followed my hunch and checked on him and that he didn't lie down in the shower; if he had, we would have needed a *lot* of help to get him up.

Back at the RV, we eat outside where he can cool off, and we go to bed early.

The next day we decide to give the river a try. I scout out a short trail to the river that's suitable for Michael to walk, and we set off, carrying our L.L. Bean beach tent shaped like a half dome, two blow-up "chairs," an air mattress, some plums and marshmallows, water, and things to read.

The trail proves to be fine, and we both get down to the river easily. Michael wears a pair of water sandals that work well for him in and out of the water. He takes the rubber covers off the ends of his hiking poles and, using the exposed metal points, is able to maintain balance well as he walks both on the uneven trail and over the pebbles and rocks on the river bottom.

We find a lovely place on a sandy strip close to the water's edge to put up our little shelter from the sun, whose direct rays would be too hot for Michael. I'm pleased we thought through what we would need and managed to bring everything with us; it looks as if we're improving in the area of preparedness. Nearby, close to shore, is a natural pool in the river, formed by a large redwood stump at one end and a little stone bar at the other. The water flows slowly, its green color echoing the green boughs of the redwood trees, their strong trunks furry with reddish-brown bark.

We spend the majority of our time in the river. Michael finds that as long as most of his body is covered by cool water, he does well. In fact, he even feels he can walk almost normally because the water keeps his legs cold and his body temperature down. He wears a hat and dark glasses to protect his head and face from the heat of the sun. The river is a fairly short distance across at this point, and Michael can easily walk to the other side on his own, without using his hiking poles.

While I'm experimenting with swimming against the gentle current and letting it carry me back to where I started, I notice Michael has been standing at the opposite bank for quite some time. I go over to him.

"What are you doing?"

"I'm watching the dragonflies," he tells me.

I notice there are a host of dragonflies flitting among the reeds that grow along the bank. We both stand transfixed, watching their transparent wings reflect the sunlight, transforming them into prisms of iridescent color. They're creating a miniature light show as they dart and twist, abruptly turning and changing direction.

There, standing side by side in the still water, our bodies touch, and our love flows gently between us. Despite his disability, he has walked across the river on his own, and he's excited to share his reward with me—the wonder of dancing dragonflies.

In the years to follow, dragonflies will become a powerful symbol for Michael—a transformative symbol of strength and renewal, a symbol of being whole.

When we get back to the RV, I take my chair to the far end of our campsite. It overlooks a creek, and beyond the creek, the redwood trees become a forest. I put my feet up on the split-rail fence and write in my journal, reflecting on the day and listening to the blue jays squawk as they flit from tree to tree. As I write, I recall with wonder the flickering dance of the dragonflies.

I'm grateful we've found this place, that there was a space for us, and that we're here, right now, enjoying this beautiful spot. Michael emerges from the RV and brings a bowl of granola and soymilk over to me; he's just discovered the granola hiding in the cabinet. His gift is like the cherry topping on an ice cream sundae.

"Thank you," I say, taking the bowl and smiling up at him.

# Chapter 19
# Omens and Endings

The next day we return to the river, but it isn't the same. Michael experiences more trouble with the trail, and the sun gets to him as he attempts to cross a sunny stretch of river rock that fronts the river. The water is nice, but not nice enough to revive him. With my help, he gets back to our campsite. I'm beginning to wonder how much longer we will be able to do these trips.

Earlier today, something strange happened that I now take to be an omen. About seven in the morning, we heard a loud bang, as if something had hit the RV. Startled, I got out of bed and opened the door. Looking up into the tree nearby, I noticed a gang of blue jays squawking frantically. Looking down, I saw a lone blue jay lying on the ground. It apparently had slammed into the side of our RV. It was dead.

Later, when I walk to the office to pay for three more nights, I ask the ranger what to do with the bird. She says to let nature take its course, so that's what we do: Michael picks it up by its little feet and puts it on a redwood stump partially hidden by the bushes at the back of our campsite.

Around one o'clock, Michael is napping in the RV, recovering from the heat and the trek to the river. I decide to go for a hike on a nearby trail through the redwoods. It's a gorgeous day, and I don't meet a soul along the trail. About a mile and a half in, I begin to feel a little uncomfortable about being alone. I remember the poster in the visitors' center warning of bears and mountain lions. Trying to put this out of my mind, I continue on a bit and then decide to head back. At this point, I hear a *woof* sound somewhere in front of me. I instinctively freeze and then begin to back up slowly.

*Probably just the trees creaking,* I tell myself.

Nevertheless, I pick up two large sticks and pound them together to make noise as I start walking again. The fact that I've been reading *The Tibetan Book of the Dead* probably figures in here somewhere because I never do see a bear and probably look pretty silly walking along making a racket.

Safely back at camp, I decide this experience is cautioning me to be more mindful. It's amazing how a little shot of adrenaline can wake you up.

Michael tells me that while I was gone, he took the RV into town and drained the tank. I'm glad he was feeling better and also glad I hadn't returned earlier to find an empty campsite. I go to the office for firewood, which I drag back with some difficulty. (Later, I find out I should have pushed the hauling contraption ahead of me instead of pulling it behind.) After dinner, we make a roaring fire with some of the wood, and I discover in Michael a talent he has kept hidden from me throughout our marriage: he is an excellent roaster of marshmallows!

"You didn't know that, did you?" he kids, flashing me his teasing smile.

After I gorge on these, possibly my favorite treat in the whole world, we do the dishes, and I write in my journal. Then we go to bed.

The next day, my arthritis kicks up from lugging the wood, and my back hurts. Michael suggests we take it easy and visit the big trees in Founders' Grove. After a short drive, we're there. Seeing Founders' Grove involves taking a beautiful short walk that includes the gigantic Founders' Tree and an even bigger downed redwood trunk that dwarfs Michael as he stands in front of it for a picture. The only disturbing part of the adventure is hearing the logging trucks continually passing by. I envision the trees quaking in dread, unaware they're safe and protected. (Somehow, I don't really believe they are safe.)

After a lunch of chips, salsa, and apples, we go west to the Federation Grove, where we find people filming a commercial for Mitsubishi. I think we passed a sign telling us the road was closed, but Michael doesn't think such signs apply to him; I'm guessing he passed many with impunity during his years as a truck driver. When we park in the picnic area, we find a Japanese film crew eating catered box lunches under the redwoods. We talk to the caterers, who are from a restaurant in the Arcata Hotel. The food looks good, and we vow to go there for a meal but somehow never do.

It's a short walk to the beach just below the picnic area, and Michael finds a shady place to sit near the water. When he ventures into the river, he feels good, and we end up spending hours in the water. It's deep and still enough that I can do some real swimming. I have my air mattress with me, and in a little while, I decide to blow it up and do some floating. At one point, the mattress flies off in a gust of wind and is caught by a little girl playing at the water's edge. She climbs aboard during the process of trying to get it back to us and looks like she's having so much fun that I let her use it for the rest of the afternoon. She's delighted, and we have fun watching her.

Michael does some water walking and also some snorkeling. There are lots of fish swimming around our toes for him to see. Sitting on a rock to rest on the far side of the river, he discovers a fish nursery and calls me over to see.

"Look, there are all different sizes of fish swimming around," he marvels. It feels a little too warm and swampy over here, so I nod and leave him to his wonderings.

After cooling off in the river, Michael feels good and makes it back to the car with no difficulty. We go into Garberville for coffee and supplies. Over my protests, Michael makes the mistake of walking in direct sunlight to a store that catches his eye. He gets hit hard by the heat but still insists on doing the driving up to Redway for dinner. He isn't thinking clearly and drives through a parking lot we could easily have avoided. He also doesn't see a car backing out as we drive behind it. It takes four seconds for him to react and stop the car. All the while I'm saying, "Watch out!" Then I shout, "Stop! Stop!" when he doesn't react. Fortunately, the woman backing out sees our vehicle and stops just as we do. Again, I vow to myself—as I have many times before—to do the driving whenever he's tired or weak from being out in the sun. I know only too well how his judgment deteriorates at times like these—along with his perception, awareness, and ability to respond. Fortunately, I was paying attention this time. I resist the temptation to make him wrong and let the incident pass.

One might wonder why I don't just insist on driving. I try sometimes, but it always ends up in a fight. Michael has a strong personality and sees himself as someone who can't be "messed with." He doesn't take no for an answer, and he's used to getting his way. It will take many more years, many more arguments, and many more near-accidents before he'll realize that sometimes he has to relinquish the wheel—after all, being a truck driver was a big part of his life and his self-image, and none of us relinquishes parts of ourselves easily. No longer being able to work was a big blow, and I know driving his own vehicle will be hard for him to give up.

Fortunately, the restaurant is air-conditioned, and we stay there for a while after eating to be sure he's cooled down. Again, he drives, and we make it home okay.

The next day, July 15, we go back to the area where they were film-ing and spend a long time enjoying the water and staying cool in the river, even though the day is hot. I have my air mattress all to myself. Michael seems to be doing really well and enjoying himself. We stay for about four and a half hours, just having fun.

As we leave, Michael walks up the incline from the river more quickly than I do. He's been careful, wearing a hat and a T-shirt to avoid the sun, and even letting me put some sunscreen on him when he was in the water. When he gets to the picnic area, he goes into the bathroom, and I continue on to the RV. After a while, when he doesn't show up, I go to the bathroom to check on him. He has diarrhea, he tells me, and when he exits he goes back in the water. That helps him some, but he looks awful. He drives back to the campground all right, but after eating some chips he feels terrible again and goes to bed.

In bed, he gets what he calls convulsions: the muscles along his ribs and sides contract violently, and his whole body goes into spasms. He's cold, even though it's stifling in the RV, despite my attempts to cool it down. He tells me later his neck tightened up and felt like it was in a vise. I wrap him in a blanket and remember he'd had just half a bottle of iced tea at the beach and, before that, only morning coffee. I encourage him to drink water, but he will not. I let him sleep but wake him up an hour or so later and finally get him to drink a cup of water.

The water goes right through him and brings on diarrhea again. We're just happy to have the toilet in the RV so close to his bed. But he can't get there quickly, and by the end of the night, there is quite a mess on the floor. I clean it up as best I can, and he stops refus-ing my help. I refresh him with some wet wipes and a damp, warm washcloth, and fashion a urinal out of an empty gallon size spring water bottle.

He can't stand it if I touch his legs; he says it sends shock waves throughout his body. He finally goes back to sleep but continues to moan every once in a while. I don't know if he has a fever, as I hadn't thought to bring a thermometer—I guess I didn't think of everything, after all. I want him to take small sips of water every ten minutes or so, but he resists. After a while, he turns from feeling cold to feeling hot. Then he loses all coordination and strength and just sleeps.

Later, I realize he was having an exacerbation, during which a new MS symptom—one that won't go away—appears, along with increased weakness and fatigue. I imagine that being in the sun so long and getting dehydrated brought it on. After this, Michael will continue to suffer from tension and pain in his neck.

The next day is one of much needed rest for both of us. Michael is very weak, but he gets progressively better. He takes a shower, eats a little, and abstains from coffee. I can tell he feels embarrassed and ashamed about losing control of his bowels, but we don't talk about it. He sleeps most of the day, and I read in my chair outside the RV, keeping the door open in case he needs something. We both have just a salad for dinner, because the tempeh and stir-fried veggies I also made were horrible. I guess I'm just not into cooking right now.

I suggest we go home the next day, but Michael is determined to finish our vacation. He's sure his getting chilled in the water is what caused him to get sick, and he insists he's getting his strength back. I'm worried, but I'm also excited to see what's ahead, so I agree to push on.

We drive to Eureka, where Michael empties the tanks, and I vacuum the floor at a car wash. We decide to go on to Arcata and check into a motel for the night. We end up staying in Arcata two nights, grateful to have a real bed and a full, handicapped bathroom. Michael recuperates, resting on the bed and watching TV. I buy some rug shampoo and toilet cleaner and thoroughly clean the RV, surprised at how good it looks when I'm through.

After we leave the motel, we head out to Patrick's Point State Park on the coast off Highway 101. While standing on top of Wedding Rock, I see a whale swimming not far from shore. Michael sees it too, from the parking lot; we've actually remembered to take the binoculars, and he has them.

Back in the RV, Michael gets sick again. I can't believe this is happening after my major cleaning, and I'm feeling a bit discouraged. Fortunately, I still have some rug shampoo, and it isn't as bad this time. This is all part of being a caregiver, I decide, and it's a job I accept with love and hope for the best.

On the road again, we head for the Smith River after stopping in Crescent City for breakfast. We're amazed when we see the river, and I'm glad we took time to enjoy the Eel River first—because if we had seen the Smith first, we would not have thought the Eel was so beautiful. The Smith is the only undammed river in California. Its water is crystal clear, and it moves rapidly, creating white water above its sparkling surface. I imagine the Eel must once have been this clear, before the lumber companies devastated the mountains and erosion brought silt to the river.

We check out Panther Point Campground and find it too hot; we're moving out of the redwoods into a warmer climate. In fact, we find out the entire country is experiencing a heat wave, and we've been in the coolest area in the country during our trip.

So we scramble back to the cool of the redwoods and try for Jedediah Smith Campground, where we're lucky to get a spot. This turns out to be a popular campground with great facilities, and most spots are reserved in advance. We're considered "drive-in" users and have to register before ten each morning to keep our handicapped place. The river is gorgeous, and we have easy access close to where we're parked. The weather is foggy until about noon, and, while we're there, doesn't warm up much during the day. This proves to be just the type of weather Michael needs. We bring our chairs down to the river and soak up its beauty even though it's too cold to go in. Once more, Michael seems to thrive.

On our last day, the weather turns warm enough for us to get into the river. The current is a little stronger than it looks, and much stronger than in the Eel. Also, it's colder, so we don't stay in long.

On July 23, one month after our twentieth wedding anniversary, we're told no campsites are available, and we decide to set out for home. Characteristically, we do it in one day. But still, we're mindful: During the hottest part of the day, we stop, and Michael takes a nap. We get back about two in the morning—starving. We stop at a supermarket, where I buy eggs. After a couple of tasty omelets, we finally go to sleep in our own comfortable bed, dreaming of rivers and redwoods and watching for dragonflies.

# Chapter 20

# Endings

In August of 1998, a month after our journey up the northern coast of California, we make another trip in the RV. It's a short one; we go down the coast to see *Othello* at Shakespeare Santa Cruz and spend the night.

Michael discovered his love of Shakespeare years ago, shortly before we were married. He had signed up to take classes in Administration of Justice at our local community college. On his way to his first class, he saw a professor sitting cross-legged on top of his desk reading aloud from a book. Intrigued, Michael went in and sat down. The class was reading Shakespeare's plays aloud, and Jerry, the professor, encouraged Michael to join them. Needless to say, he kept going to that class and never signed into the other one. He probably never actually registered for this one, either. (His favorite play was *Richard III* and mine, *Hamlet*.) As soon as we returned from our two-week honeymoon in Maui, we went to the Shakespeare Festival in Ashland, Oregon, with Jerry and his wife, beginning a long-term friendship for the four of us.

For me, the high point of this trip to Santa Cruz is swimming in the ocean at Sea Cliff Beach State Park. Unfortunately, as I bodysurf in on a wave, the current pulls off a ring Michael bought for me several years ago at an art fair in Berkeley, and I feel terrible about losing it. (Of course, I can't find it in the sand.) Michael takes the loss in stride. I guess the loss of a ring is not so important compared to all he's lost through MS. He assures me he'll buy me another ring just like it the next time we go to the art fair.

Michael overheats at the beach while I swim, but he doesn't go in the water to cool off because he can't keep his balance in the sand and the waves. Fortunately, there are showers in the camping area, and he uses one to cool down.

Michael sleeps most of the way home as I drive. During this hour, I have time to reflect. All in all, this has turned out to be quite a pleasant trip. I love it when we can share new experiences and have fun together. Yet, once again, he overheated, and I could see his energy draining away like sand in an hourglass. Questions and self-doubt assail me: *How much longer can we be out and about when the weather is warm? How damaging are these trips for him? Are they hastening his decline even as they lift his spirits by letting him be as active as possible? Am I failing as a caregiver?*

Soon after we return home, Michael goes to bed, exhausted and withdrawn. When he wakes, I sit on the bed next to him and take his hand in mine. As we look into each other's eyes, it becomes obvious to both of us that Michael's condition is deteriorating. No words are necessary. We realize this was probably our last trip.

"It's time to sell the RV," Michael tells me without emotion. As always, when he feels threatened, he appears stoic, his face an impenetrable mask. "I know I wouldn't be able to climb up into the driver's seat again. In fact, I can barely walk," he states.

"We're in this together," I tell him, squeezing his hand and offering a reassuring smile.

From this point on, Michael begins using forearm canes for more support, and our activities become more limited. We have to say goodbye to one of the happiest times in our lives together, but we know we have no choice. We'd come close to realizing our dream of traveling the country in a motorhome, at least as close as we could ever get.

One day at the end of August, Michael goes to Berkeley to go water walking at the Y and comes back with a manual wheelchair; he just went into a wheelchair store, let a salesman sell him one, and rolled out in it. He was able to collapse it, put it in the trunk, and drive home. I bring it up the stairs and into the house for him.

"Why?" I ask. I'm feeling a bit blindsided. I hadn't expected this.

"I just couldn't struggle with those canes anymore," he says. "I put it on the credit card."

It was expensive, and it's too small for him. I wish he had talked it over with me; I could have at least helped him pick out one more suited to his large frame. I'm aware that one of his biggest fears was to end up in a wheelchair, remembering his vow to end his life if it ever came to that. Now he's confronted his worst fear and accepted it as reality. I think buying the chair on his own, without consulting the doctor or me, allowed him to feel that he was still somewhat in control.

To accommodate the wheelchair, we try to make the largest bathroom upstairs more accessible. In order to get the wheelchair into the bathroom, we have someone cut back the lower part of the door frame and take the knobs off the cabinets and drawers across from the tub. We also buy an elevated toilet seat.

Because Michael has kept many items from his trucking days, he comes up with a creative idea for using one of them: a load lock, which is a long, extendable metal pole that can be fastened across the width of a truck trailer to keep the load from shifting. His idea is to place the load lock vertically next to the tub, extending from floor to ceiling, so he can hang onto it for support when he steps in or out of the tub. Whenever he has trouble, which is often, he emits sounds of distress that stab at my heart like ice picks. They're almost animal in nature, reminding me of a creature caught in a trap. I always rush in to help. It frightens me that I can't always be there. Soon I'll have to go back to work; summer vacation is almost over.

Because climbing into the tub has become treacherous, we buy a shower seat. Now, with the shower seat in place, it's safer, and I can help him get his legs over the side of the tub. Still, I worry because he insists on showering alone when I'm at work.

In October, we have a stair lift put in so Michael can go up and down the inside stairs from the bedroom on the lower level, just off the garage, to the rest of the house. He can no longer manage the stairs on foot, but now he'll be able to transfer from the wheelchair to the lift. On the other end, he either uses his forearm canes or I bring the chair to him.

I'm worried now because he's home alone all day while I'm at work. He assures me he'll be fine, but still I'm anxious. So far, at least, he's been able to cope on his own.

Although we put grab bars along one side and at the head of our bed upstairs, he spends most nights in the downstairs bedroom because of the spasticity in his legs. The constant jumping and jerking keeps me awake when we're sharing our bed upstairs, and I have to have my sleep so I can function at work. We're not happy about this, but even though he takes medication for the spasticity, it's worse at night. I hate to ask him to go downstairs when I can't sleep. Sometimes I go to the futon in the guest room, but he doesn't want me to do that. He'd rather be the one to move.

About this time, I have the following dream:

*I'm high, high up on a tropical mountaintop. Below me is a green, lush valley, but as I look down, I feel the sharp chill of fear in my stomach. Then the scene changes, and I'm looking at lots of things to eat spread out on a buffet. Everything is overpriced. I get a cup of coffee in a fancy cup with chocolate decorations on the outside, but it is overfilled, and I get a second cup to put the overflow in. Someone gives me a tiny hot dog on a long stick (like a corn dog), but it costs $7.00. Someone warns me it's too expensive, but I eat it anyway.*

I don't know whether or not this dream is related to Michael's decision to buy a wheelchair and the other expenses, like the stair lift, but it seems as if it might be. Money is getting tight. And I'm frightened when I see how rapidly Michael's needs are changing. We seem to be looking into an abyss of needs and expensive solutions. Things are overpriced, not only in terms of money, but also in terms of physical and emotional costs. My cup runneth over—not with good things, but rather with things that are ominous and costly and impossible to contain.

Yet not all is bleak. Michael agrees to join me in seeing a psychologist, Dr. Jones, for weekly couples' therapy because he realizes our relationship has to become more inclusive if we're to meet all the demands of his illness. Also, he's willing to go because he loves me and wants to support me and our marriage. This is no time to engage in power struggles or waste energy over petty disagreements; we need to become more aligned and focused on meeting the challenges of this disease. Again, I'm reminded of my dream image. We need a larger container to hold what's happening to us. We both have to stretch and grow. Michael is open to change, and Dr. Jones establishes good rapport with him and gains his trust. We're making progress.

I also continue my work in individual, Jungian-oriented therapy, and I'm paying close attention to my dreams. The feminine goddess energy appears to be coming more to the forefront for me. I see goddess energy as feminine power—power *with* rather than power *over*—the latter being the distorted application of masculine power manifest in the patriarchal model, the one that came forward in our power struggles. This emerging feminine energy will help me work collaboratively with Michael as we move forward. Also, the hermaphrodite—half masculine and half feminine—has appeared in my dreams as a strong, positive symbol of wholeness. The coming together of feminine and masculine energies inherent in this symbol gives me more internal resources and positive power.

Yet no change is without its regressions. One day in November after we finished dinner, Michael is struggling at the top of the stairs to transfer from his wheelchair to the stair lift. I'm standing near him, waiting to help.

Suddenly Michael shifts his anger and frustration onto me and pokes me forcefully in the solar plexus. "You're just standing there staring at me!"

I feel shock and a cold stab of pain.

I walk into the kitchen, and my own anger hits. I throw a bowl in the sink, shattering it. The fury passes, and I sit in the dining room—where he can't see me—and listen to him struggling and making those awful noises he makes when he can't do something and won't stop trying. I feel numb. A few tears fall, but no more. At that moment, I feel no compassion or concern for him. Instead, I feel oddly detached.

Soon I break my silence and tell him evenly that I can hear him having trouble. After a little bit, my head, not my heart, tells me I should ask him if he wants my help.

"No."

I start doing the dishes. I'm just a few feet away from where he's struggling at the top of the stairs. I'm ready to help if he calls me, but I keep my distance. He finally gets himself downstairs, and I can hear him continuing to struggle for a long time as he tries to get undressed and into bed. I'm unable to go downstairs; I feel a door has been slammed shut between us.

I fall into bed upstairs, sad, confused, and exhausted. Only once before, very early in our relationship, had he ever expressed his anger physically. At that time we were able to work through the pain and confusion and renew our loving promise to each other. I realize that now, suffering from MS, sometimes Michael will not be able to keep this commitment. I will have to be very careful not to provoke his anger. There may be times when he'll be unable to deal with the extreme frustration this disease brings, and he may transfer his anger away from the disease and onto me. Letting the bed support the heaviness of my body, I take a few deliberate, deep breaths. Slowly the tension begins to leave my body, my muscles loosen, and sleep seems within reach.

With Dr. Jones's help, Michael comes to understand I'm not just "staring" at him in situations like this; it's his self-consciousness and frustration that make him see me that way. Sometimes I don't always act spontaneously to help him when I see the need because often he snaps at me and tells me to stop or to go away when I do. I've learned to wait for him to ask for what he wants—but often he doesn't, and situations like this arise. In therapy, Dr. Jones suggests that perhaps Michael expects me to read his mind. Over time, Michael comes to realize that I can't, and he becomes more able to let me know what's going on with him and to tell me what he needs. He also learns things aren't always as he perceives them to be. There will still be times when he thinks I should do something differently and becomes accusatory, but, all in all, things get much better.

A month after the painful incident with the stair lift, I note in my journal that Michael is learning how to communicate his feelings and needs to me and that he's becoming more open to hearing mine. He's beginning to trust more in my good intentions instead of seeing my mistakes as purposeful. "Give her the benefit of the doubt" is one of the messages Michael takes to heart from our therapy sessions.

Going to therapy is a big step for Michael. It's a big step for him to realize some things in him need to change, as well as some things in me. He will need to become more aware of his assumptions, and I will need to become more aware of his emotional limitations, as well as my own. As Michael's caregiver, I'm learning I no longer need to fight for control, and, because of MS, so is he. More and more we're learning to work together and to put our power struggle behind us.

As we move toward the end of the year, I have a dream that threatens to be prescient:

*Michael and I are living in a room in some type of living unit. Michael is hooked up to a lot of tubes. It seems this might also be my mother. The tubes get blocked. Fluids back up. He/she goes into a coma. I panic but can't fix things. Someone there is supposed to help, but doesn't. I try to call 911. The phone doesn't connect me. I go to a dining room and ask someone to call. A woman tries on her cell phone, but it doesn't work. I'm beside myself with anxiety.*

My mother really had been hooked up to tubes and a respirator during her last days. It's as if I'm seeing the same fate for Michael—and, as with my mother, I'm helpless to stop it.

I know Michael has such fears too. The doctors deal with his immediate needs; they don't tell us what the future will hold. Since MS is such an unpredictable disease, different for every patient, most likely they really don't know. Yet, questions begin to plague me: *Where is he headed? What's going to happen to him? How much will he lose? How can I help him deal with all the changes that appear so ominous and imminent? And how will they affect me?*

# Chapter 21

# Loss and Rehabilitation

It was important that we had our RV adventures precisely when we did because now, in early 1999, Michael's condition is rapidly deteriorating. His urinary problems have reached the level where he has to perform intermittent catheterization; whenever he needs to relieve himself, he has to insert a sterile tube through his penis into his bladder. Nevertheless, since his diagnosis in 1996, he has rigorously striven to stay as active as possible. When I'm at work, for instance, with the aid of his forearm canes or his wheelchair, he's grateful he can do most of the grocery shopping and cook most of our dinners. "I'm not going to have you work all day and then come home and cook," he insists. I'm happy he feels this way—and besides, he's a good cook!

But I have my share of worries, too, when he tells me about incidents such as the following, which he described in his journal:

> I was leaning over the cart in the grocery store, dragging both legs. People were staring at me . . . out of the corner of their eyes. Kids openly looking. I'm becoming self-conscious . . . can't let that one stop me. Besides, I can still send the little ones scurrying back to Mom—and, with luck, fill their dreams full of creatures and bogeymen. Hope so anyway.

At least he still has his sense of humor, I think, even though the scene he's painting is pretty grim. Michael loved to tease little kids when he drove his truck on local runs. He used to keep a teddy bear in the cab beside him. When he came to a stop behind a car with a child in it, if the child turned around to look, he would hold up the teddy bear and tilt it back and forth. Invariably, the child would tap—or sock—his mother on the shoulder and point to Michael's truck. When the mother turned around, however, the bear would be gone, and all she would see was a truck driver staring blankly ahead. When she turned back, Michael would repeat the scene for as long as traffic allowed.

Around this time, Michael experiences several falls, though he's fortunate never to break a bone or seriously injure himself. Sometimes it's his dignity that's injured.

"I fell this afternoon in the front yard," he tells me one day when I return from work. "I was trimming the bushes in the front, and I just lost my balance. I got up, and I felt embarrassed. I don't know why I should. I kept snipping away for a while but didn't feel steady and hung it up."

We buy a window air conditioner for downstairs and qualify for special gas and electrical rates because of Michael's medical need to avoid the heat. Still, he often falls into what he calls "stupid mode." The heat or a drug reaction or just the fatigue that comes out of nowhere can cause this. Prozac helps—but it doesn't prevent him from slipping into darkness, and depression continues until he becomes mobile again.

"I was going to do the bills today, but I just went into the tank," he tells me after one difficult day. "I just felt it slipping away and was unable to pull myself out of it."

That summer we tell ourselves things will be better when the weather cools, but when the weather cools and they're not, we say things will be better after Michael gets a good night's sleep or after he rests . . . after, after, always after.

Talking about the need to water the front lawn one day, Michael tells me, "I was afraid to go down the front steps. I've come to depend on a railing, and without one, it looks way too dangerous for me right now."

And then he muses, "When did it come to this? It just sneaks up. One day I realize it isn't worth the chance of falling, and things get a little smaller in my world. Time to get out that walker of your mother's. Hey, it's better than falling down."

Those times when he has energy—and there are many still—he continues with his water walking at the Berkeley Y. But as he needs to use the wheelchair more often, his water-walking days are numbered. Soon it becomes quite difficult for him to lift the chair into and out of the trunk. Gradually, he becomes chilled in the water and shivers uncontrollably. The pain in his neck that started with the exacerbation on our RV trip up the coast increases. His balance and gait become erratic, his legs feel stiff, and his movements are uncoordinated. When he can no longer manage undressing and dressing—let alone making the drive—and becomes unable to climb the gently sloped steps into and out of the pool, he gives up the only sport he had left.

With this loss of activity, I remember the discussion from my MS caregivers' support group in which I learned about a rehabilitation hospital run by our HMO. On our next visit to Michael's neurologist, Dr. Nichols, I ask him about it.

"It has a wonderful reputation for helping people function again after strokes, spinal cord injuries, and accidents," he tells us. "They also help people with MS." To qualify, we learn, the patient must be able to improve.

At our request, Dr. Nichols refers Michael to this facility, and he's accepted. His intake evaluation reveals that Michael has difficulty swallowing, a condition known as dysphagia; at this stage, it's mild. His other problems include impairment of his bowel and bladder functions and weakness in his left upper and lower extremities. The doctor also notes that Michael has a "very superior range [of] intelligence." This prompts his social worker to ask whether Michael engages in meaningful projects or activities so as not to become bored; he wants to be sure Michael's doing things to keep his mind active. "I read a lot," Michael tells him, and I'm quick to add that we go to plays and cultural events whenever he's able.

So, for seven days in August of 1999, Michael is immersed in a rigorous program of physical therapy, occupational therapy, speech therapy, and group therapy with a licensed clinical social worker. He has a written schedule that hangs in a plastic sleeve from his wheelchair, and he's responsible for being at the right place at the right time. He has the benefit of excellent medical staff, who carefully select and track his programs and therapies, and his admitting doctor oversees his treatment and progress. Although he has a regular hospital bed in a four-man ward, he is rarely in it except to sleep at night and sometimes to rest for a couple of hours in the afternoon. He takes his meals in a group room and participates in the activities and movies that are provided for patients during their free time. I'm able to visit him whenever I want, but because the facility is quite a distance from home, I don't come every day. At last, I'm able to take some time off for myself, secure in knowing that he's well taken care of.

Michael gets more cheerful while he's here. The hospital is laid out to accommodate wheelchairs, and the wide hallways make it easy for him to wheel around to the various rooms.

"I thought I was getting better," he tells me when I visit one day. "But the doctor tells me my MS isn't disappearing. It's just easier for me here. Everything's laid out for a wheelchair, and I have all kinds of support."

He does make progress, however, and as his functioning improves, he sees new possibilities opening up for him. His balance and walking get better. He becomes independent in upper-body dressing, only needing help with pants, socks, and shoes, and his confidence improves. Physical therapy increases his strength and range of motion, and when he leaves he'll go home with an exercise program designed to maintain his gains.

Two caring women in the occupational therapy department get Michael out of his ill-fitting manual wheelchair and approved for a customized, electric power chair. It has mid-wheel drive, which makes it highly maneuverable, and Michael loves it. When he takes it out for a test drive in the parking lot and garage, he puts it through its paces, taking risks he was told not to take—but being a professional driver and stubborn, he doesn't listen to anyone but himself. The chair passes the test and, thanks in large part to Medicare (which Michael has received early due to his disability status), he's finally outfitted with what he needs. I think the two women who made this possible felt they needed to rescue him from his unfortunate manual chair and take him under their protective wings. We're so grateful for their help and guidance.

Michael likes and appreciates all the people who work with him. He jokes with them and makes small talk, enjoying himself as much as he possibly can. His spirits lift as he learns to strengthen his leg and arm muscles and increase his range of motion and stamina. It's time well spent.

Sometime before this but after the sale of our RV, we purchased a used van with money Michael's father sent us. His gift was unexpected but much appreciated. The van had been modified with hand controls, a wheelchair ramp, and a driver's seat that swiveled around to make it easier for Michael to use. He was able to transfer from his manual chair to the driver's seat and operate the vehicle using the hand controls—quickly becoming adept with them. Although most people must have training to use hand controls, Michael took to them effortlessly—no doubt the result of his many years of driving a truck. This allowed him to continue driving even as his disability increased.

He often had a hard time getting up and out of the seat, however, especially when he was tired. I remember one time going into the house and leaving Michael in the van as he was transferring to the wheelchair. When he didn't appear, I hurried into the garage to check on him. He was repeating the same, futile motion over and over, trying to get up from the driver's seat and into his wheelchair. When I spoke to him, he seemed in a daze. With my help, he finally made it. I never again left him to make the transfer alone.

Now that he has a power wheelchair and hiking poles are a thing of the past, we have an EZ Lock installed so he doesn't have to transfer when he drives. This consists of a lock on the floor that receives a bracket affixed to the bottom of the chair when he drives into place. This often takes a few tries, but it works well. Using the button and lever on the dashboard, he can release the lock, lower the ramp, and wheel out. Once outside, he can retract the ramp and close the automatic door with a remote device on his key chain. We had the original driver's seat removed from the van to accommodate the wheelchair.

So that he has enough room, we removed the passenger seat too. This was easily done, as it's on wheels and snaps into and out of place.

As a passenger, I now ride in the back—but sometimes, when Michael is tired, I do the driving. I position the passenger seat in the driver's position, lock it down, and he wheels into the passenger space. Then comes the hard part: I have to crawl around on the floor, loop the four tie-downs around his chair, and clip them into the metal slots on the floor. The whole procedure proves extremely hard on me because of my osteoarthritis. It's also pretty dirty on the floor, due to the wheelchair's coming and goings. Sometimes when he can't drive, we forgo outings altogether because Michael thinks it just isn't worth the trouble. After I help him with bathing and dressing, get ready myself, and then get him situated in the van, we often have very little energy left.

Nevertheless, the van makes it possible for us to do a lot of things we would otherwise never be able to do, and it allows Michael to be independent when he has the energy to drive. We're grateful for this, and for all the new and emerging technologies and laws that make it easier for people with disabilities to live their lives in ways they choose.

# Chapter 22

# Mishaps and Cruising

As 2000 begins, Michael's world is opening up for him again. He has a wonderful new electric wheelchair and a van with hand controls. The things that give him this new mobility, however, may also bring him close to disaster.

With the loss of the RV, Michael fears his traveling days are over. Dr. Jones points out that we live in an area that provides wonderful and varied opportunities for day trips, and we begin to take advantage of travel and sightseeing close to home—the wine country, San Francisco, and the nearby coast and parklands. The power wheelchair and van make this possible.

Michael continues to be active despite his growing disability. He can no longer lift his legs by himself, but I am able to help him with all the activities of daily living: bathing, grooming, dressing, etc. He becomes adroit at self-catheterization, and he is able to wash and sterilize his catheters in the microwave according to the instructions from his urologist. It's extremely important to Michael that he does all he can for himself.

Michael and I have begun making adjustments to our sexual life. We love each other, and we approach this situation without judgment and in our usual creative and exploratory style. Sometimes, when he's lying in bed, he'll just ask me to lie down on top of him, and we hold each other that way—just being close and quiet and calm.

We frequently take BART to San Francisco to go to plays or concerts, out to dinner, or just to enjoy the sights. When I'm at work, he often goes to the city on his own, driving the van to and from our local BART station. Because he has his handicapped placard, he always has a place to park.

Michael often comes home from these trips to the city with reminders of the time he walked across the Eel River all on his own and stood in the cool water, watching those dazzling dragonflies. He has found a myriad of dragonfly art to buy, including a sterling-silver necklace that has a smooth-winged dragonfly hanging from a linked chain. This has become his good luck piece and is always around his neck. Another time it's a small painting of a dragonfly from one of the many arts and crafts booths on the Embarcadero near the BART station. This goes up on the wall in his downstairs bedroom. Another small, pewter dragonfly finds a permanent home on one of his hats. He is always watching for dragonflies—real or artistically fashioned—to appear in his life. In making them his own, he holds onto his past and his ability to walk—to continue moving through life. I think he's brave to go out alone in his wheelchair, but he refuses to make a big deal of it. He's confident and determined to do all he can, and he's still adept at using the hand controls on his van. He always travels with his portable CD player and headphones, listening to his favorite music as he goes about his adventures. Currently he's enjoying *Everything But the Girl*.

Sometimes I do worry, especially if he doesn't come home until ten at night or later. My gentle reproaches and his well-meant promises fail to bring change, and I finally realize Michael simply no longer has a sense of the passage of time. He becomes enthralled with exploring a store or looking at paintings in a museum, and then is shocked when he looks at his watch and discovers that the minutes he spent were actually hours.

Despite my worry when he goes off on his own, I know it's important he do so. One time in particular, however, my worries are justified.

Michael spends the day on a solo trip to San Francisco, where he visits the Museum of Modern Art, a place he dearly loves. Often, he loses himself in the paintings, and he likes to analyze the artists' techniques and incorporate some of them in his art journal when he gets home. On this occasion, it grows late, and I become anxious when I don't hear from him. Eventually, I get a call, and he tells me the museum has closed and he has been locked inside. The night watchman is letting him use the phone.

"I was catheterizing in the handicapped stall in the men's restroom," he explains. "I heard someone ask if anyone was in here, but I ignored it. I figured I was almost finished."

As often happens, he was not almost finished. It sometimes takes him as long as an hour to catheterize. He has to get the hand sanitizer out of his bag and use it, open the Ziploc bag that contains the catheter, make sure the catheter touches nothing so as to remain sterile, apply lubricating gel to its tip, insert the catheter, and position the free end inside the Ziploc bag before urine begins to flow. He does all this with diminished motor coordination in his hands and with everything piled on his lap. No wonder it takes forever.

"When I wheeled out, the museum was dark," he goes on. "There was a night watchman. I think I scared him, but he was really helpful."

Michael assures me he'll be able to drive the wheelchair to BART, which is just a few blocks away, but he doesn't think he'll be able to drive the van home from the station. He's weak and weary.

Ordinarily, it wouldn't be a problem to drive my car to the BART station, switch over to the van to drive him home, and get a ride back to the station in the morning to pick up my car. The problem is, there's no driver's seat in the van, because Michael drives from his wheelchair—and we removed the passenger seat to give him more room to maneuver his chair. I'm at a loss as to what to do, until I decide to ask my neighbor for help.

Fortunately, Bob, my neighbor from across the street, comes to my rescue. We put the passenger seat in the back of his pickup. When we get to BART, he gets the seat down for me, and I push it up the wheelchair ramp and lock it down in the driver's position, all before Michael arrives at the station. (Thank God for the extra set of keys!) When Michael shows up, he wheels right into the van, and I tie down his chair on the passenger side. He's mightily relieved to see me and so grateful for our wonderful neighbor's help. When we get home, both of us exhausted, I spend the next forty-five minutes helping him undress and get into bed.

This isn't the only time our dear neighbor helps us out. The hand controls on Michael's van are used for both accelerating and braking. When I drive the van, I switch the mechanism over to regular floor controls using a hidden, hard-to-find, little switch buried inside the hand-control unit. Also, when I drive, I install the passenger seat in the driver's position. One time, after driving the van and then removing the seat, I forgot to switch the control unit back to hand control. I was at work when Michael got into the van to go somewhere. As soon as he started the van and put it in reverse, it took off and shot out of the garage, across the street, and straight into our neighbor's garage door. Michael was powerless to step on the brake because he couldn't move his legs, and he was too shocked and surprised to shove the automatic gearshift into park. Fortunately, no car or person or pet was on the sidewalk, in the street, or in either driveway. Michael wasn't hurt, but the unfortunate garage door was seriously damaged, as was the back of our van. Our neighbor and his wife were understanding and forgiving. Our AAA insurance paid for a new garage door quickly and without question—and without raising our rates. The only lasting result was my guilt for having forgotten to switch over the controls.

These mishaps do not deter us in our quest to discover modes of travel that will accommodate Michael's situation. We decide to take a cruise up the Inside Passage of Alaska. This looks like something Michael can do. We embark on the final voyage of an old Princess Line ship, which, conveniently, sails into and out of San Francisco. In fact, our ship is the original Love Boat! We take our local bus company's accessible shuttle (East Bay Paratransit) to and from the dock, saving us the hassle of parking.

Taking a cruise turns out to be a good decision. Although Michael isn't able to go on all the shore excursions due to accessibility issues, he does go on most of them. The high point of the trip for him is a historic narrow-gauge rail excursion on the White Pass and Yukon Route out of Skagway. The train is wheelchair accessible, and we board just a few feet from the dock where our cruise ship is anchored. This rail system, the Railway Built of Gold, was constructed between May 1898 and July 1900 to provide a lifeline from British Columbia to the Yukon, opening up the Yukon Territory for settlement and commerce following the gold rush of 1898.

As a truck driver, Michael has always been fascinated by the history and varieties of transportation. Now he can actually ride the historic rails through verdant gorges, along sheer cliffs, and over death-defying trestles. The gorgeous, scenic journey takes us 2,865 feet from sea level to the summit of White Pass and back down again.

Our cruise ship is fairly easy for Michael to transverse, and during our time at sea, we enjoy all the amenities it has to offer: observation decks, cocktail lounges, floor shows, the spa (for me), and food, food, food. Many times, when he's tired, Michael can rest in the cabin while I go off to explore the ship. I'm always nearby and never gone for long, so we feel comfortable with this arrangement. The times we have the most fun, though, are when we're enjoying the cruise together. We are lucky to have beautiful, clear weather and smooth water the whole way.

Not long after our cruise and when we've purchased cell phones, I decide to give Michael a call on my way home from my therapy appointment in Oakland. I'm startled when an unfamiliar voice answers the phone. The voice identifies himself as a fireman and tells me Michael has been in an accident and is being taken to the hospital. At first, I think I have the wrong number—even though I pressed the button for my "favorite" number—or that someone is playing a joke on me. I soon realize this is no joke. I learn Michael was visiting a neighbor who was working in his yard up the street from our house, and, as Michael turned his wheelchair around, he hit a rock and tipped over. The paramedics don't know the extent of his injuries, so they've taken him to the hospital by ambulance.

When I get to the hospital, I find Michael in an exam room in the ER; he seems dazed. He looks at me and appears to pass out for a second. Then he looks at me again and asks, "Who are you?"

Frightened, clutching his hand, I say, "I'm Suzanne. Your wife."

Then he looks at me and laughs! He has a sick sense of humor sometimes. He thinks this is very funny, but I am not amused, although I'm extremely relieved he's okay. He does have a black eye and a cut on his forehead that needs a few stitches, so I don't reproach him. I'm reminded this is the same Michael who found it hysterical when I thought he had fallen off a cliff and into the ocean on our trip up the coast in our RV. Actually, I'm glad it's the same Michael, as one of the things I love most about him is his sense of humor. We laugh together a lot—and, thankfully, not always at my expense.

I'm reminded of the many times I've picked up a book, only to find that Michael has written an "inscription from the author" inside. In a book of art reproductions by Toulouse-Lautrec, I found the following inside the front cover, written in the flourishing penmanship he loved: "Michael—Your work has always been an inspiration to me," followed by a line-drawing of a smiling face and a flourishing signature, dated 1895. Inside a book of photographs by Helmut Newton I found: "Michael—Thanks for all the ideas you've given me over the years! It's been fun!!" It's signed, "Hemet Newton 11-17-75." Not confining his fun to art books, inside my *Chez Panisse* recipe book he wrote: "Michael—You've taught me so very much over the years. Love always, Alice Waters." Inside *A Brief History of Time* I found: "Michael—I'd still be in a black hole if it hadn't been for your insights. Thank you, Steven Hawking." This elaborate signature was followed by several small dots, a triangle, and an arrow that bent down at a forty-five-degree angle. I never know when I'm going to find one of these and break out in laughter. He does them for his own amusement, never mentioning any of his "inscriptions" to me.

Michael is soon released from the hospital, and we go home. I drive; I had remembered to go home and switch over to the van before coming to the hospital. (I also carefully checked the hand-control setting to be sure I was in normal drive.) When we get home, I switch it back to hand controls. I'm learning.

# Chapter 23

# Drugs and Desert

Throughout 2001 and the beginning of 2002, MS continues to dominate our lives. Michael has begun taking Ritalin to increase his energy. It works, and it keeps him going. In addition to the Ritalin, Michael is taking Provigil (usually prescribed for narcolepsy) and amantadine to fight fatigue, baclofen for spasticity, Prozac for depression, Valium (occasionally) for anxiety, temazepam for sleep, and Vicodin as needed for pain. His neurologist says if he were to take all of the medications Michael is taking, he would be in a coma.

Michael also injects Copaxone once a day, the only drug in this panoply that targets the progress of his disease rather than its symptoms. Studies show this drug diminishes the number of exacerbations in patients with relapsing-remitting MS, but Michael's naturally suspicious nature keeps him from really believing it will help. Consequently, and much to my growing frustration, he's careless in its use and doesn't always inject it at the same time each day, as he's supposed to. I remind him often and ask him almost daily if he has injected, but even with my nagging, he's often inconsistent. I suspect he maintains this distrusting attitude to protect himself from disappointment if the drug doesn't work. This is the pattern he established early in childhood, when his father failed to follow through on promises of camping trips or visits to the zoo. He came to know his father's plans rarely if ever materialized, and his childhood excitement seemed always to bring disappointment.

I continue accompanying him to all of his medical appointments. His short-term memory is getting worse, so he relies on me to mention any new symptoms to the doctor and to recall later what the doctor said.

For quite a while now, we've both been meticulous in avoiding germs. Because of MS, even a cold can knock him down, and he has a hard time recovering. I wash my hands assiduously and avoid being around people who are sick so as not to bring germs into the house, and he does the same. This vigilance pays off, and he rarely becomes ill.

Even so, his medical condition is worsening. Because he is catheterizing now, he sometimes gets urinary infections. I learn to watch the color of his urine in the collection bag I attach to his catheter at night and to notify the doctor immediately when it gets dark. Fortunately, these infections can be treated successfully with antibiotics. His MS exacerbations are occurring less frequently, but this doesn't mean he's getting better or that the Copaxone is working. Instead, it means Michael has entered a new phase of his disease; secondary or chronic progressive MS is what the doctor calls it. Over time, he'll continue to get worse. How long that time will be we have no way of knowing.

It's clear to both of us if we want to be active and enjoy our lives, we need to do it now. We no longer have the RV, but we do have the wheelchair van, and Michael is able to drive and get around. With this in mind, and with Christmas fast approaching, we decide to take a weeklong vacation to Palm Springs, a place neither of us has been before.

Michael drives the van from his wheelchair, and I ride somewhat uncomfortably in the back seat. Our destination is a resort called Miramonte in Indian Wells, near Palm Springs, and it proves to be the perfect choice. Just as they had assured me, there is good wheelchair access throughout, and the grounds are spacious and lovely, patterned with paths that wind through manicured grassy areas bordered by colorful flowers. Palm trees abound, and there are beautifully groomed pine trees. (So beautifully groomed, we learn, that pine needles are never allowed to litter the grounds.) Miramonte consists of a series of villa-like structures with red tile roofs. It has quite an Italian feel to it. Also featured is the promised view of the mountains. We have a large room with a terrace facing the grounds, and Michael is able to transfer to the shower bench and use the shower in our accessible bathroom on his own, with help from the grab bars. At this moment, life is good.

Unbeknownst to me, he has brought along two presents, one for Christmas and one for my December birthday. I receive a gorgeous Hermes scarf and a floral night set—tap pants, matching top, and short robe. He is always so romantic when it comes to gifts, and he has fun selecting them and giving them to me. We had agreed the trip itself would be our present to each other, so I didn't bring anything for him. I do manage to reciprocate, however—the lingerie being the inspiration, as he knew it would.

The novelty of the place and the variety of things to see and do enable us to banish our fears, and we focus on having fun. We attend the Follies in Palm Springs, somewhat doubtful that a show featuring beautiful and talented showgirls fifty and older will be worth seeing. To our delight, it turns out to be a terrific and inspiring show—a high point of our trip. In the days that follow, we visit an oasis or two, luxuriate in the large Miramonte hot tub (mostly I do that, and he watches), and cool off in our choice of two swimming pools. We love being served wine, fruit, and cheese at poolside and relaxing in the shade of the cabana.

I especially relish this rare time of being taken care of and catered to—a welcome relief from the combined stresses of work, taking care of Michael, and worrying about our future. Here, we can simply look forward to tomorrow and the good things it will bring. We love the climate too. Just as in Death Valley, we both feel rejuvenated by the warm, dry air.

Yet the trip is not entirely free of difficulties. Michael's wheelchair gets stuck in the sand at one oasis in the desert. He, of course, doesn't think I have the strength to push him back onto the hard-packed path. Ignoring his "You can't do it," as I often must, and confident in my ability to handle things, I succeed, and we continue on. In the evenings, Michael is frequently too tired to make it to the resort's restaurant for dinner, and we opt for room service. They bring us good food, though, so I can't say we actually suffer too much.

Inevitably, the time arrives when our vacation must end. We embark on the long drive north toward home, bringing our suntans and good memories with us.

Back in Castro Valley, Michael continues to remain active by doing the home exercises given to him by his physical therapist. He is determined to do as much as he possibly can, and it warms my heart to see him succeed. We continue taking day trips, exploring San Francisco, touring the Napa Valley wine country, or going down the coast or up to Point Reyes or just to our local recreation area, Lake Chabot. We both feel lucky to live in the Bay Area, where there's so much we can do.

Sometime after our trip, Michael goes through a long-hair-and-shaggy-beard phase. He eventually relents to pressure, but continues to sport a goatee—his last holdout.

As we continue to be active, we become more and more aware of how being in a wheelchair changes the way a person is perceived. When we are out together, more often than not, people talk to me and ignore Michael. Many times it's as if he isn't even there. Having been so tall, never ignored and always obviously "there," it's difficult for him to adjust to this. One extremely annoying thing happens frequently when we are being seated for dinner. Ninety-nine percent of the time, the waitperson will ask me where Michael wants to sit or if the table is okay. Sometimes, when Michael becomes really annoyed, he will say in a demanding voice, "Talk to *me!*" Then, as if noticing him for the first time, the waitperson will talk to him and ask him the questions. Sometimes I just say, "I don't know. Ask him," when the waitperson asks me what Michael wants.

Many of the simplest tasks for ordinary people have become challenges for Michael. Elevators will start to close before he's completely inside; sidewalks will suddenly run out of curb cuts, or the incline will be too steep to maneuver unaided down or up a poorly made cut; people will block wheelchair routes; heavy doors will impede his entrance to buildings; and a million other things will happen that an able-bodied person would never have to navigate.

Michael gets livid when he rolls into an "accessible" bathroom or stall only to find a table or chair blocking his path. The ADA specifies a required amount of space for a wheelchair turning radius, and putting something in that space makes maneuvering a wheelchair impossible. I've even seen so-called accessible bathrooms in restaurants used as storage space or decorated with chests and cabinets. And, of course, how many people have no idea what those striped lines mean next to a handicapped parking space? More than once, Michael finds he is unable to lower his ramp on the side of the van because someone has parked carelessly and blocked part of the striped area. A few times, he's been able to get out of the van only to find, on his return, that a car has blocked his access back in. If I'm driving and he's a passenger, I can back up enough to lower the ramp, but this is risky, and it can put him into traffic.

I know books have been written about what it's like to be at knee level to others in the world. Things are different from that perspective. And, more often than not, people act differently toward people in that position. The other side of the story is there are many, many people who offer to help. People hold doors open for Michael, help him to find the accessible entrances to places, ask whether he is all right, and offer assistance in countless other ways. Sometimes a person, usually a woman, will hold a door open for Michael when he's gone ahead of me, thinking he's on his own. When I catch up, I'll get a nasty glare for being so insensitive as to let him fend for himself. Michael always finds this most amusing. In fact, he attracts scores of women who want to help him. "The only problem with this," Michael says, "is they want to mother me, not flirt with me."

What an ego-downer that can be for an attractive man who suddenly finds himself perceived as helpless. On the upside, Michael notices when he encounters a woman alone at night on a darkened street or in an elevator, she doesn't appear nervous or frightened. "They see me as harmless," he says, with some ambivalence.

As Michael learns what it means to cope with a chronic disease and be confined to a wheelchair, his compassion for others increases. He always has a good word for homeless people on the street, and, more often than not, gives them money; being at eye level with a homeless person who's also in a wheelchair gives him a new perspective. I notice a "How ya doin', brother?" or a similar phrase from Michael often seems as welcome as spare change to a street person.

Michael becomes more sensitive to my needs, too, and what it means for me to be a caregiver. He worries, for instance, I might hurt my back when I tie down his wheelchair in the van when he's the passenger or help him roll onto his side in bed. Once he felt quite bad when, trying to get his pants off him when he was lying in bed, I tugged so hard I sprained my wrist. He often says, "I want you to be my wife, not my caregiver." But the reality is I need to be both, and he comes to accept that.

And so things go. We are coping. We are managing. We do all we can to keep living our lives in the best possible way. More and more, we're working together and meeting challenges head on. Michael continues to have pretty good upper-body strength. He continues to draw in his art journal, although sometimes he can't, and to read and keep up with the news. We travel as much as possible, go to movies, plays, museums, and restaurants, and enjoy just being together. If anything, our marriage is growing stronger. What began as a power struggle is transforming into a collaboration based on love, trust, and acceptance.

# Chapter 24

# Salvation and Shock

As time goes on, I'm forced to acknowledge that I can't do it all alone—I need help taking care of Michael. He is no longer able to manage many of the tasks of daily living. He needs help getting in and out of bed, bathing, catheterizing, and dressing. It has become dangerous for him to attempt these things when I'm at work and he's alone. More than once, he has fallen or become stuck, unable to move or complete a transfer to or from his wheelchair. When I'm home, the physical act of helping him is becoming too much for me; I lack the strength and stamina to do the job well, let alone safely. Fortunately, I'm put in touch with a wonderful woman who is to become our lifesaver.

Una has a generous and competent nature. She's from Tonga, and she brings us not only a cheerful and loving presence but also a glimpse into a fascinating culture so different from our own. A devout Methodist, she works with Michael untiringly for three hours each morning, but her Sundays are dedicated to church and bingo. We learn her island has a benevolent king as its ruler, and family bonds there are strong. There is no end to the tough love of a mother's discipline, and even grown and married children who stray from acceptable behavior accept a physical rebuke without question. Children are cherished and, in turn, take care of their elders when the need arises. Una doesn't understand why such familial obligation doesn't hold true in this country, and she protects her own three children from the harsh realities of American culture as much as she can. She is here for no other reason than to better their lives; there is no room for economic advancement at home.

Now that Una is here to help Michael each morning, my home life is much less stressful. I no longer worry every time I leave the house for work. I know he will not be alone in the mornings, struggling to shower and dress. My worry was always he'd fall and be unable to reach the phone to call 911. Now he's covered, and I can leave the house with increasing peace of mind.

Michael enjoys his mornings with Una. Through their conversations and interactions, he is helping her with her English. She, in turn, entertains him with stories of her children, her culture, her plans, and her challenges. She has a sense of humor, too, and often they laugh as she busily attends to his needs. I can't imagine trying to manage without her.

My major stresses now come from work. Early in the 2001–2002 school year, I have the following dream:

> I am driving in the mountains to a destination. Nancy, my supervisor at work and a good friend, is driving. She is going too fast; she's in a hurry. She pulls into a rest stop, and I get out. She doesn't realize I have gotten out and drives away without me. I decide I'm not going back in the car even if she returns for me. I know I would face great danger if I do. I walk down the mountain on the road next to the inside lane.

*It's pretty here: It's a rural area with green grass, flowers, and trees. I keep going. I follow a country road through the green valley. Evening is approaching.*

I see this as a dream of transition, and it offers me direction and hope. I decide it's time to make the separation, get out of the car that's going too fast, get back on my feet, and take a different route—one that will put me back on my true path, my path of spiritual self-discovery. A large part of this path is service to others. The need to pursue this through my work is over; I want to devote my time to Michael and to our marriage. I make plans to retire in 2002.

In 1992, I began graduate studies in transpersonal psychology at the Institute of Transpersonal Psychology (now Sofia University) in Palo Alto, California. Studying at ITP was life changing for me. The school offered an experiential and transformative program of personal growth coupled with a rigorous academic curriculum presented in the context of a supportive and safe community. It was a time of finding my own voice and embarking on a spiritual path of self-discovery.

According to Robert Frager, founder of ITP, "The core of transpersonal psychology includes the premise that wisdom, creativity, and intuition are essential qualities within each individual. The goal of transformational education is to facilitate our access to our own rich inner resources." Arthur Hastings, ITP professor emeritus, wrote, "Transpersonal psychology is the study of human experiences that transcend the normal boundaries of personality—including higher states of consciousness and holistic levels of human development."

In my course of studies at ITP, we explored the psychospiritual aspects of the individual, including profound spiritual and mystical experiences, the nature of consciousness, altered or transcendent states of consciousness, psychic phenomena, and more. I was engaged in activities of self-exploration such as creative expression, dreamwork, somatic work, shamanic journeying, breathwork, and meditation. Those studying to become therapists acquired knowledge and techniques based on transpersonal research and practices. I was on the academic track, more interested in research than therapeutic application.

While at ITP, I learned rituals and practices that allowed me to access higher states of wisdom. They now provide me with spiritual guidance and inspiration as I care for Michael and for myself. It was at ITP that I was drawn to the psychology of Carl Jung. In studying his theories and discovering the knowledge hidden in the unconscious, through dreams and creative expression (such as writing and collage making), I was able to grow in ways that allowed me to know and express myself more fully. This is proving invaluable to me as I help Michael in his struggle with MS, providing me with a powerful toolkit of resources from which I can draw.

It hadn't been easy for me to make the decision to enroll at ITP. I spent months in therapy agonizing over whether or not I should "follow my bliss," as Joseph Campbell would say. My inner critic insisted it would be unforgivably selfish for me to spend time and money just on myself. Michael, too, was initially skeptical and unsupportive of my decision. I had yet to learn that to be of service to others does not mean denying my own needs. At ITP, I learned that true service comes from doing what one is called to do. Self-sacrifice isn't a part of this; in fact, it's counterproductive and can only lead to confusion and resentment. Acting from a centered place within, making decisions that are best for me, as well as for others, leads to true service.

Most of my life, I had been both absorbed by and in rebellion against the judgments of others as they defined who I was and what I did. At ITP, I made tremendous growth in this area, growth that later proved essential in helping me build the confidence to be a competent caregiver for Michael. In a self-reflection paper, I wrote the following:

> I realized that I deserved and was entitled to my own per-
> ceptions and sense of self, and that this sense of self included
> intrinsic value. I have become more and more aware of my
> own inner guidance. I feel I have a reliable and accurate inner
> sense of what's right and wrong for me, and I have gained
> enough confidence in my own self-worth and intuitive feelings
> to allow me to confidently choose to do what I feel is right. I
> was taught early on to doubt my own experiences, perceptions,
> and power, so this shift is a major accomplishment for me.

As self-doubt diminished, I began to trust my inclinations and follow my intuition. During my years at ITP, I was immersed in a program that challenged me academically and provided me with the culture and community support to grow psychologically and spiritually. I earned my master's degree in transpersonal psychology by going to school at night for two years, and I spent another year on sabbatical completing coursework for the PhD.

When I returned to work, I requested a split assignment. I was assigned to teach two classes of psychology at the high school, and the rest of my day would be spent at the district office as the grant proposal writer.

I was able to transform my career in education; I was teaching a new subject I loved and acquiring new writing skills through pursuing funding for education. Writing was another of my passions. As my work become more consuming, it became evident that I didn't have the time to complete a dissertation and finish the PhD program. Perhaps I already had all I needed to feel fulfilled.

To my delight, I was able to integrate much of what I had learned and practiced at ITP into my psychology classes at the high school. I found teaching these classes kept me in touch with my process of personal growth and allowed me to provide similar opportunities to my students. I loved watching them expand their concepts of reality and discover new aspects of themselves. I remember one student who, after completing a collage representing herself, looked at the finished product—which contained pictures of clothing, sexy boys, cars, and alcohol—and commented in alarm, "Oh, my God, I'm superficial." After that revelation, I noticed she began to be more serious and self-reflective.

Over time, my dedication to my district job outweighed my enthusiasm for teaching psychology. When my supervisor asked me to do grant proposal writing full-time, I could have declined, but I felt it would be irresponsible to do so; I had been instrumental in bringing a number of excellent programs into the district that had helped many students and teachers. I was, so to speak, a victim of my own success.

In developing programs for grant proposals, I grew in many ways; I developed leadership skills and learned to work collaboratively with other educators and outside stakeholders. Yet I was also aware that, because I was no longer teaching my psychology classes, I had strayed far from the path I had begun at ITP. Teaching psychology had given me a way to keep my own personal growth alive. Through guiding my students in their own inner explorations, I got back far more than I gave.

Now, in the fall of 2001—after working hard the previous year, including straight through the summer—my change in direction has taken its toll. It's okay, I tell myself, because I'm going to retire soon anyway, and I'm conscientious about my health. When I retire, I'll be able to concentrate more on my psychological growth and spiritual discovery, and I can devote much more time to Michael. I've got it all figured out.

Then, on March 4, 2002, I am diagnosed with colon cancer.

# Chapter 25

# Reaching Out and In

I'd been feeling tired for some time, but I attributed it to the stress of work and our ongoing battle against MS. Many months before March 4, I went to my primary care physician complaining of fatigue. He determined I was depressed but suggested a "wait and see" period before considering medication. Although I eventually began to feel better, my energy remained low, so I decided to change primary care physicians. I wanted more help than he could provide. In February, my new doctor ordered a blood test that showed I was anemic. Since I was no longer menstruating, she suspected internal bleeding to be the cause. A fecal occult blood test revealed blood in my stool. The next step was to have a colonoscopy.

On March 4, Michael drives me to the clinic for my colonoscopy. They require me to have a driver, and I'm glad Michael is up for making the trip. Also, they tell me I will need someone there to hear the results, as I might not remember what I'm told due to the anesthetic.

The night before, I religiously follow the long purging procedure to prepare my colon for its close-up. I feel weak and not a little nervous. Lying on a bed in the clinic before the procedure, I'm given IV hydration for an hour. This gives me plenty of time to imagine the worst. It turns out that undergoing the tests, which include both a colonoscopy and an endoscopy in which they insert a tube down my throat and into my stomach, is not all that bad, thanks to the IV anesthetic.

Once I'm back in the recovery room, the doctor and Michael appear. The doctor tells us he's discovered a polyp he believes is malignant. He's visibly concerned and expresses his sorrow at having to give us such bad news. He tells us he'll order a biopsy, but he's pretty sure it's cancer.

Right now, everything seems surreal. An image of Dali's melting clock slides into my mind. I'm so glad Michael is here with me now. He appears strong and steady as he takes in the news. I know he's here for me now and that I can lean on him.

"Don't sign any contracts or make any major decisions for twenty-four hours," the doctor cautions. "The anesthetic will affect your judgment, even if you don't realize it."

Sure. That's the least of my worries.

Stunned but calm, I return with Michael to the van, which is parked in a handicapped space in front of the clinic. As we approach, we notice a large pickup truck parked in the space next to the van, and it's intruding into the white-lined area reserved for lowering the ramp. The driver of the pickup is sitting behind the wheel. Instead of nicely asking the man to move his truck, Michael yells up from his wheelchair, "You'd think someone who drove such a big car would know how to drive!"

This remark does not engender a polite response. The man looks down defiantly at Michael and refuses to move. Suddenly, I become enraged. I shower the offending driver with a screaming litany of ADA parking laws, using plenty of swear words for emphasis. He and his truck remain unmoved. Finally, I convince him to unblock the ramp area by threatening to get the parking attendant and call the police. He moves, and Michael is able to lower the ramp.

Michael is surprised and amused by my outburst, and we both start laughing, breaking the tension. Later, my therapist will tell me to mentally thank the man for unknowingly taking the brunt of our anger at my diagnosis.

Thus begins my preparatory path for surgery. As I rest at home after the test, lying in a hypnagogic state between wakefulness and sleep, pleasant images appear of things I enjoy: mountains, the sea, rock 'n' roll, dancing to songs like "Simply Irresistible." I begin a dialogue with the tumor. I ask it what it wants. A message filters back to me: I want you to take time for yourself.

I reflect on the ways I've forgotten myself, one of which was to put my work in transpersonal psychology off until retirement, when I would have more time for it. Now it's a life-and-death situation—me or death, and maybe death anyway.

I don't realize it yet, but I will be using all the knowledge and resources I gained at ITP—and more—to get through the next few months. There will be nothing but time for walking my spiritual path.

I take out my journal and make a list of things that are important to me: Michael, friends, Michael's children and grandchildren, visualizations, dreamwork, travel, creative writing, research, holistic health, transpersonal psychology, parapsychology, spirituality, nature, god/goddess. Then I add "Me" and put a circle around it. I realize I must take care of myself, both for my own sake and for Michael's. I realize, too, I need help, and much of that help lies within. I think of ways I can become healthier: yoga, swimming, meditation, eating well, imaging. I intentionally turn my focus away from fear and toward healing. This turning seems to come naturally, and it feels right.

The next day I have a dialogue with my Wise Old Person, or WOP. The WOP is an aspect of my own higher wisdom. I learned this practice when I was involved with psychosynthesis, a spiritual and holistic psychology developed by Roberto Assagioli, and I still find it illuminating. In my imagination, I enter a peaceful and beautiful valley. There is green spring grass and an abundance of golden and purple wildflowers. I easily find the path leading up the mountain, but soon I realize I don't need to make the steep climb. Instead, a tram pops up and carries me to the top. I become aware that the mountain is Mt. Diablo, which has been visible to me for most of my life, first from my hometown and then from most of the places I've lived in Northern California. My WOP appears to me in the form of Jesus, and he welcomes me. He looks like a rabbi in traditional dress. From his accent, I take it that he's from New York. A thought forms in my mind: "Through him I can heal." Deep inside me, my inner child seems to be awakened. (My mother had often taken me to the Christian Science church when I was young, which emphasizes healing through Christ Consciousness.)

Then Buddha and Padmasambhava appear. I realize I can also heal through them. They are there for my adult/intellectual/ feeling self, and both have a heart connection to me. I bow down in thanks, and a red heart appears in front of me. I think of rose crystal and its power to heal the heart, and I feel tears of gratitude streaming down my cheeks. It's time to leave the mountaintop, and I turn to descend, bringing these visions back home with me. After ending my inner dialogue, I write about my experience to ground it in this reality.

I tell myself I must go to Mt. Diablo this spring. I think of all the other places that are special to me: the ocean, the Stanislaus River, the Sierra Nevada, Lake Tahoe, Point Reyes, and the farming valley of my childhood. I see them all as my special homes in California.

Some of the messages I take away are: accept; don't judge; follow what comes up; there is no conflict between Jesus and Buddha; compassion and healing are the links.

I accept that I am not in control, but I believe I can influence my life toward healing. My intuition is telling me I cannot remain passive on this journey. It's also telling me that all will be well. This last message comes to me not as a belief or an affirmation or something I am actively willing to happen; it comes as an inner knowing.

A few days later, I go to the hospital to get a CAT scan. The severity of my diagnosis really hits me when I see "colon cancer" written on the scan request. I'm immediately afraid of the CAT scan machine, and I suddenly realize I know nothing about it. Nervous and anxious, I seek reassurance from the technician.

"You'll be fine," he says, "and if anything were to happen, all the resources of this hospital would descend on this room like gangbusters."

That makes me feel better.

Michael is with me when, soon after the CAT scan, I meet my surgeon. I like him immediately. He appears to be quite competent, and I'm reassured to find out he's also a professor at UC Medical Center in San Francisco. From his impeccable dress and confident manner, I decide he meets my requisites for perfection. (Michael later swears that when the doctor left the room, he clicked his heels as he turned and that he was wearing Armani shoes. I wasn't aware of either and wouldn't have known an Armani shoe from a Buster Brown.)

I'm relieved to find I have confidence in my surgeon, but I also realize I have a long-held fear of doctors and anxiety about being in hospitals. These feelings probably started when I had my tonsils removed when I was two, and, as I lay on the gurney screaming for my mother, a nurse told me my mother wasn't there. She'd gone shopping, the nurse told me. Of course, that wasn't true, and the nurse didn't succeed in shutting me up. In fact, I was doubly terrified after that. I can still remember screaming "No!" while rejecting the toys they offered me and feeling completely helpless, confused, and abandoned. And then, when I was six, I had an appendectomy and experienced being "suffocated to death" as an ether mask was held firmly over my nose while I kicked and struggled to breathe. That time, they told me, I kicked the doctor in the stomach.

I make two appointments before my surgery to help me deal with my fears and anxiety. The first is with a healer in Marin County, recommended by a friend who survived cancer, and the second is with my hypnotherapist.

The healer does energetic, hands-on bodywork. As I lie on the table in his office, I can feel warmth radiating from his hands as he sends healing energy to my lower abdomen. He suggests I dialogue with the spirit of my cancer. He also gives me a much needed gift in the form of a parable. He tells me the story of a man who couldn't get his donkey to move for three days. Finally, his neighbor hit the donkey over the head with a two-by-four, and a few seconds later, the donkey moved.

"Why did you do that?" the donkey's owner asked. "How did you get him to move?"

"I just whispered in his ear," the neighbor said, "but first I had to get his attention."

After the session, I sit in my car for a while and feel centered and aware. I notice a city park nearby where redwoods are growing. I get out, walk on a path into the park, and sit on a bench, looking at the strong and long-lived redwood trees. I listen to the wind blowing through the tops of the trees and a feeling of peace comes over me. The sky is clear and blue, the temperature in the high sixties, and I decide to do the dialogue.

The spirit of the cancer appears to me as a messenger—perhaps Hermes. Hermes is the herald, or messenger, of the gods, and it's his duty to guide the souls of the dead down to the underworld. Hermes's arrival is serious business, comparable to being hit over the head with a two-by-four—he has my attention. He "whispers in my ear" that I must get back on my transpersonal path, and I must make that my first priority. To do so, I have to trust my intuition. I must follow my intuition without having to know why I am being called to do certain things or where it will lead or how things will turn out. He tells me I often do something for myself only if I can see it will also benefit others. I need to act for myself now. I don't need to justify it.

I remember back to my decision to do graduate work at ITP. In making that decision, I learned to trust my inclinations. It was the right thing then, and it will be the right thing now.When the dialogue is complete, I walk up a little path and ascend some steps that appear to lead nowhere. When I get to the top, however, I realize from here I have a different perspective on the park. I sit down on a nearby bench, and, feeling the warm sun on my skin, I slip into a brief meditation.

When I get back in the car, I write this message to myself:

*My intuition seems much more accessible to me now than before I studied at ITP. Don't ignore it. Access and follow it. I have permission now from everyone to take care of myself because I'm in a life-and-death situation. If I do, the cancer won't need to be here. When I went back to work after my sabbatical at ITP and gave up on the plan to finish my PhD, did this encourage the cancer? Did it increase when I stopped*

*teaching my psychology class? I can't grow through Michael
or through his illness right now. My growth has to be for and
through myself. My growth will help him, too, but that can't
be my main focus.*

The second place my intuition leads me is to hypnotherapy. I
have a long student–teacher relationship with the hypnotherapist
Dr. Arthur Hastings, who was one of my professors at ITP, and I
trust him completely. Arthur headed the master's program, and due
to his gentle, caring guidance, I always felt recognized and heard.
One of my favorite classes was the one he taught on hypnosis. I feel
relaxed and safe with him. I go to two sessions in which he induces a
hypnotic state and gently suggests that I may now have a shift in my
feelings about doctors and hospitals; I may begin to think of doctors
and nurses as allies, people who are on my side.

I listen to the tapes of these sessions many times as I prepare for
surgery, and my feelings do, indeed, make this shift. My attitude
toward the healthcare staff and the operation becomes genuinely
positive and cooperative, and I begin to see the medical staff as being
here to help me.

Everywhere I turn, I seem to find validation and support. Dianne,
a friend from ITP, sends me some of her books and tapes on healing, helpful resources that arrive at exactly the right time. Cards and
phone calls from friends and coworkers let me know I'm supported
and not alone. Another friend, Sally, a colleague from the high school
where we both taught psychology, gives me emotional support and
hands-on healings. Most importantly, Michael is there with me every
step of the way. He never shows his fear. I receive only constant love,
concern, and support from him.

I'm especially touched by the support I receive from people in my school district; the assistant superintendent, who is my supervisor at the district office, and Elaine, who is the director of human resources, make sure I'm given immediate leave to prepare for surgery. And to my eternal gratitude, other teachers in the district donate some of their sick leave to me.

My surgery is scheduled for March 26. On March 12, I read a magazine article that proves to be quite helpful. It cautions against rushing back to usual activities in times of crisis and warns that, if we do, we risk closing our eyes and ears to clues that might lead us to more fruitful actions. It speaks of living, for a time, "empty" and receptive to inward messages in order to gain guidance now that our world has changed.

I can go back to work before my surgery if I choose. My supervisor encourages me to do this only if I want to; it's my choice. This article comes at just the right time. I realize I must turn my energies inward for healing. Fortunately, I'm able to do this.

I make a list in my journal of all the positive, healing things I can do. The list includes seeing a Christian Science practitioner; doing healing visualizations; meditating; working with my psychotherapist; spending time in nature; laughing; petting animals; surrendering to a higher will; writing in my journal; and, of course, spending time with Michael.

I have a dream during this time that is set in my windowless work area at the district office:

> *I'm outside my cubicle where I work, looking in. It's dark inside, windowless, covered with spider webs. My Mac laptop is there, and I'm supposed to be working on it. I complain about the working conditions. I see Judy, a good friend and an administrator in my school district, knocking down cobwebs*

*with a broom. I ask her why they told her to do this, and she*
*just smiles a knowing smile. I see the faces of two women with*
*cobwebs behind their head. I try to warn them that, when they*
*move, the cobwebs will stick in their hair. I go to leave, and a*
*cobweb sticks to me. I remove a maggot from my top lip. "This*
*is gross," I say. "I'm going to call OSHA!"*

What do the cobwebs signify? I'm not sure, but I think a lot of yucky stuff is sticking to me right now, a web of work and unfinished projects, for one thing. Also, I've always been afraid of spiders, so their webs may point to my fear of being entangled in cancer's web and my unknown fate. Judy was known as one who liked to clear clutter. Maybe she, or the part of me she represents, is trying to help me get unstuck—get all the work responsibilities "out of my hair" so I can get on with the work of facing my cancer. The disgusting maggot must be the insipient cancer itself, and OSHA the higher power I'm calling in.

Now, in the third week of March, I'm feeling frustrated. I'm trying many different modalities of healing and not going deeply enough into any one of them. Besides following the activities on my list, I'm also doing shamanic journeying and the tarot cards, and I have requested twenty-four-hour prayer through Silent Unity. The Unity movement was founded by Charles and Myrtle Fillmore in 1889 as a healing ministry, based on the power of prayer and the power of our thoughts to create our own reality, and Silent Unity offers round-the-clock prayer support to everyone who requests it.

On top of coping with my own feelings about the impending surgery, life must go on. I have Michael to assist and a million other "has-to-be-done" chores. I want to be outside in nature, yet here I am inside with bills, one of which is paying for an accessible patio for Michael. This will be a place of refuge for us both, but right now it entails disruptive construction and mounting cost. I envision needing outside care for both of us and not having enough money to pay for it. I'm also worried about Michael. I know he has too much to handle, with my being sick and the ongoing work on the patio. As if this already weren't more than enough, his dad, who lives in Colorado, is in medical crisis. March 18 is Michael's fifty-eighth birthday, but we don't have much of a celebration, and I tell myself I should have done more.

Yet, despite day-to-day frustrations, Michael and I are aligned, and I know I'm not alone. Michael supports and encourages me as I explore alternative ways of healing. In the back of my mind, I hope I can inspire him to do likewise.

I decide to do a shamanic journey, following the drumming from a CD. This steady, slow drumming induces an altered state of consciousness in which my imagination runs free. I am delighted when an eagle appears four times. As I embrace him and climb on his back, he takes off in majestic flight through the blue sky. I can feel his enormous power permeate my body as he soars. When I ask for a gift, eagle gives me a golden nugget.

Later, after the journey, Michael tells me he had a dream in which he saw my aura as iridescent blue and the cancer as gold and black. He awoke feeling I would be okay.

Our images have, indeed, overlapped, both presenting the pure element of gold. Suddenly I feel a shift in perspective, as if a hidden door has opened. I recall the work of the ancient alchemists and their goal of transforming base metal into gold. Perhaps my cancer, too, will transform from its base state into a golden opportunity. I can only hope that it will.

# Chapter 26

# Healing

By the time I go into surgery, I feel I'm ready. I'm certainly cleaned out—that's for damn sure! I drank the "cleansing potion" on schedule, but was unable to keep the last dose down, depositing it directly from my stomach into the toilet without benefit of a journey through my intestines. I'm also chock-full of antibiotics.

I haven't seen the inside of an operating room since the 1960s, so I'm surprised when I'm instructed to walk into a seating area and wait to be called. I've always spent the night before surgery in the hospital, so this procedure is new and a bit unsettling.

When contemplating the surgery, I've usually felt trepidation, especially about the anesthetic. Now, however, because of the hypnotherapy, the prospect no longer seems as frightening: I've come to believe that the medical staff is there to help me and that we're all on the same side.

When I'm finally on a gurney and stationed just outside the operating room, I'm surprised to find I feel completely trusting. The anesthesiologist and anesthesiology nurse are both women, which is reassuring. They bend over me and include me in their discussion about how to best address my particular needs. I feel seen and acknowledged as a real, whole person rather than as just a body to be dealt with. I sense they are warm and caring women—and, most

importantly, I sense they are on my side. They solicit and acknowledge my feelings and concerns. I feel calm and taken care of. After all
this time of being the caregiver, now I can be the recipient. I feel so
very grateful. That's the last thing I remember.

When I wake up, the first thing I see is Michael sitting in his wheelchair by the side of my bed. He is smiling reassuringly and holding
my hand. This is the best sight in the whole world. He tells me later
he sat there for quite some time, watching me go in and out of sleep,
and was surprised by how well I was doing. He said I had good color
and I appeared relaxed.

During my hospital stay I receive flowers, phone calls, cards, and
visits from family and many friends. Michael is able to drive himself
to the hospital every other day to visit me. He tells me he's doing fine
and has made good friends with the ladies in the deli department of
a local supermarket. They see his needs are well met. Una gets him
up, showered, and dressed in the morning, and she helps him get
undressed and into bed at night.

I find out from my doctor that he removed most of my right
colon—which I don't really need, he assures me. He also took out my
gall bladder because it was slightly inflamed and seven lymph nodes,
just to be sure. One of my pre-surgery hypnotic suggestions was I
would have minimal bleeding. I ask him if this was the case. He tells
me it was but assures me that was most likely due to his excellent skill
as a surgeon.

I had asked him, before surgery, if he could arrange for me to have
a room with a window. I knew I would heal faster if I could look
outside and see nature. He said he had no control over that, but now

I find myself in a private room with a view of my beloved Mt. Diablo! When I'm strong enough to walk the halls, clutching a pillow to my belly, I discover many post-surgery patients are in dark, four-person wards with only a viewless window at one end. I feel extremely lucky not only to have a view but a private room as well, and I spend many hours in my hospital bed looking out my window, gaining strength from seeing the natural world beyond. I know it helps me to heal.

On Easter Sunday I awake early, at six o'clock, and write this in my journal: "Today begins my new life as a cancer survivor."

As I gaze out the window, I contemplate this special day, seeing it as a symbol of spring's renewal and the beginning of a new cycle of life. I feel connected to Persephone and her yearly emergence from Hades; I, too, have survived possible death and am awakening to a newly blossoming world, fresh with deeper meaning and welcoming gifts.

Just beneath my window is a section of the red roof that extends out from the floor below. It creates a broad ledge that falls away to reveal the mountain in the distance. As I gaze out, two mallard ducks fly in and land on the ledge. I watch—as do they—as the sun begins to rise behind Mt. Diablo. As a child, I was able to see this mountain from my rural home in Brentwood, and I often watched the sun set below its crest. Now I am resting in its protective shadow, seeing it from another perspective as the sun rises above it.

I remember my father telling me stories of when he was a young boy and he and his friends would explore this mountain. "I used to find arrowheads on its rugged slopes," he told me, his voice full of sadness at how depleted of history his boyhood world had become. I learned that before the invasion of the Spanish, Mt. Diablo had been a sacred place for early Native Americans. Then, in 1804 or 1805, a Spanish military expedition visited the area in search of runaway mission Indians, a term used for Native Americans who were con-fined to Catholic missions throughout California and subjugated to "civilizing" influences that stripped them of their freedom, beliefs, and culture. At a willow thicket, the soldiers encountered a village of Chupcan people and surrounded it. But when night came, all the Indians escaped, unseen. Angry and confused, the Spanish called the site "Monte del Diablo," or "Thicket of the Devil." Later, English-speaking newcomers mistakenly assumed the word "monte" meant "mountain," and the name became "Mt. Diablo."

According to Native American legend, Mt. Diablo and neigh-boring Reed's Peak were once surrounded by water. The creator, Coyote, and his assistant Eagle-man made the world and Native American people from these two islands. Mt. Diablo, which was called "Tuyshtak"—"at the dawn of time"—by the Ohlone people, was considered to be a sacred place of transformation.

On this morning, the mountain is a dark purple-blue silhouette against the soft yellow-orange of the sunrise. Close to my window, the hospital pines rise high above the mountain's profile. The morning is still, the hospital sounds not yet in full swing—the insistent electric beeps, the urgent loudspeaker announcements, and the rushing and tumbling of the ice machine are all in subdued withdrawal, awaiting the activities and needs of the day.

*This is my own private Easter,* I think, *one I share in spirit with all those who gave me their support and love throughout this difficult process.* With that thought, the mallards rise and fly away.

Lying here, I have plenty of time to watch my thoughts rise and fall. One thought I wonder at is: *Sometimes, I'm almost glad I have cancer.* Why am I thinking this? It seems a strange and alien idea, yet it is there.

Examining this thought more closely, I notice it contains no fear of death or even any acknowledgment of its existence. It seems to be more about affirming life. I've been so stressed at work and at home these last few years. Now I'm finally the one being taken care of.

It looks as if I'm back on a transformative path; I guess life takes you where you need to go. Didn't Jung speak about the symptoms of an illness also being a natural attempt to heal?

Despite my thoughts of Easter and renewal, as I lie here in the hospital, I feel as if my insides are dead. My body's life-sustaining system is not functioning. Nothing moves in my body; nothing moves in my life. No nourishment is taken, no waste or toxins eliminated. I have reached a dead end.

With the help of a friend, I contact my hypnotherapist, Dr. Arthur Hastings, by phone from my hospital bed. I'm frightened: *What if my functions don't come back?* He tells me how peristalsis works through gentle tightening and releasing of the gut. He suggests I repeat this clutching and releasing with my hand, alternately tightening and loosening my fist and imagining my system doing the same. I do this. And finally, there is movement. And then, once again, there is life.

As the days go on, my pain lessens and my body begins to work. Finally, I'm hungry! I have never realized before the staggering importance of the digestive system. I never dreamed I would celebrate my ability to pass gas! But this is my most important accomplishment, one that signals my body's ability to initiate peristalsis. This complex internal system was cut open and shut down—and yet, by itself, it's come back to life. I'm in awe of what my body can do with no conscious direction from me. I do believe, though, that my preparatory hypnosis sessions, positive visualizations, and intentional shift toward healing have helped.

I get excited about returning home and eating. With great relish, I look forward to a preliminary diet of eggs, yogurt, whole wheat bread, organic milk, chicken or fish, brown rice, vegetables, fruits, and soup. It sounds divine.

I begin to work on healing again. I do white-light meditations, seeing healing white light permeating my body. I visualize my white blood cells as an army of white knights on white stallions with alert white unicorns as helpers. The knights are armed with lances and laser guns, à la Star Wars. The unicorns point out cancer cells to the knights via two-way radios. The cancer cells are dark-gray hedgehogs, stupid and slow. After the knights kill the hedgehogs, the unicorns pile them up, using their horns, and the horses pound them to pieces with their sharp hooves. Then the unicorns clean up and take away the debris. Sometimes, in the process, they throw a white fishnet over the dead cells.

I do this visualization once or twice a day, just in case there are some cancer cells still in my body. Sometimes I change it and have little white Pac-Men—or white sharks—gobble up the cancer cells, but the white knights are my favorite.

Reading *Bones: Dying into Life* by Marion Woodman is also inspiring. This is one of many passages that stands out for me:

> *The images that come from my spiritual womb hold the energy that can destroy or heal. They hold the transformative power that connects body, soul, and spirit. Internalizing the images, breathing, dancing, writing them into my body, giving them time to radiate my cells with new energy—that is healing.*

I begin to plan for the future—which means I believe I *have* a future. I make lists of how to rearrange furniture in the house, what flowers to plant outside, and where Michael and I can go for weekends or a vacation.

About this time, drawing again from the practice I learned in psychosynthesis, I set forth on another journey to meet my Wise Old Person. In my imagination, I walk across the rooftop outside my hospital room window and fly over the trees, houses, and freeway to Mt. Diablo. I walk up a dirt trail on the side of the mountain. There are areas of bright green grass decorated with poppies, lupines, and mustard splayed out in bold splashes of orange, purple-blue, and yellow. A puppy and cat appear in my arms to accompany me. Later they walk on their own. I think I'm wearing lederhosen.

At the top of the mountain is the observation ring, and next to that an expansive open area. The Christian cross appears low down in the sky, along with the tomb. Then Jesus in spirit appears, looking like the traditional representations of Christ, but transparent. At times, there seem to be many of him. He tells me to look at the North Star. Where he points, it's clearly visible in the daytime sky. He tells me to gauge every action I take by whether or not it furthers my progress to the North Star, my soul's destination. He says my mother's diamond ring (which I always wear) will serve as a symbol and reminder of this. Then he brings over a hot air balloon. I get in with the puppy and the cat. He accompanies us, and it's clear that there are indeed many of him; he can be many places at once. He will be with me. Along the way, the two ducks I saw on Easter and some geese hop on board. We sail over the San Francisco Bay in the balloon, and at one point I look down and see my father's fruit trees in blossom in our long-ago orchard in Brentwood.

I come away feeling that everything I've done to heal, all the people I've seen, and all the actions I've taken were representations of him in his multiple forms.

With my returning health, I begin to value simple things much more than I had before. For instance, I love my standard-issue lunch in the hospital; it's so delicious to me right now that I want to come back when I've been discharged and buy it as takeout! I love having an appetite! Dinner is great, even though it's ham—and I dislike ham. I even relish the broccoli and the rice and the salad. When satiated, I carefully squirrel away a plastic bowl of fresh strawberries and a packet of two graham crackers to enjoy as a snack later in the evening.

Gratitude fills my heart. In my journal I write:

> *I feel that I fell and there were a hundred hands to catch me. I so appreciate what my surgeon has done for me . . . and the anesthesiologist . . . and all the nurses . . . and all my friends! I had no idea I was surrounded by so much love and compassion! I am humbled and thankful. My heart is full.*

I begin to live more and more in the moment, in present time. One day I write in my journal:

> *I've been totally present to this day. The sun is now gone, and it is evening. I miss the day, the sun, being with Michael. I see the metaphor, and I don't want to go into the night. But I know I will—tonight to sleep and one day to death. I will miss this life, these friends, my love Michael, and his children.*

The next day, when Michael comes to visit, we sit outside on a patio. I feel how much he loves me and how much I love him. I see how deeply my illness and this whole experience have touched him. I'm aware of how wonderful it is not to be alone through all of this, how comforting it is to have him by my side. I think he, too, is touched by all the love, prayers, and support that people have shown.

The day I leave for home, I notice my compulsion to tidy up is particularly obsessive. I arrange and rearrange everything on my bedside table. I put the freshest flowers together in a vase for the nurses and throw away the rest. I fill out numerous "appreciation forms" for the many nurses and aides who have been so kind and helpful—and one, of course, for my surgeon. I think of balance, and, for ten minutes, I meditate on a poster of the Tibetan Blue Medicine Buddha that I brought with me. I look at the azure blue Buddha sitting in lotus pose, and I feel his blue healing energy permeate my body. I have read that, if one meditates on the Blue Medicine Buddha, one will eventually attain enlightenment, but in the meantime one will experience an increase in healing powers, both for oneself and others, and a decrease in physical and mental illness and suffering. I see the white snow lions near the Buddha become my white blood cells, intent on devouring any stray cancer cells. They will fiercely patrol my body to protect me. I see them eating the cancer cells and see the cancer cells coming out the lion's anus, transformed now into gold nuggets.

Before I leave the hospital, I take some time for reflection. In doing all I've done to overcome this cancer, I'm developing a stronger belief in my own self-worth and my right to live out my life. As much as I appreciate Michael's support—and the support of others—my sense of self-worth doesn't depend on what others do or think. And it doesn't come from loving and caring for Michael. It comes from within, and that makes me stronger. It means I can be there for Michael without the overwhelming need for his constant approval and validation. It means I will be a better caregiver for Michael because what I give to him I will give unconditionally. It means I will be a better caregiver for myself.

On April 2, I come home from the hospital. Earlier I'd purchased a hospital bed and had it placed downstairs next to Michael's hospital bed so that we could sleep together in the same room. Zoie had been the inspiration for its purchase. On one of her visits, she had been appalled to see me sitting in a chair below the side of his bed while we watched TV. "You two were always touching," she said. "You need a bed down here to be close to Dad."

Now I'm grateful to have this bed here, waiting for me, when I arrive. A wonderful friend, Nora, and her husband, Dick, bring me home, as this would be too difficult for Michael to manage.

Michael is so glad to have me home. The first night, he goes to sleep holding my hand, and when he awakes in the middle of the night, he pulls my arm slightly as he turns. I feel a brief, sudden stab of pain in the area of my incision. I groan a little, and in his grogginess, he apologizes. It's a minor price to pay, I think, to have him next to me again.

The next morning, I awake to the sound of Michael rattling his pills as he takes his morning drugs—which sounds to me like a demented shaman shaking his rattle in my ear. He soon transfers to his wheelchair and attends to washing his catheters and sterilizing them in the microwave. I'd been doing this chore for him for some time due to the difficulties he has with motor coordination, but I see he's able to manage now, albeit with difficulty. Shortly thereafter, Una arrives. We'd planned to have her help me, too, but most of her time needs to be spent with Michael. I'll have to convince him to let her take over the catheter detail.

I discover I can no longer watch violent or gruesome scenes on television. I truly don't have the stomach—or intestines—for it. It's a strange feeling, as if I take the violence into my body and it attacks me in the parts that are wounded. I'm not strong enough to take it, especially the violence in the news. Michael doesn't understand at first—violence in movies or on TV doesn't bother him—but, by remaining calm and focused, I'm able to explain it to him, and he finally understands. A big part of my healing, I believe, is saturating myself in positive, life-affirming images, and I'm determined to keep doing this. So Michael, always in charge of the remote control, picks shows for us that will be pleasant to watch and, at the video store, rents comedies for my amusement.

I meditate often on the Blue Medicine Buddha, letting his blue-white energy enter my body. I also repeat affirmations to counter any negative thoughts. One is: "My immune system is healthy, active, and strong. My white blood cells are vigilant." The most profound thing I do is read *Getting Well Again* by O. Carl Simonton, MD. I follow all of his exercises and listen to his tapes faithfully. Dr. Simonton also has a residential program, through which he has helped many "terminal" cancer patients live longer and healthier lives. His patients have a survival rate twice the national norm, and, in many cases, have experienced remissions or total cures. He uses a mind-body approach to healing that's in line with what I'm doing already. As time goes on, I will complete his entire program using his book and tapes. It helps me immensely and will be especially important in the next phase of my journey: chemotherapy.

Chemo is ordered as a prophylactic measure to catch any cancer that might have evaded the surgeon's knife. My surgeon told me when I left the hospital that, as far as he was concerned, I was cured. My oncologist, it seems, has a different opinion. I'm in for quite a ride, but I'm ready.

# Chapter 27
# Chemo

Weak from surgery, I'm not sure what I will and will not be able to do to help Michael. I'm so grateful we have Una to help us. She spends three hours six days a week—every day but Sunday—assisting Michael with toileting, bathing, and dressing. She does all this with love, compassion, and unwavering attention to detail. Michael has always had immaculate personal hygiene, and now he claims never to have had such a clean back. Una spends a lot of time scrubbing Michael down with washcloths and a shower brush and then rinsing him off and patting him dry as he sits on his shower bench. Several years ago, we converted the downstairs bathroom to make it accessible and installed an open, roll-in shower that's easy to access from a wheelchair. Despite all this, he has a crisis, and Una calls 911 without even telling me.

Around eight thirty in the morning, Michael transfers from the bed to his wheelchair. Knowing Una will soon be here to help him, I go upstairs to listen to a guided meditation tape and put on the headphones. For some reason, and unbeknownst to me, Michael decides to transfer from the wheelchair to the shower bench by himself before Una arrives. Transferring is becoming increasingly difficult for him, as his legs have gotten weaker and his balance more uncertain. He misjudges the positioning of the wheelchair and the bench and gets stuck between them, not fully sitting on either. Fortunately, Una arrives, but she can't get him situated properly. On Michael's instruction, she calls 911. Three paramedics rush in and manage to get him back into his chair. Upstairs, oblivious to the uproar downstairs, I peacefully continue my meditation.

Later, when I do go downstairs to see how Michael and Una are doing, he tells me what happened.

"I wish you'd told Una to let me know what was happening," I say, shock running through my body.

"Why should I?"

Suddenly I feel as if he has slammed a door in my face. I don't know what to say and go back upstairs, feeling diminished and inadequate.

Upon reflection, I think he probably called to me for help and, of course, I didn't hear him. I guess in this instance, I really wasn't there for him at all. The weight of our situation suddenly comes pressing down on me. The plug has just been pulled on what little energy I have, and I go back to my upstairs room and lie down.

Michael rests in his chair for the remainder of the day, too weak to get back into bed. I venture downstairs to lie on my hospital bed and be close to him. I wonder how we are ever going to survive my recovery.

The next day, we realize Michael was having an exacerbation. It's no wonder, since my surgery must have been stressful for him, even though he managed to maintain a supportive and positive attitude. He must have been afraid of losing me and worried about what might happen to him if I didn't pull through. On top of it all, he's constantly dealing with all the symptoms of MS, and I'm in no position to be of much use.

Fortunately, when it's time to see my oncologist and find out about chemotherapy, Michael has recovered and is able to drive me in and accompany me to the appointment. My oncologist isn't as reassuring as my surgeon was. According to her, I have a 60 percent chance of nonrecurrence after chemo. That means, of course, a 40 percent chance of recurrence. I wonder why outcomes have to be stated in the negative. I guess nonrecurrence is a safer prediction than "cure" or "getting well." I decide I'll rephrase all this for myself when I get home and do my meditations.

She tells me I probably won't lose my hair—but I do—and I probably can drive myself in and out—but I soon can't—and my main side effect will be diarrhea—which it is.

Not surprisingly, I'm depressed after this visit to the oncologist. I decide to give more weight to what my surgeon told me previously: I'll be in the top percentile for survival. For me, it's 100 percent.

After accompanying me to the oncologist, Michael again becomes quite fatigued and stays in bed the next day. At one point he does get up, and as I lie in my bed, unable to physically assist him and watching him struggle back into his bed from his chair, the thought comes to me that we just can't live this way.

With that thought I begin to hyperventilate, my lungs uncontrollably straining for air. Michael quietly tells me to go upstairs, and I do, my lungs still heaving. I sit down and put my hands over my mouth, breathing in carbon dioxide. That finally stops it.

I know Michael didn't have the energy to deal with my pain right then. I probably frightened him as well as myself. I rest for a few minutes, and I go back downstairs and help Michael a little to shift his legs in the bed.

"I realize you're too vulnerable right now to cope with everything," he says gently.

"I am," I say, relieved he understands.

We talk about our situation, and he agrees to let Una wash and sterilize his catheters and empty his bottles for urine catch. He's aware that this has become too much for him and that it would be too much for me, too, at this point.

"You should just leave the room when I'm struggling to transfer," he says. "There's really nothing you can do, anyway."

This episode begins a pattern in our relationship. If I'm overwhelmed, Michael withdraws for his own survival—because he is literally unable to deal with me in the moment—and I leave the room. I no longer have that compulsion to pursue him and reestablish communication. It has been replaced by cooperation and understanding.

I know Michael's inability to deal with stress, mine or his own, is an unavoidable symptom of MS, yet I'm frightened and worried. I call my doctor, intending to ask for a prescription for some tranquilizers. But the advice nurse who answers the phone instead tells me to get more support and to be sure to arrange a break in my activities to balance the stress. She also suggests I make an appointment to see about taking an antidepressant. I will eventually do this but not right away.

About mid-April, I begin to feel more fear. I don't want to handle this new crisis alone anymore—and I feel really alone—but I don't want to burden Michael with my fears. Since the operation, I've felt stress physically, right in my gut. I've lost my physical strength and stamina, and I don't know what's going to happen to either of us.

At least I don't have to try to drag myself to work. Thanks to the wonderful people in my school district, I have enough sick leave to last to the end of the school year, at which time I'll be officially retired—certainly not the retirement I'd planned, but a blessing, nonetheless.

On May 9, I have my first chemotherapy appointment. My friend Sandy takes me in, and afterward we go out to lunch.

"This chemo is no problem," I tell her. I even eat more than she does.

I have no side effects, except I sleep thirteen hours that night and eleven the next. On the third day after treatment, I'm able to go for an hour's walk. Gradually, I begin to feel more awake in the morning and more interested in the day ahead. I also join a cancer support group in town that proves to be a wonderful place to share my feelings and receive and give support as well as a rich source of information. A clinical psychologist runs the program, and she provides us with a safe space where we all feel heard and understood.

I join a local fitness club just for women and hire a personal trainer from the club to give me a customized workout plan. I schedule time for walking, yoga, and swimming, along with appointments to get blood drawn and my weekly dose of chemicals at the clinic. I participate in classes for patients undergoing chemotherapy at my HMO and have a private session on visualizations with an RN who took classes from Dr. Jeanne Achterberg, who was an author and scientific researcher in alternative modes of healing. I continue faithfully with my visualizations, adding a wonderful tape by Bellaruth Naperstek in which she guides me to envision the chemicals as a healing blue liquid. I also continue with my own visualizations and psychotherapy. In uncovering resources, I discover both the Wellness Center, which offers classes, books, and tapes, and the American Cancer Society, which provides wigs and a wonderful free class on makeup that helps women look and feel more attractive during chemotherapy.

I keep track of my symptoms from chemotherapy—which, as it turns out, does not continue to be a great pre-lunch event. The symptoms include: fatigue, diarrhea, nausea, loss of appetite, weight loss, sweating and chills, sores inside my mouth, numbness in some fingers, vomiting, stomach pain, and, eventually, dehydration and hair loss. There are pills for everything, but they don't work after a while. Soon I'm forced to cut back on my activities and eventually give up my exercise program altogether.

It turns out my body isn't able to tolerate the type of chemotherapy I'm being given. I become extremely weak, only able to walk from my upstairs bed to the bathroom over and over each day, sometimes staggering around due to extreme weakness and dizziness. I don't stay downstairs with Michael. I decide to suffer through this on my own. My incessant trips to the toilet and my violent diarrhea and vomiting would be too much for him to bear. He just doesn't have the strength or stamina. But I do, and, thanks to Una, I only have myself to manage right now; I couldn't possibly take care of us both.

The chemo nurses are wonderful and always available by phone when I call. After several weeks, during which some of my wonderful friends take turns driving me to the clinic for hydration, my oncologist finally puts me on another type of drug. But she doesn't do it soon enough, and I continue to suffer excessively and, perhaps, needlessly. The final drug they give me to treat nausea is tincture of opium. It helps. Before taking me off the initial chemo drug, my oncologist tells me, "This shouldn't have happened with prophylactic chemotherapy"—so why, I wonder, did she let it? But I'm too weak to ask. I took a chemical I couldn't tolerate from May 9 to June 24—forty-six days.

With all that's going on, my hair loss is the least of my worries. The hardest part is seeing clumps of my long hair appear on the shower floor after I shampoo, scooping them up in a wet mass, and depositing them in the wastebasket. When I've had enough of that, I go to my hairdresser, and she shaves my head free of charge. I opt to acquire lots of hats and head coverings rather than those hot and uncomfortable wigs. The good ones are too expensive anyway. Michael always wanted me to try wearing my hair short; now I can accommodate him when my hair grows back, as I'm sure it will. But I miss my shoulder length hair. Soon after we met, I had my hair permed, and I have worn it that way ever since. I've gotten lots of compliments, and I know Michael likes it this way. When it grows back, I guess I'll wear it short and straight again—at least for a while.

The new chemical cocktail—Comptosar, or CPT11—requires a ninety-minute infusion once a week for six months (the months I spent on the first drug don't count), rather than the two hours required for the first one. I'm able to tolerate it better, although I'm still weak, too thin, and often have diarrhea and nausea.

Fortunately for both of us, Michael's brother, Steve, knowing my situation, travels from out of state to help for a week. He does some shopping and cooking and gardening for me. I will always be grateful for his help during this difficult time. Also, it's nice for Michael to visit with his brother; they don't see each other much anymore.

Even with Steve here, I still try to do too much. One late afternoon when I can drive again, on my way home from a doctor's appointment, I realize there's nothing in the house for dinner. I stop and pick up a couple of pizzas, bring them home, and go to lie down. When I get up, ready for pizza, I discover that Michael and Steve have eaten it all. I'm incredulous, even though I had given them the pizzas to eat.

"How could you not have saved me some?" I ask with some accusation in my voice.

Michael and Steve apologize profusely, but I tell them it's all fine and open a can of soup. And it is; I really don't care. I'm tired and not all that hungry.

As time goes on, I begin to feel better and am able to resume my

exercise routine. By the end of the year, I'm finished with chemotherapy, and soon my hair begins growing back.

Things have gotten more complicated, though, for Michael.
Everything he does takes longer. One day it takes a total of five hours
of morning preparation for him to get ready to leave the house for
the day. It's getting harder for him to do even the simplest things.
Spending a day out means being sure we have all the necessary equipment and pills, catheterizing in the van or finding a place to catheterize, disposing of the urine—usually in some plants—positioning the
wheelchair in exactly the right place on the passenger side of the van,
tying down and untying the wheelchair, and on and on.

Eventually, Michael becomes unable to transfer, and we purchase
an electric ceiling lift. To use the lift, I must get him into a sling.
While he's in bed, I push him over on his side—he helps by pulling
on the straps I've attached to the bed frame—and I fold the sling in
half lengthwise and push it under him. Then I go to the other side
of the bed and pull the other half of the sling out from under him,
so it's underneath him, and he's lying flat on his back. The sling has
six loops—two pairs for the upper body and one for the legs. (It ends
in two long strips of material with loops at the end that crisscross
between Michael's legs.) All the loops hook into the bar that drops
down from the ceiling track. With the remote-control mechanism, I
raise Michael up off the bed. If the sling is positioned correctly, he's
now in a sitting position and ready for the lift to carry him where
he needs to go—which has to be in a straight line. The ceiling track
goes directly between the bed and the shower/commode bench in
the bathroom. It can stop anywhere in between, so we also use it to
transfer him to and from his wheelchair as well as the shower bench.

When Michael goes back to bed for the night, the process is
reversed. I get Michael back into the sling while he's sitting in the

wheelchair. This involves a lot of pushing and tugging, but we learn to do it. Once he's on the bed, I get him out of the sling and undress him (more rolling from side to side and pushing and tugging), put in a new catheter and set up the urine-collection bag, help him with his nighttime pills, heat up his neck warmer in the microwave, and get him warm and comfortable for the night.

Our HMO provided a manual Hoyer lift for our use, but it didn't work out. That lift is an awkward contraption in which the patient is again raised up in a sling. The caregiver must use muscle power, however, to crank the patient up in the air, turn the contraption around, and push it to where the patient needs to go with the patient hanging in midair. The instructions warn that it takes two to operate, but Una isn't here at night when Michael needs to transfer to the bed. Even before surgery, I didn't have the strength to operate it. I tried to make a case for an electric ceiling lift to our HMO, explaining the situation and suggesting that if I injured myself using the Hoyer lift, it would probably cost them more to treat me than to install a ceiling lift. My case was denied on the basis that Medicare would only provide a Hoyer lift. (Michael signed over his Medicare to the HMO as a condition of coverage, and the HMO itself would not cover an upgrade.)

The electric ceiling lift was expensive, but it was absolutely essential.

They say having cancer is life changing, and that's certainly true for me. I come to appreciate everyone and everything more following my cancer ordeal, and I especially value my time with Michael.

Frequently, Michael tells me how much he appreciates all I do for him. He has such warmth in his voice and love in his eyes when he tells me how much he loves and values what I do that I feel immensely grateful I can be here for him. He has become so patient with me now that I sometimes wonder whether he's suppressing his anger. I worry that if this is the case, it might cause him stress—which, in turn, might cause an exacerbation or hasten his rate of decline. But the truth is he has learned to share his feelings in a non-blaming way, and he has become a kinder, more compassionate person than the man I married.

Multiple sclerosis has taught us some hard lessons. We've come to value and cherish our growing interdependence as the only way to cope with this disease. And as we've come to trust one another, we seldom resort to criticism and we no longer feel the need to control. Michael has learned to ask for and accept my help when he needs it. He has softened and become more compassionate and understanding of the needs of others.

When Michael worries that I'll come to resent him because I have to take care of him, I realize I don't feel resentment and I don't think that I will. I've chosen to be where I am, and I've learned how to take care of myself. Michael has changed too. He's learned to listen and to care about my feelings, rather than close himself off or assign blame. We communicate much better now than we ever have, and we can talk about and process our problems rather than letting them fester and grow. We know, more than ever before, that we need to be here for each other, and we are. We no longer have room in our relationship for blame and reciprocation for perceived wrongs.

I remember back to a time earlier in his diagnosis when Michael was pretty sure we would divorce. He felt I was overburdened taking care of him—that it wasn't fair to me—and he doubted our marriage could survive. A conversation he had with some men in his MS support group after a member and his wife had divorced helped him see things differently. They all wondered whether their wives really loved them enough, whether they would be able to stick it out. One pointed out that since all of their wives were still with them, they must love them enough and would stay. Now, as Michael sees me by his side each day, he has learned to trust that I will always be there.

I'm increasingly aware of the existence of lightness and darkness in ourselves and in our lives now. I'm learning to hold both, knowing that acceptance and balance is key. I'm reminded of a quote from Dr. Carl Jung: "Even a happy life cannot be without a measure of darkness, and the word happy would lose its meaning if it were not balanced by sadness. It is far better to take things as they come along with patience and equanimity."

All in all, I believe we are doing this and managing well together, and my patience and endurance usually hold up. At the heart of all the changes in our lives is a growing respect for and appreciation of each other, a dawning sense of our own mortality, and complete and total commitment to our marriage. Most of all, there is love.

# Chapter 28

# Hassles and Errors

As 2004 begins, life has settled down, and we're attending workshops on transpersonal topics, going to movies and museums, and generally being as active as possible. We know we'd better do as much as we can while we still can, as it's apparent that Michael's condition isn't getting any better. I, on the other hand, have recovered my strength, and my ordeal with cancer and chemo is now a thing of the past. My renewed appreciation of life continues to expand.

At a recent return visit to the rehab facility, Michael got a new wheelchair that's more comfortable and supportive. We think this will make travel much easier for him. The new chair can better accommodate his weakening condition; it's larger than his old one, allows him to stretch his legs out, and tilts all the way back so he can recline. It comes with a ROHO cushion, which facilitates blood flow by fitting, matching, and tracking a person's shape. This makes sitting comfortable for him and protects his bottom. In addition to a headrest, it has side pads that hold his upper body in place so he can remain comfortable in the chair for longer periods.

While I was visiting him one day at the facility, the physical therapist asked Michael if he would like to stand up. "You bet!" he said. So the physical therapist strapped Michael onto a standing board. This device gradually raised him from a prone position to almost vertical.

The first thing he said when he was "standing" was, "I want to hug my wife."

I moved close and embraced him, and he put his arms around me. It was the first time we had held each other this way in years. I was a little self-conscious being in a room full of people but feeling the full length of his body against mine was sublime. I closed my eyes, rested my head on his chest, and savored the moment. We held each other until the therapist came to crank Michael down.

I come up with the idea of going on a vacation to San Diego. Before he got sick, Michael discovered the San Diego Zoo on a trip to Southern California. He was intrigued by it and wants to visit again. I, in turn, am looking forward to swimming in warm ocean waters and just getting away for a while.

We have high expectations for a fun, relaxing vacation. I reserve a handicapped room in a nice hotel, using the hotel points we've accumulated, and choose a place that looks lovely in the pictures. It's on a marina, and I think Michael will enjoy being near the water.

I know, for our vacation to be a success, we'll have to do much more than just reserve a handicapped-accessible hotel room—and we'll need to prepare early so all of Michael's needs will be met. Three weeks before we plan to leave, I call the company that provides the equipment that Michael's condition requires. Our HMO administers Michael's Medicare benefits, so we receive his durable medical equipment at no additional cost to us, including what he'll need for this trip. I order an oversized shower seat/commode, a hospital bed, and an electric lift and a sling to be sent ahead to our hotel room, then notify the hotel of their impending arrival. To our medical-equipment supplier, I specify that the lift must be electric and explain in detail why an electric—as opposed to a hand-cranked—lift is needed. The woman on the other end of the phone assures me that this will be no problem; they'll fax the order to their San Diego office immediately.

I call back several times over the next few weeks to check on the order. Each time the same woman tells me she has the papers and is just about to fax them. She insists I have nothing to worry about.

On the day before we leave, I still haven't received verification and am at my wits' end; I had been promised a prompt call once the papers had been faxed. My stomach in knots, I make yet another call and am told the woman in charge of making these arrangements is out right now.

"Put the manager on the phone," I demand.

"You can leave a message on her answering machine, and she'll call you back." The disembodied voice is calm, politely transferring me to a machine.

Finally, just before the end of the business day, I receive a call from the woman in charge, telling me the papers had been faxed just a few minutes earlier and everything is set. I'm relieved to hear this—but furious at the company for their inefficiency. I decide to let it go, however, and somehow manage to relax, trusting that what we need will be waiting for us when we arrive.

I had contacted the airlines weeks in advance to be sure everything would be available and ready to get Michael on the plane safely and efficiently. They had a lift, I was assured, and trained personnel to help with Michael's transfer. I also contacted the company that maintains Michael's wheelchair to find out what needed to be done to prepare its two fifty-pound batteries for flight. The man who has come out to the house many times to adjust or repair Michael's chair informs me that airline personnel will remove the batteries before the flight and replace them as soon as the wheelchair is manually rolled back onto the ground. He assures me the wheelchair will be safe and happy in the cargo hold. I'm glad to hear this but still a bit anxious.

We had attended a travel workshop on flying with a wheelchair some time back at a convention called the Abilities Fair, where we heard a man's story of looking out the airplane window and seeing the plane about to run over his wheelchair, which someone had apparently left on the tarmac. He arrived at his destination without the wheelchair and at the mercy of an inept airline.

Despite this worst-case scenario, I anticipate a positive experience because I've carefully arranged everything in advance. Following the advice of our wheelchair repairman, I even affix a note to the chair explaining how to remove and replace the batteries in the unlikely event that airline personnel don't know how to do this.

The day before we plan to leave, I pack our clothes and all the necessary paraphernalia—catheters (we will use disposable ones for the trip), a multitude of pills, straps to tie to the bed frame for Michael to pull on to help him move in bed, bed pads, rectal syringe, hand sanitizer, and more. I secure his pills for the day in a carry-on bag, along with everything else we can think of that we might need.

We have plans to take our van to our local BART station and take BART to the San Francisco Airport. We get up in plenty of time on our departure day, but Michael isn't feeling well; he's weak and definitely not energetic. I have an ominous feeling that we should cancel, but no, he's determined to go.

We manage to get ourselves and everything we're taking into the van, onto BART, and to the airport. No sooner do we get there, however, than Michael has to use the men's room. There's no way for me to accompany him into the huge airport men's room, so I sit outside and wait . . . and wait . . . and wait, sure that we're going to miss the plane.

When we finally arrive at the counter, I expect the agent to have advance knowledge of Michael's condition and to assure us someone at the gate will be prepared to assist him onto the plane—but he has no such knowledge and has made absolutely no preparations.

"But I called ahead of time and was told you'd be expecting us!" I exclaim, incredulous. "Do you at least have a lift?"

"Yes, of course we have a lift," he says, and assures me he'll call ahead to the boarding area, and everything will be fine.

Somewhat relieved, we continue to security, where they decide to search Michael. They have no enclosure that can accommodate his large wheelchair, so they proceed to pat him down and around and under, right there where everyone can see; the agents are not at all sympathetic or even polite.

"Can't you lean forward?" they demand.

*He can't move by himself,* I want to scream, wondering at their lack of consideration. I could help, but I haven't been cleared; I can only watch from a distance.

"Can't you rise up a little so I can check between your butt and the cushion?"

Michael says nothing and remains calm. I cringe, knowing he must be feeling helpless and humiliated.

Finally satisfied that Michael is not a terrorist cleverly disguised as a paraplegic, we're told we can continue on our way. We have just enough time to grab a bite to eat before we go to the gate—but when I finally find a table in one of the crowded restaurants, I realize we don't have enough time to eat after all.

"Then why are we here?" Michael asks.

I don't know why we're here and give in to silent tears. But there's no time to break down; we have to leave the restaurant and go to the boarding gate. When we get there, I check in with the woman behind the counter and ask whether the lift is ready.

"What?" she asks.

"The lift," I repeat. "The lift to get my husband out of his wheelchair and onto the plane. The man at the front desk told me you'd have one ready for us."

"We don't have a lift like that," she says. "He must have been referring to the elevator."

*This isn't England. What the fuck is going on?*

In response to my piercing and incredulous stare, the woman calls for a manager. A nice woman arrives and takes control of the situation. She gets the lift—there really is one; I guess only a select few are privy to its existence and location. Then she calls several employees to get Michael out of his chair.

Three very short men appear. Michael is six-five and 260 pounds, and he outweighs and is much taller than all three of them together. I look at the manager in disbelief.

"I know," she says, "They're outsourced."

When I attempt to greet them, I discover I don't speak their language and they don't speak mine. Nevertheless, we proceed down the jet way to the area just in front of the door to the plane. The men try their best—even though they have no concept of what to do, let alone training to do it, and can't even begin to budge Michael. They're supposed to get him into a sling, raise him up with a Hoyer-style lift, and transfer him onto a narrow, wheeled chair that will take him onboard. To roll down the aisle of an airplane, this chair is so narrow it resembles a solid thong that Michael will have to straddle with both cheeks.

Since I can't explain to them what to do, I put the sling on Michael myself, as they have no idea what it's for. They attempt to raise him up but can only get him slightly above the aisle chair seat, and then, instead of positioning him in a sitting position, they try to position him horizontally as if to shoot him through the door.

I'm concerned that Michael may be suffering and will be injured if this continues. Yet, remaining amazingly patient, he tries to tell the men what to do, even though they can't understand a word he says. It's an impossible situation, and the pilot—who must have realized takeoff might be delayed—appears from the cockpit. He doesn't know what to do, either.

Then, like a guardian angel alighting from the sky, another pilot, who's hitching a ride to San Diego, comes to our rescue. He's a former paramedic and gets Michael onto the aisle chair and into the plane. I don't get to witness that triumph, however, because as soon as his wheelchair is empty, I'm told to accompany the men downstairs; they don't know how to operate the wheelchair.

I leave Michael and motion to one of them to sit down in the seat so he can drive the chair. He uses the footrest as a step, putting all his weight on it, which can damage it.

"No," I yell, but to no avail; he's already seated.

The next hurdle is to get the wheelchair into an employee elevator. I show him how to use the joystick and follow him to the elevator— which, I assume, is as far as I'll be allowed to go. When the elevator door opens, he shoves forward on the joystick and rams the right armrest into the side of the elevator doorframe.

That's it. "Get out!" I yell, motioning wildly.

He gets out, and I get in. I'll drive the damned thing myself wherever it needs to go. After a short ride, the elevator opens to reveal a dreary ground-floor room. I'm directed to a bank of lockers and summarily abandoned. I look around and see an "Employees Only" sign on the wall.

Only one of the men comes back; apparently, the other two have something more important to do. Pointing his finger, he directs me out a door and onto a sidewalk bordering an interior airport road, where I face a curb. I stop and look at my guide. I shake my head. He looks distressed. Then he has an idea. He directs me to a curb cut.

Now I'm out on the tarmac, looking up at the nose of the airplane.

*Oh, my God,* I think. *Isn't this a violation of security?* Suddenly, two airline employees dressed in jumpsuits come running toward me.

"Do you speak English?" I ask them. "Can you operate a wheelchair?"

Ignoring my questions, they tell me to get out of the chair. Then, with great skill and confidence, they drive the wheelchair alongside the plane. The manager reappears and rushes me up the steps they've brought out and onto the plane. As I get on, I see Michael smiling at me from an upgraded front-row aisle seat in first class. The seat is large enough for him, and he looks fairly comfortable. I look up and see rows of passengers glaring at me. I look down and am quickly ushered into the first empty aisle seat in coach, from which, thankfully, I can see Michael. The plane takes off at last, twenty minutes late.

By the time we land, I'm sick to my stomach. I attribute this to not having had lunch and ingesting only the meager salted treats offered by the stewardess. I know things will be just fine when we land— or, anyway, as soon as we can get Michael back in his wheelchair.

Certainly, I tell myself, the airline will have notified San Diego of our impending arrival and of Michael's special needs.

There are indeed some able-bodied men ready to assist Michael when we land; the problem is with his wheelchair. He has to wait on the plane until it can be brought to him. After a while, an employee appears and tells us the chair isn't working. Could I come down to assist?

I'm led to an area where three male airline employees are fiddling with the chair, unable to figure out why it wouldn't work.

"Did you put the batteries in?" I ask.

"Yes," they reply.

"Did you follow the written instructions on the paper taped to the battery compartment?"

They say they did.

I ask to see, so they take off the battery cover. I point out that the batteries have been installed backward. They take them out and reinstall them and are amazed when the chair springs to life. I am amazed, too, but not at the wheelchair's return to life. I'm amazed at how inept they are.

As soon as Michael's safely back in his chair, we go to an office where I fill out a damage report for the broken armrest. Then we call the hotel for the shuttle that runs every twenty minutes between the hotel and the airport and go outside to wait.

San Diego typically isn't hot; it's known for consistent, pleasant weather that's usually in the seventies. Today, however, it's hot, and the heat affects Michael as we wait for the shuttle—which seems to be taking an inordinate amount of time. It finally arrives, but it's not wheelchair accessible. Somehow, this doesn't surprise me as much as it would on any normal day.

I go inside and call the hotel again. They tell me they'll call a local shuttle service that's wheelchair accessible, which should arrive shortly—and they will, of course, reimburse us for the charges.

It doesn't arrive shortly, and we wait outside in the heat for more than two hours. When it finally does arrive and we disembark at the hotel, we're greeted with lavish apologies and are quickly reimbursed. Their wheelchair-accessible shuttle isn't working, we're told, but it should be fixed by the following day.

At that point, all we want to do is go to our room and relax. When we finally open the door to our holiday hotel room, however, the first thing we see is an unmade hospital bed and a manual—not electric— lift. In the bathroom, inside the roll-in shower (at least something's right) is a regular-sized shower chair, not the oversized one I ordered. But it's after five o'clock and too late to call the company. Dejected and beaten, we call for a bed makeup and go downstairs to eat what turns out to be a mediocre dinner with one bright spot: sliced fresh tomatoes in balsamic vinegar.

When night falls, I eventually manage to get Michael safely into his hospital bed using the manual lift, and then we fall into an exhausted sleep. He will have to wait until tomorrow for his shower. Thus ends the first day of our San Diego vacation.

The next day we look forward to going to the San Diego Zoo. In the morning, I decide to get Michael out of bed, showered, and dressed before I prepare myself for the day. Very carefully, I position the sling under him, hook it up to the manual lift, and manage to get him up in the air. Next, I attempt to turn him in the correct direction. Suddenly, he's falling—the whole lift is falling! Stunned, I watch it fall on its side and dump Michael onto the floor, and I'm falling too. I quickly get up, unhurt, but Michael remains motionless on the floor. Terrified, I call out his name. He doesn't respond. I run to the phone and dial the hotel operator, because I don't know for sure how to dial out for 911, and I think this will be the fastest way to get help. But when I tell the operator to call 911, she asks me why. I tell her there's been an accident in the room and my husband is unconscious on the floor. She responds that hotel procedure is to send security up to check on a problem before they can call 911. Unable to convince her to call, I remember my cell phone and dial 911. As soon as someone answers, there's a knock on the door and I rush to admit two security men. They quickly assess Michael's situation and call for an ambulance.

The ambulance arrives immediately, hardly giving me enough time to throw on some clothes while the security guards stay with Michael and watch him intently. Michael is conscious as the paramedics lift him onto the gurney, and we ride together in the ambulance. He says he's okay, but his neck hurts. He assures me it isn't my fault that the lift tipped over, but still I feel awful.

And so we spend the second day of our vacation in the emergency room. Somehow, Michael has a sense of humor about the whole thing and insists I take pictures of him on the gurney. "They'll be souvenirs of our San Diego vacation," he says.

After various examinations and X-rays, which take several hours, he's declared to have no major injury and given some pain pills for his neck. Fortunately, we have a wonderful discharge nurse who takes a special interest in our case. She asks me how this happened, and I explain, including the fact that the wrong type of lift was delivered. Livid, she calls the San Diego branch of our medical-equipment supplier (which is connected to both our HMO and this hospital) to find out why we were not sent an electric lift as promised. The woman tells her our request did not specify an electric lift. Our nurse then talks to the company manager and asks her to read back the original fax. It shows that I did, in fact, specify an electric lift, but the manager tells her they don't have one in San Diego. Our nurse suggests they'd better find an electric lift or they'll be liable if any more injuries occur, and the company manager assures her that when we return to our hotel room, a real electric lift will be waiting for us.

Our nurse then asks me whether I need help taking care of Michael. I realize that I do, and she recommends a home-healthcare service and offers to call them for us. For the rest of our trip, we make good use of this competent service and the elusive electric lift.

Our nurse then turns her attention to our hotel. When I mention the nonexistent wheelchair-accessible shuttle and the delay in calling 911, she's appalled and says the hotel should "comp" us for our stay. Since we're already using points, I'm not sure whether this will count for much. She mentions a popular local TV personality who specializes in uncovering evidence of local incompetence, and suggests I mention to the hotel manager that Ms. X of Station Y might be interested in hearing about our experiences at his hotel.

When we get back to the hotel, I follow the nurse's suggestion. The manager immediately arranges to comp us for the rest of our meals and any other hotel expenses we might incur.

I wish I could say that from here on our vacation goes smoothly. We do have some fun together; Michael and I do get to the zoo, and I enjoy the ocean's warm waters. The hotel's wheelchair-accessible shuttle never materializes, but we find an independent shuttle service that takes us everywhere we want to go. This is fortunate, because we discover that even though we can see downtown from the marina, where our hotel is located, we can't actually get there by walking and rolling. We are, for all intents and purposes, stranded.

Michael and I especially enjoy our day at the San Diego Zoo. The paths are wide and, despite the crowds, Michael can zip along nicely in his wheelchair. We get to see the adorable panda bears, and Michael buys a child's umbrella bedecked with images of the furry creatures, which he uses to shield himself from the sun. At one point we get separated, but I soon discover him so engrossed in checking out the sights and enjoying himself that he isn't worried at all.

The high point of our trip, for me, is the day I go swimming in the lusciously warm, clear waters of La Jolla's marine preserve, where I delight in watching the brightly colored fish darting around me. It's magical.

Amazingly enough, the plane trip back to San Francisco goes smoothly. Perhaps we've raised the consciousness of the airline—or, more likely, we're just luckier this time. The only disturbing part is there's no first-class seat available for Michael, and he has to squeeze into a much too small seat in coach. If we ever do this again, we'll have to book first class—but I can't, for the life of me, imagine ever doing this again. No way.

# Chapter 29
# Life Goes On

Summer gives way to fall, and we recover from our "trip from hell" and get back to our regular activities and short excursions.

Michael's having more and more difficulty catheterizing. His hands are getting weaker and his motor coordination is poor, so, more often than not, I help him or do it for him. I don't mind doing this, nor does he mind letting me. Whenever possible when we're out, I accompany him into single-toilet public bathrooms, and we laugh, remembering times we both used to go into these facilities just because we wanted to stay together. The first time this happened, just a few weeks after we met, we were at a restaurant in Berkeley, and I left the table to use the women's bathroom. As I came out of the stall, I was shocked to see Michael entering the bathroom. With a self-conscious smile, he confessed he had missed me so much he had to come and find me. Surprised, I quickly ushered him out. Fortunately, we had been the only ones in the bathroom at that time. This was just one example of what I came to accept as Michael's disregard of rules; he often felt they didn't apply to him. As time went on, we often used a single, unisex bathroom together just for convenience, rather than waiting in line. I learned to be amused rather than embarrassed by people's surprised expressions when we both exited, so now I don't have any inhibitions to overcome (Michael never did). Our search for large, unisex bathrooms with doors that lock is unending.

Despite these inconveniences, Michael is ready to go out for entertainment, and since I'm now retired, we go to Berkeley, Oakland, and San Francisco often, visiting coffee shops or bookstores, going to movies or plays, or just walking and rolling through the UC Berkeley campus, where I used to be a student.

Michael's arms are still working, even though his legs are not, and he loves to take photographs with his new digital camera, especially when he takes BART to the city on solo adventures. My main worry now is that he might become dehydrated; he avoids drinking water so he won't have to catheterize. Riding along Market Street and listening to music on his iPod, he's drawn to photographing buildings and people. Recently he purchased a Mac and spends hours at home working with his photos—cropping, enhancing, and playing with color.

We now have an EZ Lock installed in the van on the passenger side as well as the driver's side, so Michael can roll in and lock down whether he's the driver or the passenger. This makes it much easier for both of us. When I'm driving, it saves me from crawling around on the floor of the van to tie down his chair, a task that was getting more and more painful due to the arthritis in my left knee and back. Maneuvering his new, larger wheelchair into the passenger position takes some work and the carpet in the van is getting some rips and tears, but all in all, we're pleased with the arrangement. Often, if we're out for the day, at dinnertime I'll buy food at a restaurant and bring it out to the van, where we eat before driving home. This saves Michael from having to maneuver out of and back into the van, something that is always more difficult for him in the evening.

Michael's snoring is becoming intolerable, although he keeps insisting he doesn't snore. At night, he makes a racket followed by a long pause—no sound at all. Then there's a gasping, sharp intake of breath. The cycle repeats endlessly, and sometimes I leave my hospital bed next to his and sleep upstairs.

When I finally get him to go to the doctor, he's tested, diagnosed with sleep apnea, and outfitted with a CPAP machine. Our nightly ritual now includes my putting Michael's sleep mask on him, adjusting the straps of the head gear so the mask is comfortable, and then adjusting the airflow. There's also a special procedure I do weekly to wash and disinfect the mask and hose. With everything in place, he sleeps much more soundly, and I don't have to flee upstairs. Sleeping with his mask on isn't comfortable, but his sleeping pills quickly knock him out. Added to this discomfort is his ongoing neck pain, made more severe by the onset of osteoporosis.

Michael's internal thermostat is way off. Most nights I put a neck warmer in the microwave for him and then place it around his neck, which helps him get more comfortable. Still, often he becomes exceedingly cold, and I get him his wool hat, microwave his warming mittens, and place extra blankets on top of him. He's a most bizarre sight with all this paraphernalia piled on, the CPAP mask with its plastic hose snaking out to the machine on the bedside table, the catheter nighttime-collection bag attached to the bed frame, and the flow tube stuck secured to his leg so it won't pull out. It breaks my heart to see him this way.

Minor disagreements and hurt feelings over simple things continue, as in any marriage, and I'm finding it difficult to maintain a life of my own outside our relationship. Anytime I'm away from him, especially if I'm doing something he loves but is no longer able to do, I feel guilty. He, on the other hand, is beginning to feel resentment.

In November of 2004, I accompany my friend Nora to a conference in Berkeley about the possible establishment of a Peace Department in Washington. Michael encourages me to go, but when I come home in the late afternoon about three hours later, he's no longer in a supportive mood.

"I hope you had a good time while I lay here helpless in bed," he says.

I'm stunned and awash in both guilt and the feeling that I'm being sabotaged. I had tried to convince him to let me ask Una to stay with him, but he insisted he was going to be fine—he could always call 911, he said, in an emergency.

"I understand it's hard for you when I go off and do things we used to do together," I tell him, fighting back tears and trying not to become defensive and counter accusative.

He nods, and after that we're able to talk and work through our feelings.

I'm grateful we're able to communicate about things like this and to hear what the other has to say. We both realize that communication is the key to understanding and accommodation.

Nevertheless, ensuring coverage of Michael's needs when I'm away from him continues to be a problem. I always try to convince him to let Una come and stay with him when I go out—and he always refuses. Thank God for cell phones! When I do leave the house, I've learned to call and check on him frequently, and he can always call me if he needs to. As time goes on, however, the times I go out and he stays home alone become fewer and fewer—yet when he feels well enough to go somewhere on his own, he thinks nothing of leaving me behind.

These are some of the issues I bring into my weekly therapy sessions. My therapist points out that according to Jung, the goal of therapy is not to end suffering but to make it meaningful. Troubling patterns don't necessarily disappear, but we can learn to have new relationships with them by bringing them into consciousness. Both dark and light exist, and we cannot escape the dark. That's where the gold is hidden, in the unconscious, and shining the light of consciousness into the dark brings insight and change.

She's also fond of pointing out that if I don't take care of myself, I won't be able to take care of Michael. This is a hard lesson for me to learn because, even after my battle with cancer, I still have a little critic who sits on my right shoulder and often tells me I'm being selfish or wrong or not enough.

As an example of how to deal with the critic, my therapist says, "Tell her, 'Thank you very much. You're often quite helpful to me, but right now I choose to go out for coffee with my friend.' And don't let her beat you up for making a mistake. Part of being human is making mistakes." This proves to be valuable advice as I begin to make conscious choices, accept responsibility for my errors, learn from them, and move on.

During this year in therapy, I also work on getting in touch with my animus, or masculine positive energy. I need this take-charge, organizing energy to take care of the multitude of details connected with Michael's condition and state of mind and to continue to care for him out of choice rather than obligation. This masculine energy is very different from the aggressive masculine energy I learned from my father when he and I had our fights. That was the only model of power I knew. Now gentle and caring animus figures begin appearing in my dreams, replacing the more dangerous, negative masculine figures of old. One dream in particular indicates that the energy I need is gaining strength in my life:

*Michael is a young man, and he is sitting next to me in a movie theater. He puts his arm around my shoulders, and I feel cared for. He is kind. The sling is somehow showing on the side of his seat next to me. I am sexually attracted to him and feel love for him.*

I see the dream-figure Michael as being my emerging (young) animus figure here. He's taking care of me and is by my side as we watch this movie that is our life. As is often the case in dreams, the sexual energy symbolizes spiritual energy and union. The sling, of course, is, on one level: the sling that the real Michael sits in as the lift moves him at home. On another level, it reminds me of the "slings and arrows of outrageous fortune" that we are now encountering. The sling also reminds me that Michael himself needs support, as does my developing animus energy, and it is this energy that will help me support Michael and take care of myself.

In October, I dream of a strange goddess. I see a young woman who has been enchanted; eyes appear all over her head and in her long, dark hair. She is beautiful. I sense that this dream is showing me that my awareness is increasing now and that I'm also becoming more conscious of my nurturing feminine energy and intuition and the collaborative power it brings.

This goddess is powerful in her femininity. She is self-contained and aware of both herself and others. Her eyes see all. I am aware that the aggressive, confrontational manner that characterized my power struggles with Michael have given way to a much more supportive and collaborative power—a power that allows us to work together as we face the ups and downs of Michael's disease and my experience as his caregiver. This is the feminine power that Michael always valued in me, the one he hoped I would find when he withdrew from our arguments, unwilling to support my aggression by joining it to his own.

These two dreams are a source of inspiration for me. It looks as if I have both yin and yang energy to help me out—as long as I can stay in touch with their beneficial aspects and keep doing my inner work.

At Christmas Zoie and her son come out for a visit. Michael has fun letting his grandson ride on his lap in the wheelchair. The lad is quite mechanical, and often Michael will let him take the joystick and steer by himself.

As 2004 draws to a close, though Michael's condition is worsening, he gains a new lease on life being around his grandson: playing with him and reading him stories—the pop-up dragon book being the favorite. We look forward to a brand-new year and hope it will bring us all good fortune.

# Chapter 30

# Slippery Slope

How can I begin to describe 2005? It's a year filled with heartbreak and stress, challenges and victories, and unimaginable change, all of which seem to be foreshadowed by a dream I have at the beginning of the year. Though I write it down in my journal, I soon forget its ominous message.

*There has been a gruesome accident in my childhood hometown. I can see it across the railroad tracks. I walk away, not wanting to look. I notice a young boy, maybe nine or ten, and walk with him. I know I should know his name, but I don't remember it. I ask the boy. He says his name is "Mc" something. He's a cute boy with a full head of light brown hair. I feel protective of him. He is going to visit his father. I join him, and we find we have to cross a large, flat bridge over water. We cross and come to an island. The boy's father is there, and he takes him in but takes no notice of me. I think I should speak to him, but he is busy doing something with the boy, and I have to find a way off the island. I inquire at a little establishment about ferry service. Next, I find myself on another island, still trying to get to the mainland. People give me advice, and I have a lot of baggage to deal with. I'm in a hurry to get back because*

*there's a man I must see. Next, I'm back, and when I see the*
*man, he is dissatisfied with me. I need to fix something about*
*myself, he tells me. Someone places three pieces of plastic tape*
*across my spine just below the shoulders. This strengthens me.*

I've been watching Michael grow weaker and weaker until finally
he's unable to move his legs at all and his arms hardly work. He
begins to choke when eating his food. Sometimes he coughs violently
when drinking liquids, especially water. On this particular morning
in mid-February 2005, when he chokes drinking a glass of carbon-
ated water and continues to cough and gasp for breath, I dial 911 for
an ambulance.

He is admitted to the hospital with a high fever and diagnosed
with aspiration pneumonia: Liquid has entered his lungs and caused
an infection. He remains delirious most of the time he's in the
hospital.

"Ants are crawling all over my face and body," he tells me. "Don't
you see them?"

"There aren't any ants," I reassure him.

He doesn't know where he is or what's wrong with him. On one
level, he believes me that there are no ants, but another part of him
sees them and experiences them crawling all over him, moving in
black trails on the white hospital sheet. Much of the time he's so sick
that he isn't aware of anything and is not communicating at all.

Michael sleeps most of the time at first. He is unable to eat, and
the doctor orders a feeding tube to be threaded through his nose and
down into his stomach. On this day, I stand helplessly at the foot of
his bed, watching the procedure begin. It wakes him up. He has no
idea what is happening to him, and he becomes fighting mad. "Get
away from me! Get that goddamn thing out of my nose!" he yells as

two people hold him down while the doctor tries to insert the tube. I'm amazed that suddenly he has the energy to protest and yell. I try to calm him and explain what is happening and why it must happen, but it's no use. I can only stand there with tears streaming down my cheeks as I watch him suffer. My instinct is to protect him from these torturers, but I know the procedure is necessary, and I let it happen. I feel as if I'm betraying him.

A bag of liquid "food" hangs on a pole by his bed, its contents measured and dispensed directly into his stomach via a machine to which the nasal tube is attached. I spend every day with Michael, always on the watch to see that the nurses take proper care of him. He is unable to put on his call light by himself. Repeatedly, I ask the nurses to be sure that he is checked on frequently, but this rarely happens. I have to be there.

Because Michael doesn't understand why he has a tube stuck in his nose, he tries to pull it out. He does this over and over, and each time I stop him and try to explain that it would be dangerous to pull it out because if the liquid "food" is released in the wrong place, he could choke and aspirate again. He could even drown. I have to keep continual watch over him, and I have to monitor his feeding times because the nurses don't always keep to the schedule. I have to be sure that the head of his bed is kept at the right angle so the food won't come back up. All too often, following a bath or after being turned, the head of the bed is left too high or too low. At first the turning team doesn't understand why he doesn't "help them," not realizing his legs are paralyzed and he's too weak to push with his arms. I have to explain the situation over and over, as the turning teams change with each shift. I have to be sure he's comfortable after being turned, that all his tubes and urine bag are in the right place. Sometimes they leave the bag on the bed instead of hanging it on the rail underneath, and then his urine can't drain and might back up.

I drive the twenty-odd miles to the hospital every day and back each night. For some reason, I don't even think of getting a room in town.

Finally, because Michael keeps trying to pull out his feeding tube, they put restraints on his wrists—"bracelets" with straps tied to the bed frame. I have to give permission for this. It breaks my heart to see my husband's hands tied to the bed, to see him unable to lift his arms and unable to understand why. By now, thanks to the intravenous antibiotics he's receiving, he's stronger and more alert. He pleads with me to take off the restraints and doesn't understand when I won't. Sometimes he promises not to pull his tube out, looking me directly in the eyes with an oh-so-assuring stare. I learn I can't trust him. He probably just forgets, feels the tube irritating his nose, and makes a grab for it. One time I see his hand going toward his tube, and I grab his forearm with a quick and solid movement.

"You hit me," he says, his eyes widening in surprise.

Thanks to friends, on February 12 I'm able to rest at home for a day after spending twelve days in a row with Michael, days when I only left him to grab some lunch or to purchase my daily "reward"—a soy decaf latte. I write my thoughts in my journal:

> *It's so hard. I love him so much. It's an emotional roller coaster. I realized yesterday I couldn't stay on top of things—too tired and exhausted. Mistakes happened. Michael partially pulled out his tube the day before yesterday when I turned my back*

*for a second. His neurologist was in the room, and we were standing talking next to Michael's bed. The doctor hadn't retied Michael's hand restraints after he examined him, and I hadn't caught it. I'm losing it—not on top any longer due to exhaustion.*

Back at the hospital the next day, I continue to anguish over having to restrain Michael's arms. February 14, Valentine's Day, is an especially difficult time. As is often the case, that night I come home from the hospital and weep. I'm afraid he's going to die. Sometimes when I go home I cry because I miss him so terribly, and sometimes it's just because I love him and feel so helpless.

This night I come home and cry because I'm afraid I've broken his will. Today, he didn't protest when I retied his hands. MS has taken away his ability to move his legs, and now, it seems, I am taking away his ability to move his arms. God, I don't want to do that, but even more I don't want him to hurt himself. I begin to doubt everything. I wonder if he thinks he's been kidnapped and brainwashed. I wonder if saving his life by tying his hands has taken away his will to fight and to live. I pray he will forgive me if I've done the wrong thing. And yet, the next day, in a moment of clarity, he suddenly begins to plan for the future. He asks me if I think there are wheelchair trails in Yosemite. Maybe he's willing to go through all this to find those trails. Maybe I haven't betrayed him; maybe I've saved him. Maybe, I think . . . maybe.

Since I can't spend twenty-four hours a day with Michael, he does finally succeed in pulling out the nose tube. Someone forgets to retie the wrist restraints after turning him over. The doctors have a difficult time reinserting the tube, and eventually they call in a nose and throat specialist to do the job. By that time, I'm with him again at the hospital, watching the procedure. I'm impressed by this specialist's ability to thread the tube smoothly through Michael's nasal passage and down into his stomach. But they waited way too long before they called him in, and, for almost a whole day, Michael went without food or water.

A feeding tube can only remain in the nose for a short period of time. Soon it's necessary for Michael to have a stomach tube inserted. When the doctor tells him this, Michael doesn't seem concerned. Since he's better now and more alert, I try to explain what's going to happen, but he just nods. He will tell me later that he thought they were putting him on, trying to con him or scare him so he wouldn't pull out his nose tube anymore. As I walk by his side as he is being taken to the procedure room on a gurney, he continues to nod and smile at me enigmatically. He pretends to be asleep when he goes in. He doesn't really believe they're going to cut a slit in his stomach and insert a tube—not until he feels the knife. He thinks he hears the technicians say, "This guy is really out of it. He won't need anesthetic."

I have no idea what really happens in that room, but when Michael comes out he has a tube protruding from his stomach. It's called a G-tube.

Before Michael comes home, I learn how to change the dressing around his G-tube, how to apply antibiotic ointment to the incision with swabs, how to handle the sterile gauze strips, and what tape to use. I learn to check the protruding tube length with a ruler to determine whether it's worked its way out too far and am taught how to administer the nutrients. I learn to measure the liquid food by pulling it into the plastic plunger before pushing it slowly into the tube. I learn how and when to put water in the tube to flush it, with what pressure to push, what schedule to follow, and how to keep everything clean. This is what's called bulbous feeding, as opposed to drip feeding from a suspended bag, and I feel awkward, at first, performing all these tasks.

Once Michael is home, he receives home healthcare. A speech therapist comes to evaluate his swallowing, an occupational therapist to ascertain what new equipment he needs, and an RN to take care of the necessary medical procedures. I continue Michael's bulbous feeding, becoming more and more adept.

On the recommendation of his speech therapist, he switches from drinking sparkling water, which he prefers, to plain water; she explains the carbonation makes it more likely he'll aspirate. She also recommends he give up using a straw, but he refuses to do that. He feels the straw makes it easier for him to direct the water to the right part of his mouth. Even so, she maintains it isn't safe; air can get into the straw and increase his chances of aspirating. I stay out of the controversy. I know Michael doesn't believe rules apply to him, and he'll do what he wants. Maybe, I think, he's even right about this.

Gradually, Michael goes from tube feeding to taking puréed food and finally onto a mechanical soft diet. With the latter, Michael can eat most foods as long as I make sure they're easy to chew and swallow. We leave the tube in as a fallback safety measure.

During Michael's ordeal, I'm surprised to find I feel his pain quite physically. My heart actually aches. "I love him more than I love my own life," I write in my journal. "I ache, I doubt, I wonder, I plead, I want—Michael."

And I ruminate on what it would be like if our life together is ending. *Is this what my dream portends?* The symbolism evokes the realm of the dead, a place where Michael is welcome, a place I must leave. I'm reminded of the ferryboat that takes souls across the River Styx to the Underworld in Greek mythology. I took the ferry back; he stayed. I know I will need the strength I'm given in this dream—the plastic tape placed across my spine—as I go forward on this uncharted journey that we're on.

And so, the year 2005 begins—all this, and it's only late February.

# Chapter 31

# Roller-Coaster Ride

My journals this year are full of notations that chronicle all the medical tasks I need to perform for Michael, lists of the foods he eats and the quantity and protein counts, lists of supplies to buy or items to request from the home healthcare nurse—mouth swabs, catheters, adult diapers, bed pads, skin-care products to avoid bedsores, medication to treat bedsores, and on and on.

Early in the year, Michael switches from doing intermittent catheterization to having an indwelling Foley catheter, and I learn how to change it while maintaining a sterile environment. It's necessary that the catheter and all the accompanying paraphernalia be sterile to avoid urinary-tract infections. Changing catheters is difficult, intense, and frustrating for me, yet I'm grateful I'm able to do this for Michael. I'm learning to do new things that I never, ever thought I could do. Along the way, I'm gaining new confidence and a determination to meet new challenges as they appear, as I know, and fear, they will.

Still, this new challenge proves to be difficult to master. Even though the home healthcare nurse trains me well, more than once, in a fit of frustration, I throw catheter and paraphernalia out and start over. We use antibiotic silvertip catheters to minimize infections; nevertheless, Michael's rate of infections, which are unavoidable with indwelling catheters, goes up. A side benefit is we become well known to the urology nurse and are able to get the supplies we need easily. She's a helpful person whom we like and appreciate.

The speech therapist who visited Michael after his hospital stay encouraged him to eat nothing but soft foods after he was able to end tube feeding, but, much to my dismay, Michael ignores her warning now and insists on eating whatever he wants. Still, we do make some changes. I give him his pills in applesauce rather than with water, and he eats more soups that have a thick texture. Even in restaurants, I cut his food into small pieces for him, and he chews longer and eats more carefully.

We make some changes in the way Michael drinks liquids to make the process safer. He was given small boxes of nectar-thick juices to take home from the hospital, and I purchase more of these at a local drugstore. He drinks some but doesn't particularly like them. He hates the granulated additive I use to thicken his water, and often refuses to drink it, insisting I bring him plain water.

On March 18, 2005, Michael turns sixty-one. Our celebration is low-key; he's never been big on birthdays. Attempting to make the occasion one of renewed hope and change, I urge him to look into alternative healing.

"I saw what you did when you had cancer," he tells me. "I just can't do that."

I'm disappointed but not surprised. It's just not his thing.

The next big event of 2005 is another episode of aspiration. After drinking some unthickened water, Michael can't stop coughing. When I realize he's in peril, I call 911, and soon we're back in the ER. It's the same thing all over again.

Once admitted to the hospital, Michael goes back on tube feeding, and I'm thankful we left the tube in rather than having it removed before he left the hospital last time. He remains sick for quite a while and is unconscious for much of the time. He's unable to press the call button for the nurse, and, again, I have to explain his condition to the staff repeatedly and keep vigilant watch over his care.

For some time now, Michael's body has been unable to regulate his temperature, and he often becomes extremely cold. During one of those times during this hospital stay, some nurses bring in a machine that blows warm air into a plastic blanket they lay over him on top of a sheet. The blanket has a series of tunnels for air circulation. He had one of these the day before, when he was in the intensive care unit, so I'm happy to see it brought in. I'm not, however, happy to see several nurses puzzling over the machine, trying to figure out how it works. They finally succeed, setting the temperature selector on a high number to warm him up quickly. When I question the high setting, they assure me that, since they are going off shift now, they'll leave a note for the next shift instructing them to adjust the temperature. For some crazy reason, I take them at their word and leave for home, feeling happy that Michael is sleeping comfortably now. Just to check, that evening I call in to see how he is doing, as I often do. The nurse who answers the phone assures me everything is fine.

The next morning, I walk into the following scene: Michael is extremely agitated, turning his head wildly back and forth and moaning, "No one will come. No one will come," in a voice full of despair.

Immediately, I see what's wrong. I pull the suffocating hot-air blanket off him and shout for assistance. I grab some towels, quickly dampen them with cold water, and put them on his brow.

"You're going to be all right, Michael," I tell him. "Everything's going to be all right."

I yell for assistance, but no one appears. I step out of the room only to see three nurses intent on their paperwork at the nurse's station, oblivious to any needs of their patients. I demand that everyone in the nurses' station ". . . get in here and do something!"

Suddenly people come flocking in, including the nursing supervisor.

"You have to lower Michael's temperature," I tell them, but no one seems to grasp the situation. Michael is still moaning, "No one will come. No one will come," as people stand by the bed and stare at him.

With composure that comes from absolute necessity and with contained rage, I demand to know how this could have happened. At that point, someone with some ability bends over Michael and begins taking care of him, cooling him down.

"Don't you know he has MS?" I ask incredulously. "Don't you realize overheating is very dangerous for someone with MS?"

Michael finally calms down and goes into an exhausted sleep. I talk at length with the nursing supervisor, again demanding to know how this could have happened and telling him what transpired before I left the night before. He acknowledges that this shouldn't have happened and says the nurse who came in on the morning shift is responsible. He calls her in. She says she hasn't had time to check on her patients yet. The supervisor makes it clear to her that her first responsibility is to check on her patients and that she was in the wrong not to have done so. But, I wonder, what about the night shift? Why had no one, during the whole night, ever corrected the situation? Had Michael not been checked at all during the night, let alone the next morning? I remind the supervisor that Michael cannot turn on the call light and that his voice is too weak to be heard when he calls out.

"I requested he be checked frequently," I protest. "Why wasn't this done?"

He has no answer. He does, however, send someone up to take an official report, a cheerful older woman with white hair who looks like the archetypal grandmother.

I relate the whole incident, and she takes notes. When we're finished, I sign the report. She assures me the matter will be dealt with immediately. Relieved, I feel I've done all I can to prevent anything like this from ever happening again, to Michael or to anyone else.

Once I get home, I collapse in Michael's big leather chair in the living room and I reflect on what happened. Today, seeing Michael lying helplessly under that suffocating, hot blanket, I felt an upwelling of outrage surging through my body, and I got in touch with an assertiveness that I hadn't felt before.

As a child I was brought up to view doctors and nurses as saviors, unquestioned authority figures whose instructions were to be followed without question. The doctor always knew best. And often they did, and I'm grateful for their care. But today I learned that *I* can take charge when the medical profession fails me and I discover a situation that is not only wrong but cruel. When my mother was dying, contrary to what I knew she wanted, I blindly followed doctors who placed her on a ventilator in the ICU when she had no real hope of recovery. Eventually they moved her to a regular room and allowed her to die naturally, but only after a week of prolonged agony. When I entered her room that last time, I found her lifeless body lying on the bed, uncovered, her knees drawn up to her chest. She was gone. I should never have allowed that to happen the way it did, but I didn't have the confidence to defy the doctors. Not then. But I am no longer that person.

Although I appreciate all that the doctors and nurses do for Michael, I am not blind to the mistakes that medical professionals can make, and I'm not going to accept them. I'm drawing from a new reservoir of strength as I care for Michael, and my confidence is growing. I'll be damned if I'll let things like this pass, not now, not ever.

When he's stronger, Michael is scheduled for a barium X-ray to assess his swallowing. Just before the test begins, I ask the tech, "What if he aspirates during the test?"

Her answer is a shrug of the shoulders and an expression that says, "What can you do?" *Oh my God*, I think. *How can she be so cavalier?*

But I have to assess this situation carefully. I know this test has to be done. I know he's in the hospital, so if there is an emergency, he will be taken care of. So I weigh the risk against the benefit, and I decide to let her proceed. Fortunately, the test goes well. It shows he has to swallow several times to get his food down, but he doesn't aspirate during the test. It appears he can swallow safely, and he's put on a soft diet again.

Michael is a little stronger now, and he's so happy to be eating again. He talks with me and, when he's alert enough, with anyone who comes into the room. Even so, it appears that he feels like he's been set down on an alien planet; he doesn't seem to know the customs or understand what's expected of him. He asks me many questions, trying to find out what's acceptable behavior in this strange new world.

One time he asks, "Is it all right to talk to the nurses? Is it all right to ask them to do things for me?

"Yes, of course," I reassure him.

"Is it all right to ask one to get in bed with me?" This question is asked seriously, in the same innocent voice.

"No," I have to inform him, and I try not to laugh. He nods, calmly absorbing this important information. He really doesn't know what's acceptable behavior and what's not.

About this time, I learn he's concerned about the welfare of the people caring for him. Referring to a nurse's aide who has just left the room, he asks me, "Is she from a country the US exploits?"

"I don't know. Why do you ask?"

"Because if she comes from an exploited country," he explains, "she might be angry and take it out on me." I see his real concern and, suppressing a smile, I assure him she wouldn't, which he seems to accept. In fact, he seems to accept all of my answers, as if I'm the most knowledgeable person in the world. He even tells me I'm very smart. He seems to be completely devoid of social memory, and, apparently, he sees me as the person who can enlighten him.

A little later, out of the blue, he asks me if mentally retarded people are taken care of; he's concerned they might be left to fend for themselves. Another time, he asks if we're free.

"What do you mean?"

"Can we go wherever we want? Can we do whatever we want to do?"

"Pretty much."

"Do we have to work?"

"Yes."

"Then we aren't really free," he concludes.

I have to admit that I guess we aren't. He nods sagaciously, taking this in.

On another day, he becomes concerned about his books at home.

The nursing supervisor is in the room and hears Michael asking me about the work by Plato and other philosophy books he's been reading recently.

"Is he a professor, perhaps at UC?" the supervisor asks.

"No," I say, a bit amused, "He just reads a lot. He's a truck driver."

"Really?" he says, raising his eyebrows. "I have a new appreciation for truck drivers."

*Well, good for you*, I think, stifling a sarcastic reply.

During his hospital stay, Michael is given a variety of antibiotics intravenously. He ends up with a potent cocktail, and, eventually, it works; he gets well. There have been times when the doctor in charge wasn't sure whether Michael would recover, and now he and others on the staff are impressed with Michael's resiliency. We, in turn, are impressed with the doctor's ability to bring Michael through this crisis, despite the mistakes made by some of the nursing staff. Apparently, the current nursing shortage has forced the hospital to bring in nurses from outside the system, which, in large part, is responsible for the problems we've experienced. Fortunately, the majority of the nurses have been competent and helpful. I'm impressed by one young woman who stayed well beyond the end of her shift to make sure Michael's needs were met.

Once we're home, Michael remembers none of his confusion, such as the discussions of how to behave or the episode of the overheated blanket. As I recount these things, he finds my stories most interesting and some even entertaining.

As recommended, Michael continues eating a mechanical soft diet. Against recommendations, he continues to use a straw. I make repeated attempts to thicken his water and other liquids, but he often refuses these and demands plain water or juice.

I don't think Michael or I ever really understand how dangerous eating and drinking can be for him. Over the course of this year, he'll get conflicting messages about food from a string of speech therapists, ranging from "Stick with tube feeding" to "Eat whatever you can tolerate." Concerning liquids, one speech therapist tells him, "You can no longer drink thin liquids safely"—but that message never fully sinks in.

Eventually, it will become clear to me that Michael should have relied exclusively on the feeding tube after the first hospitalization—and definitely after the second. Instead, he chose to continue eating and drinking by mouth. On the other hand, after his first hospitalization the neurologist told me that even if Michael stopped ingesting food by mouth, he could still choke on saliva. I don't see how we can win.

Amazingly, once we're home from the hospital after this second stay, Michael's energy quickly returns. Within a month, we're back to our active, albeit modified, lifestyle. Again, he rides BART alone to San Francisco, driving his van to and from our local BART station. He takes pictures of the street scenes and buildings along Market Street, and visits the Museum of Modern Art. We go together to our local recreation area at Lake Chabot, following the asphalt paths for what we call our "walk and roll." His mind is clear, and he's no longer confused.

Yet we've begun a pattern that will repeat multiple times over the spring and summer of this year: a pattern of hospitalizations and near miraculous recoveries.

# Chapter 32

# The Last Resort

In August of 2005, Michael still has his feeding tube, but he's eating completely by mouth. He confines his choices to foods he can swallow easily, and I confine my cooking to the softer foods. We learn about a gel thickener we can buy online that's completely tasteless, and Michael finds this to be much more palatable than the granular thickener he rejected before. I use the new one to thicken water and other thin liquids, and it allows us to carry thickened water with us in the van. He persists in using a straw, defying the speech therapist's recommendation. I worry about this, but there's really nothing I can do. Besides, Michael insists the straw allows him to direct liquid into the part of his mouth where he can control it.

The indwelling catheter has both advantages and disadvantages. When we go out, we no longer have to hunt for a single, handicapped unisex or men's restroom where I can help him catheterize; now I can strap a collection bag to his leg and conceal it beneath his trousers. The bag isn't nearly as large as the one he uses at night, however, and I have to empty it rather frequently or his urine will back up. One time, I discover the bag is full when we're visiting Union Square in San Francisco. I'm sitting next to a planter, with Michael beside me in his wheelchair. I slip his plastic urinal out of the pack on the back of his chair, hold it down beside his leg, keeping it between the chair and the planter, empty the contents into the urinal by opening the spigot on the bottom of the bag, and dump the urine into the planter. No one seems to notice.

This month, being aware of how precious his times of relatively good health have become, we decide to go for a week's vacation to somewhere nearby (airplanes are definitely out!). Fortunately, with my retirement income and Michael's disability payments, we are doing fairly well financially. I book a week's stay at a resort near Santa Cruz and order a hospital bed, shower seat, and Hoyer lift to be delivered, making sure that we have a handicapped room that will meet his needs. I also check to be sure everything has been delivered before embarking on the hour-and-a-half ride in the van to our destination.

Before we leave, I have serious second thoughts. Michael is weaker than he was the week before, and I'm afraid if we go, he'll get worse—but despite my reservations, he's determined to go. Perhaps he feels, on some level, this might be his last trip.

I plan well and even make arrangements for Una and her children to stay at a nearby motel. Every morning Una and her strong, eighteen-year-old son drive the short distance to the resort to get Michael up, showered, and dressed; with their assistance, a mechanical Hoyer lift works out fine. This gives me time for a morning swim in the pool, and it's wonderful to have time for myself and to know that Michael is being well cared for. In the evening, a cell phone call brings Una and her son back to get Michael ready for bed.

I am so grateful to have Una in our lives. She's such a warm and caring person, always there for us and devoted to Michael. I love the way Michael and she interact—joking with each other and so comfortable in each other's presence. I'm glad I can give Una and her children a chance to have a vacation too. Although their motel is within walking distance to the beach, Una tells me her children spend most of their time playing in the pool. I guess, being from Tonga, they don't find the cold waters off the coast of Northern California all that enticing.

Michael and I enjoy the resort, with its spacious grounds, swimming pool, outdoor eating areas with a view of Monterey Bay, and fairly good food. Michael is subdued, but he's enjoying himself. We both indulge in spa treatments—perhaps the only one he's ever had. Though he's continued to have occasional hallucinations due to his weakened state after the last hospital visit, he has only a few during our time here.

The high point of our short vacation is dinner at a special restaurant in Capitola-by-the-Sea called Shadowbrook. My parents took me there as a child, and it was always a special treat for me. The restaurant is perched on the side of a cliff overlooking Soquel Creek, and the parking lot is at the top. To reach the dining area one either walks down a rather steep, winding path through lush flowers and verdant plants or takes the cable car down to the bottom. At the restaurant level, diners enjoy a stunning view of the creek. Of course, Michael can't walk down the path, and we have a horrible time trying to get his oversized wheelchair into the cable car. People waiting in line are patient and try to help, but we finally decide to give up—it just isn't going to work. At that moment the manager appears and, with a creative, albeit unauthorized, strategy, manages to get Michael down to the restaurant level by accompanying him in the open freight elevator. He continues to take care of us as we dine, presenting us with a complimentary, delicious hors d'oeuvre tray and checking frequently to be sure all our needs are met. We have a calm, romantic dinner in gorgeous surroundings and relish such a special experience.

We get back to the resort late, and Michael tells Una and her son that he wants them to put him not in his hospital bed, but in the queen-sized bed where I sleep. He wants us to sleep together this night. It feels both strange and comforting to have him close beside me during the night—strange because he can only lie on his back without moving; he can't even put his arm around me. I remember all those nights when we would sleep cuddled up like spoons, feeling warm and safe and content. This is different—but still our bodies lie touching all night, and the closeness feels wonderful.

Once again, we go to a play on the redwood-covered UC Santa Cruz campus. We've enjoyed seeing plays here in the past and are pleased we can get tickets again this time. After we're parked, however, we encounter a problem. Michael is extremely weak, and he struggles and struggles to maneuver his wheelchair out of the van. Finally, after what seems like forever, he lets me handle the joystick and guide the chair out and down the ramp. Once out of the van, we purchase a tasty lunch to eat outside before the performance. We see a lighthearted play in the inside theater and enjoy it thoroughly—a nice finish to our vacation.

On our last day, we pack up and decide to go into Capitola for a quick lunch. Parking is impossible in front of the beach, even with our handicapped placard. We find a parking space in front of the movie theater, and I jump out to find a place to buy sandwiches. As we sit in the van eating our lunch, I start to reminisce, telling Michael about the times my parents let my cousin and me off in front of this theater so we could watch Saturday matinees. This little town holds many memories for me—warm, happy days at the beach, playing in the sand with my little wooden bucket and shovel when I was two years old, or riding in on the waves with my father when I was a little older, walks along Soquel Creek at twilight, and eating the best hamburgers in the world at a little joint on the beach that's no longer there. My parents came here for their honeymoon back in the 1930s.

I feel nostalgic and wistful, holding on to this moment with Michael, watching my memories rise and fade, and pushing away the thought that we might be here together for the last time. Reluctantly, I start the van, and we silently head for home. All too soon, this brief time of renewal has come to an end. Michael sleeps all the way home.

By the time we arrive, Michael is quite ill. I think he used up all of his strength and determination to make this vacation work, and he's finally run out of energy. I worry I've done the wrong thing by allowing us to get away—as, once again, I call 911.

# Chapter 33

# Hospital Struggles

Michael's collapse after our trip to Capitola begins another string of hospitalizations. During the last five months of 2005, Michael is in the hospital almost more than he's out. One visit is for an infection at the G-tube site, one for a urinary tract infection, and several for aspiration pneumonia in combination with a UTI.

Hospital visits prove to be frustrating for both of us. I continually ask questions, try to get a handle on what's going on, and monitor the nursing care—the dispensing of medication, the turning in bed, the bathing, the level of comfort. One of the most difficult and prevalent problems involves the array of medications Michael must take. Each time I call for an ambulance and each time he's admitted to the hospital, I have to produce his complete list of medications, dosages, and schedules. I store and update this information in my computer and make printouts as needed. The hospital doctors have to order his meds anew, of course; he isn't allowed to bring medication in with him.

Getting the hospital doctors to write the orders correctly, getting the RNs to interpret the orders correctly, and then getting them to administer the medications correctly is daunting. Often the pharmacy doesn't have a particular medicine in stock, or they're woefully late in getting it up to the nurses' station. On many occasions,

Michael's daily self-injected medication, Copaxone, becomes a huge puzzle to the nursing staff. To begin with, they don't know how the self-injector works, so I have to explain that repeatedly to a changing rotation of nurses. Sometimes they deliver the dosage using just the syringe and without the self-injection apparatus. Consequently, it's often given at the wrong angle. On top of that, the injection site must be changed daily according to a specific plan, and it often proves impossible for the staff to keep track of where he was last injected. If he's lucid he can tell them, but they often don't pay any attention to him. Many times I come in, expecting him to have been given his morning injection, only to have to intervene and wait until afternoon before he receives it. Since consistency in timing is crucial to the effectiveness of the medication, I'm often extremely frustrated and angry at the inefficiency of the staff. Lately, either Una or I have been administering the shot at home, and I'd been hopeful that our diligence is improving the effectiveness of the treatment. Now I fear that's been lost.

I have to fire Dr. Palmer. Michael has aspiration pneumonia again, and after several days he's still not responding to treatment. I ask Dr. Palmer to confer with the doctor who, earlier this year, successfully cured Michael of aspiration pneumonia. It seems to me that the treatment that worked before might do so again. Dr. Palmer refuses to contact this doctor, who is located in another hospital in the system. When he switches Michael from IV antibiotics to the oral form, I know he's doing this too soon. I express my concerns, but the doctor abruptly informs me he knows best. End of discussion. Well, I know differently.

When I get home in the evening, I search through all the websites of the doctors available to Michael at this hospital and come up with one, Dr. Granton, who seems to be both caring and highly competent. Unlike most of the other hospital doctors, Dr. Granton has taken the time to write extensively about himself, his training and experience, and his philosophy of patient care. He even reveals a sense of humor—always, in my book, a sign of higher intelligence.

I'm not at all sure how to go about changing doctors, and I don't even know if it's possible to do so. Looking for some guidance, the next day I seek out the help of a hospital social worker. I'm distrustful of the bureaucracy, but, to my relief, I discover that the social workers really are here to ensure the best care for the patients. The woman who assists me is warm, helpful, and knowledgeable. With her counsel and support, I muster the strength and determination to confront Dr. Palmer and tell him I no longer want him in charge of Michael's care. It takes courage for me to challenge the system, but I have this courage now and I must act in Michael's best interest.

The next time Dr. Palmer visits Michael's hospital room, I confront him. This time, I don't have the outrage that propelled me to take charge as I did when I found Michael helpless and weak, sweltering under a warming blanket turned too high. What I have now is an abiding sense of responsibility for my husband's welfare and a love too strong to give into the assertions of an incompetent doctor. I won't let my husband suffer needlessly like I allowed my mother to do those many years ago. Seeing Michael lying on the bed, apparently unconscious and totally helpless, I know I have to act.

"I'm not satisfied with the care Michael's receiving," I tell him evenly.

He doesn't seem to hear me, so I try again, a little more forcefully.

"I've decided to change doctors."

The words are no sooner out of my mouth than he replies coldly, "You can do whatever you want." He turns abruptly and walks out of the room.

I'm momentarily stunned; I guess I expected a smooth transition. I realize I haven't yet contacted a new physician. At this moment, Michael has no doctor.

Fortunately, I'm able to locate Dr. Granton within the hour, and he's willing to take Michael's case. He readily agrees to consult with the doctor who treated Michael previously, and he explains to me in detail how he plans to treat Michael's condition. One of the first things he does is put Michael back on IV antibiotics with a new combination of drugs. At last, I feel reassured and can relax in the belief that Michael is once again in good hands.

Dr. Granton's treatment is successful. He cures Michael's multiple infections, which include aspiration pneumonia, a septic UTI, and a staph infection he most likely acquired in the hospital. After three weeks, Michael is released to a nearby acute-care facility.

This is not an easy transition. Michael has a great fear of ending up in a nursing home, and the facility sounds to him like a nursing home. Earlier, I talked to a person I met at the hospital who had family placed there, and from her reports, I believe it to be a good place. Really, I have no choice: Michael still needs to be treated intravenously for the staph infection and the pneumonia, and his blood has to be drawn and tested before each IV infusion. If his blood doesn't meet certain criteria, he can't receive the antibiotics. I'm told it's not possible to do this if Michael is at home.

Since Michael needed a blood transfusion during this hospital stay, he already has a catheter in his arm that leads to his heart. This makes it easier for him to have blood drawn and to receive IV medication. I'm nervous when I find out the catheter has to be removed when he leaves the hospital and another one inserted at the acute-care facility. That one, too, will have to be taken out before he can come home. It's a painful procedure for him and a difficult thing for me to watch. He's brave throughout it all, only wincing a little bit at the pain. I'm proud of him and wonder whether I'd be as compliant if I were having a tube threaded up though my arm and into my chest.

As Michael is being wheeled out of his hospital room to go to acute care, suddenly he begins yelling at me. "Take that tape out of the VCR. Take it out or forget about coming home."

As I stand there helplessly, watching and listening to him in dismay, I can feel the energy draining out of my body as tears start rolling down my cheeks.

Michael has been delirious and hallucinating during most of this hospital stay. A recurring hallucination has to do with the TV in his room. Often, he asks me to turn to a certain channel even though there's nothing on it but static. Nevertheless, he watches intently. One day, he tells me he's watching videotapes of me having sex with a variety of men. Nothing I say can convince him otherwise. He insists and begins to accuse me of being unfaithful. "Just look!" he says, nodding to the TV. "How can you deny it?"

According to his latest accusation, I'm enjoying sex with our governor, Arnold Schwarzenegger. I have to laugh at this one. Michael returns my smile with a glare. I attempt to reason with him and to reassure him, but my words fall on deaf ears. Now, as he leaves for the acute-care facility, he wants to make sure I take this "tape" out of the VCR so no one else will see it.

It's already dark as I follow Michael to the acute-care facility. I make a brief stop at home to gather some of the things he'll need. I finally relax, knowing acute care is ready to receive him. We waited all day for the call that told us a bed was available and he could be transferred. I hope with all my heart that this will be a positive move—and that he'll forget all about that TV and the incriminating "tapes."

# Chapter 34

# Acute Challenges

I arrive at the acute-care facility at eight o'clock, less than an hour after leaving the hospital. I inquire at several of the nurses' desks in the sprawling one-floor facility, but I can't find Michael. Finally, someone tells me to check a certain wing, where patients are kept waiting until a bed becomes available. Annoyed and concerned, I make my way through a maze of corridors.

Unlike the rest of the facility, this area reeks of urine. Tentatively, I make my way down the hall, checking for Michael in each room. At the last room at the end of the hall on my left, I find Michael lying on a mattress on the floor. His urine bag is lying on his stomach, preventing his urine from draining properly, if at all. There is no attendant, and three other patients are in the room, also on the floor. Michael is not hooked up to his IV.

"Get me out of here!" he begs as soon as he sees me.

I feel a rush of heat envelop my body. I am livid. I reassure him and race down the hall to find help. I see a woman I take to be an aide and ask to see the RN in charge. She tells me the RN is on break and I will have to wait. It is now quarter to nine.

"Get that woman down here right now or I am going to call an ambulance and have my husband removed from this facility at once," I demand. I am angry and focused.

She gets the message, and in a minute or two, the RN in charge appears and leisurely walks over to ask what the problem is.

Somehow containing my rage but speaking emphatically, I tell her, "It is not acceptable to have my husband on the floor. Either you get him into the room we were told was waiting for him or I am going to have him removed."

She gets it, too, probably because I take out a notebook and begin taking notes. She jumps into action and has patients moved around so there's a room available for Michael. Clearly, they weren't ready for him at all.

I go back to be with Michael as these arrangements are being made. I try to make him as comfortable as I can until he is moved; they haven't even given him a pillow. I feel as if we've fallen into a medieval dungeon. *What if I hadn't been here? How long would he have been left like this, completely helpless and ignored, with his urine backing up and no hydration or medication?*

At nine fifteen, they bring a regular hospital bed into the room where Michael is lying. Miraculously, eight people come in to lift Michael onto the bed! When they back away from the bed, I notice Michael is shivering. They've put him directly onto a cold air mattress without putting a cloth sheet over it first. When I point out this oversight to them, they lift him up and put a cloth sheet in place. It is now nine thirty.

He is rolled into a regular room occupied by one other man. As I follow, I'm relieved to note there is no smell of urine in the hall in this part of the building.

I take Michael's hand. "It's going to be all right," I reassure him.

I stay with him until quite late, when he finally goes to sleep. The shock of everything that has transpired seems to have brought him back to the present and away from his hallucinations.

*He couldn't have hallucinated anything much worse than this,* I think.

When I arrive the next morning at nine fifty-five, his gravity-feeding bag is empty and his feeding line is disconnected from his G-tube. The IV line is attached. He hasn't been given a bath or any attention. I try to turn on his light for the nurse. It doesn't work. I leave the room to report this, and immediately a workman comes in to fix it. At ten o'clock, I get the RN in, and she flushes his feeding line but gives him only a 33 cc flush and refuses to give him more water. She tells me the feeding will be off from eight to ten every morning, and he will get 150 cc of water every four hours.

Michael has foot wounds from being in bed without heel protection in the hospital. They began treatment there, and I made sure that appropriate treatment would continue in acute care. The problem with explaining what needs to be done is that often the next day's shift won't include the same people, so I'm endlessly checking and explaining. The correct procedure for Michael's feet is as follows: Right foot—wash with sterile water, apply ointment, then one layer of the yellow patch followed with one layer of gauze and finally tape. Leave toe loose. The left foot requires three Betadine swabs.

Fortunately, Michael does receive good treatment for the one thing that requires him to be here; he gets his blood drawn and tested on time, and he receives the potent cocktail of antibiotics he needs to treat his condition.

My friend Sandy comes to visit Michael during this time and brings him a neck scarf she knitted. She's alone with Michael for a time while I take a break. Later, she tells me Michael wondered if I would be able to keep pulling him back to life much longer. "The love between you is so evident," she adds.

"Yes, our love is strong," I tell her, "and I *will* keep saving him. I have to!"

Michael experiences a great deal of paranoia while in acute care. He's afraid of the adjoining bathroom and urges me not to go in there or even to open the door. He's afraid to be left alone at night and begs me not to leave him when night falls. I ask Una to stay with him one night when he's frightened. I tell her to do the following things: check his comfort after he's been turned; give him a shave if he'll let her; and ask the nurse for whatever she needs (towels, pillows, etc.). I show her how to use the nurses' call light and the TV remote. I assure her she can call me on my cell phone anytime if there's a problem, but Michael finds her presence reassuring and sleeps peacefully through the night. Una, however, has only an uncomfortable chair. I admire her willingness to stay and be with Michael, despite the inconveniences. I pay her well each week, but the money I give her can never compensate her enough for all the love and care she gives.

Michael is supposed to have physical therapy to help him regain his strength. We can't say that he actually receives this—or anything like it—as we find the PT program here to be inconsistent and ineffective. Compared to the care and rehabilitation he received at our HMO's premier rehab hospital, where he was previously treated, this facility is dismal. When he's alert enough, it takes a lot of convincing before they let him get back in his wheelchair, let alone drive it himself. For a while, they allow him to sit in it, but I have to tie his arm down with gauze so he won't turn it on. When they finally allow him some freedom, he drives it slowly and with extreme care.

During the two weeks Michael is here, I come to know many of the staff, and I appreciate the caring and competence most of them display. Michael even becomes friends with a few of them. I'm grateful Michael is receiving the IV medications he needs to recover, but in other respects, I'm gravely disappointed with the facility. Physical therapy is ineffective and rarely happens on schedule, and nothing can erase the horror of those first few hours. I vow this is one place to which Michael will never return.

# Chapter 35

# Aspirations of Immortality

It's only a matter of weeks after Michael comes home from the acute-care facility before he goes into crisis.

Once again, I call 911. As I see the ambulance pull up in front of our house, sirens screaming and red lights flashing, I feel as if I'm trapped in a recurring nightmare. I watch silently as three paramedics rush into our bedroom. Two of them check and record Michael's vital signs and place an oxygen mask over his nose. The other one questions me about Michael's condition and medications, and only then do I fully engage in the scene that's playing out before my eyes.

All three paramedics work together to lift Michael off the bed and onto a gurney. Once he's safely installed in the ambulance, they rush Michael to the ER. I grab his satchel of medications and a few essentials, jump into my car, and follow. I'm too numb to think; I just feel a heavy sense of urgency and dread.

I arrive and park just as Michael is being wheeled into the ER. I rush to his side and accompany him through the sliding glass doors and into the receiving area. When I see Dr. Granton talking to a nurse at the desk, my tension and anxiety subside. He recognizes us and comes over. I'm relieved beyond measure that he's here and that he can be Michael's doctor again.

When Michael is stabilized and able to talk, Dr. Granton has a discussion with him about his advance directives—his wishes concerning life support. He tells Michael that if he were to need intubation to maintain his respiratory function, which would involve placing a breathing tube through his trachea and connecting this tube to a ventilator, he would probably never recover due to his MS. Michael listens intently and decides to decline this procedure if he were no longer able to breathe on his own.

I feel as if I'm in a dream. Of course, we should have talked about these matters a long time ago, but we didn't. We were in too much denial to realize things couldn't continue this way forever. After every crisis, Michael came back. I guess we believed he always would. Now it's time to wake up and make some decisions—decisions about life and death. I'll let Michael do this on his own; they have to be his decisions, not mine.

After several hours in the ER, Michael is transferred to a regular hospital room. Again, he has hallucinations. During one of these episodes, he becomes convinced he's responsible for saving the soul of one of the nurse's aides. Her name is Elizabeth.

"Elizabeth, come forth," he commands loudly and repeatedly. "Come forth, Elizabeth, come forth."

When Elizabeth fails to come forth, Michael decides he is dying, and he wants to leave this world as he came in. He insists on having his hospital gown and all the covers removed so he can lie naked on the bed. Dr. Granton is in the room at this time, and he fulfills Michael's request with respectful compliance. I glance at the doctor, wordlessly asking him if Michael is really dying. He shrugs his shoulders and gives me a quizzical look, but he stays in the room. After a short while—and to our relief—Michael abandons the notion of dying and welcomes back the covers.

The next day, at my request, Michael receives a visit from the hospital chaplain. Rather than listening to her counsel, however, she listens to his. He speaks earnestly to her in a low voice, full of compassion. I'm nearby and can't make out his actual words, but she seems to be taking him seriously. He ends with a directive I'm able to catch as he raises his voice a bit to give his parting guidance. "Now go home and have sex with your husband," Michael tells her with a sagacious nod.

She gives us both a smile as she leaves and appears to be pleased at having made a connection. It's obvious to me that Michael is not at all lucid and will remember nothing of this conversation when he gets out of the hospital.

In fact, Michael is rarely lucid during this hospital stay, even though he talks and appears to know what he's saying and doing. One morning when I come into the room, he asks me if Simply Red, the British soul band, is performing for him behind his bed. He doesn't quite believe the group would come to the hospital just for him, yet he does hear them. He holds my gaze, his eyes pleading with me to set him straight on what's going on. I wish with all my heart they really were here, but I have to tell him the truth.

In the evening, I stop at a nearby Japanese restaurant for a quick dinner before going home. After eating I get up to leave, but I don't go home. Suddenly, I have the distinct feeling that something is wrong—that I must get back to the hospital.

When I enter Michael's room, I see he's sitting straight up in the bed and trying to get his covers off. I stand shocked for a moment, surprised he has the energy and coordination to do this.

"What are you doing?" I ask.

"I'm getting up," he answers, as if what he's doing is obvious and natural.

"You can't," I tell him.

"Why not?" he counters, continuing to struggle.

I begin to question myself. What if he really can get up? What if he's miraculously cured?

But I know if he can somehow swing his legs over the side of the bed, he will fall. He might hurt himself—even break a leg or arm. I rush out of the room and get a nurse. She takes in the situation, leaves momentarily, and returns to administer a shot of lorazepam to calm him down. Soon he is quiet and falling asleep.

"Goodnight, Michael. I love you," I tell him as I kiss him goodbye. He doesn't seem to hear me. As tears begin streaming down my face, I turn toward the door and, moving slowly, leave for home. How I wish he were able to get up and walk out that door with me.

Once more, Dr. Granton is able to bring Michael through another episode of aspiration pneumonia. One week after being rushed into an ambulance, he's able to come home, even though he's still on IV antibiotics and oxygen. This time, thanks to a different cocktail, he won't need to have a blood test before each dose.

Again, I learn to master new skills that seem beyond my capabilities. A nurse teaches me how to administer the IV medication using a battery-pack machine that carries out the procedure automatically. When we get home, I follow a sequence of precise operations to keep it working correctly. Michael is hooked up to so many machines and has so many tubes coming out of his body—including the feeding, catheter, and IV tubes, and, at night, the tube from his sleep mask to the CPAP machine—that it's difficult for Una to perform all the bathing and toileting chores. Somehow, together, we manage.

I'm so glad to have my hospital bed downstairs next to his. I need to be close by and prepared during the night in case something goes wrong.

Amazingly, after finishing this series of antibiotics, Michael seems fully recovered. He's eating soft foods and is even well enough to go to San Francisco on the night of November 27. His energy is phenomenal—no matter how many times he's rushed to the hospital, he's able somehow to bounce back. We have the giddy feeling that he's indomitable, if not immortal.

We have dinner at a restaurant on Pier 39 on the San Francisco waterfront. As has become his custom, after we order, Michael asks the waiter to bring him a tray. He explains that the tray will go on his lap and his food will go on the tray. It's easier for him eat this way because the armrests of his large wheelchair won't slide under the table.

When the waiter leaves, I stand up and take Michael's apron out of the pack on the back of his chair. I place the loop over his head and spread the bottom part carefully over his lap. This is a routine we follow both at home and when we're out; it keeps Michael's clothes from getting covered with food. His hands shake quite a bit when he eats, and he often drops his food before it gets to his mouth. I also put his pill case on the table.

The next time the waiter appears, he's carrying a tray in one hand and two plates with Michael's food in the other. At just this precise moment, Michael begins struggling to get his pills out of their case. The waiter stands rooted to the floor. He looks at me questioningly, apparently unsure of where to put Michael's tray since the pill case is now occupying Michael's lap.

"Just put the tray and the plates on the table," I tell him.

He puts the tray on the table and attempts to put both plates on the tray. They don't fit. He looks at me helplessly. Apparently, he wants me to solve this dilemma. When I don't offer a solution, he puts one plate on the tray, the other on the table, and dashes off. During this time, Michael is oblivious to what's going on and continues to struggle with his pills. He's having trouble getting the caps off and shaking out the correct number of pills. I know I should jump up to help him, but I don't. I'm experiencing a lot of back pain right now, and I just don't have the will to get up.

But I realize I need to do something. "I'd be happy to fix your pills for you if you can just wait a minute," I say. He doesn't respond. Either he is ignoring me, or he can't hear me above the noise of the restaurant.

Just then, the waiter reappears with my order and places it on the table in front of me. I begin to eat, but I immediately start to feel guilty because Michael is still struggling with his pills. Finally, I get up to help Michael find the pill he wants. Then I secure the tray on his lap. I know I should leave it at that, but I can't help asking him why he didn't ask me for assistance with his pills when I was already up for the apron.

"You're angry with me," he says.

I sit back down as tears start to flow. All of a sudden, life seems too crazy to bear. I *am* angry with Michael, and I'm angry with myself for being angry. I'm angry with the waiter. Not only do I have to take care of Michael, but, apparently, I'm supposed to take care of the waiter. I'm angry that my back hurts, and I'm angry that my food is getting cold.

We eat our dinners in silence, both of us ignoring my tears, and they soon go away. I realize the food is actually quite good, and

Michael seems to be enjoying his meal and managing to get most of it into his mouth. I find I'm able to let the whole thing go, and it looks like he is too.

As planned, we go across the landing from the restaurant to see *Menopause The Musical*. Michael turns out to be one of only four men in the audience. We both enjoy the show immensely. He laughs as hard as any of the women, including me. All is well again, and we're having a great night out on the town.

We took BART over to the city, and "walked and rolled" the fairly long distance along the Embarcadero from the station to the restaurant. On the way back, it's dark, and the sidewalks are mostly deserted. I watch Michael's chair receding in the distance as he moves ahead of me, traveling much more quickly than I can walk. Suddenly I feel vulnerable and alone. I've never let go of the illusion that he's my protector, even in a wheelchair. He's really not, I realize; I'm on my own. I'm really all on my own.

Then he stops and looks back. When I catch up with him, he says, "I'm sorry. I didn't realize you were so far behind." We stay close together from that point on. I smile down at him, glad to have him by my side and glad to be by his.

Michael goes back into the hospital on December 18, 2005, one day before my birthday. He has both aspiration pneumonia and another UTI and is assigned to an emergency room doctor who speaks to me more directly and emphatically than anyone else ever has.

"Michael has been in the hospital seven times this year for aspiration pneumonia. That's out of the realm of acceptance, even for someone with MS," she tells me. "*It is no longer safe for Michael to take food or drink orally."* She is emphatic, repeating this last sentence over and over and shaking her head until I tell her I get it. Michael is here, lying on the gurney in the ER, but he is not at all present. He doesn't hear her.

"We'll talk when he's lucid," she says. "He'll have to choose: eat and drink only via the G-tube or continue to do so orally and continue to aspirate."

This will be a huge loss. So much of our life together revolves around food—going out to dinner, eating before or after a show, stopping for a latte, breakfast in bed in front of the TV, treats, chocolate, scones, and on and on.

"As far as his urinary tract infections," she goes on, "he's already resistant to two types of antibiotics. The bacteria have taken up residence in his bladder; they live there. The host is the problem—his bladder no longer works and can't protect itself. He can go on maintenance doses of antibiotics, but eventually the bugs will become resistant; he really can't win."

After the doctor completes her intake procedures in the ER, Michael is wheeled to a regular hospital room. He's still not conscious enough to understand his situation. I am stunned, fully realizing the truth of what the doctor has told me: He really can't win—if aspiration pneumonia doesn't kill him, the urinary tract infection will. I wish someone had laid it out to us this plainly some time ago. We never realized the finality of what MS was doing to him. Michael always insisted on going back to eating when he returned home from the hospital. Although I was hesitant to give him regular food and water, even if thickened, he never took the danger seriously. Perhaps eating was his last holdout for a normal life. And we thought the UTI was troublesome, but we believed the antibiotics were doing their job. That was never one of our big worries.

December 19, my birthday, arrives. It's raining, and our street is full of Christmas lights. Instead of seeing the lights as mocking me, they remind me that joy and pain are opposite ends of a continuum. Things will change and change again. I feel numb but, in a strange way, centered. I know I'll need all my inner resources to get me through this dark time. I know I have to be strong if I'm going to be there for Michael and meet the challenges that lie ahead.

At the hospital, Sarah (the physician's assistant) and I talk about choices. Hospice. Tracheotomy if he chokes. No more oral intake of food. There will be a lot to talk about with Michael when he's lucid again. But today he sleeps, only aware of another's presence when he's being turned or needs to have the mucus suctioned from his mouth and throat. He's not really conscious.

The next day, Michael seems to be getting better. Most of the time he can lift his left arm and whisper yes or no to my questions. He's sleeping less and is more alert. My spirits are up as a result of his improvement. I'm so happy he's getting better—yet I dread the discussion ahead of us.

Michael has a different doctor this time; his name is Dr. Clarence. When I see Dr. Granton at the nurses' station, I ask his opinion of the doctor that Michael has been assigned. He assures me he's a fine physician, and I believe him. He seems busy with his paperwork, and I don't ask him to be Michael's doctor. I wish the woman we saw in the ER could continue to treat Michael, but I never see her again.

Dr. Clarence tells me Michael has been eligible for hospice care for quite some time, as this automatically occurs if one has been hospitalized more than four times in a year. I'm shocked—why didn't any of the other physicians tell me this? I tell him I'm interested in learning more about this, but no one comes to discuss it with me. The doctor doesn't counsel me to request hospice, nor does he tell me how to go about making it happen. I decide this is another thing Michael and I will have to talk about when he's more lucid. We'll have time to consider the best course of action once he bounces back, as he always does.

After a week of IV antibiotic treatment in the hospital, Dr. Clarence asks me if I would like Michael to come home. I tell him of course I want Michael to come home.

The doctor has not mentioned hospice to me again, and I assume Michael is well enough now to make the transition to home.

I'm pretty frazzled by the time Michael leaves the hospital. He hasn't been strong enough for me to begin our discussion, so I know when we get home we'll have to face some serious issues. He'll have to consider restricting his food and liquid intake to the G-tube alone, and we'll have to talk about the possibility of hospice care. We'll also have to consult his urologist about his recurring urinary tract infections.

Michael is released on December 25, and I pack up his things. But I accidentally leave one thing behind: a wall poster of the Blue Medicine Buddha. This poster accompanied Michael on his last four hospital stays, and he always wants it with him. Many, many times he felt fear in the hospital, and seeing the Blue Buddha always comforted him. It was the one thing that remained unchanged when he was hallucinating. "I can look at it and know what I'm seeing is real," he told me.

Although I immediately go back to the hospital, it's gone. Later, I phone and have the staff on two different floors look for it. I go back the next day, and even talk to the custodian, but it's never found.

I haven't had the time or energy to plan Christmas, and for the first time, we ignore it completely, except for some Merry Christmas wishes to each other when Michael gets home. When the children were with us, we did the whole shebang, though Michael would have preferred to ignore it even then. This year he's more than happy to let the day pass unobserved.

He isn't home long enough for us to have our talk. The next day, December 26, he's back in the hospital with chest pains and shortness of breath. He goes home again three days later, still on IV antibiotics, G-tube feeding, medication through a nebulizer, and intermittent suctioning. It's my job to give him his IV medicine and the medicine to inhale through the nebulizer, to hook him up to the feeding tube, to be sure to dispense the right amount of food and push the right amount of water through the dispenser to flush it, to care for his G-tube site with daily applications of antibiotic ointment and gauze secured by porous tape, to perform frequent suctioning of mucus from his mouth with the suctioning wand, to dampen those pink, spongy plastic swabs and twirl them in his mouth to clear out the mucous, and to use the lemon swabs for some refreshing moisture.

Michael remains weak after this hospitalization. Although he was diagnosed with aspiration pneumonia and received oxygen in the hospital, Dr. Clarence does not order oxygen for Michael at home. Even though he's always had oxygen ordered in the past, I'm too busy with all the other tasks to wonder at this.

Zoie is concerned about Michael's repeated hospitalizations. On the twenty-eighth, she arrives for a visit, bringing along her new baby daughter. During their visit, Michael is able to see and hold his new grandchild for the first time. He's lucid and takes delight in seeing his daughter and her adorable baby.

Michael seems to be on a healing journey—but on a spiritual level, not a physical one. He has a wonderful phone conversation with his brother, Steve, that's filled with warmth and humor. He even brings peace to the disharmony between his first wife and himself in another phone call.

"I love you," he tells her before hanging up.

A bit surprised, I ask him what that means.

"It means I don't hold anything against her anymore," he explains.

I nod my head, understanding that he is seeing his life as a whole, no longer split in two, black and white, as he so often tended to do. He is moving toward wholeness.

"I need to connect with you," I say, feeling a strong urge to hold him and to be held.

He looks up at me, his gaze both inviting and quizzical. I lean over the bed and rest my head on his chest, inhaling his scent—which is so familiar to me, so exciting and so comforting. When I arise, he smiles and goes back to reading. He seems to be at peace with himself.

I marvel at how far we've come in our life together and how differently I can react now to hearing him tell her that. Thirty years ago, I would have felt threatened. Now I can ask for what I need instead of reacting from old patterns of fear and insecurity. We've both grown so much over these years of struggle. There's a calmness and peace that, despite adversity—or maybe because of it—pervades and abides with us now. I know there's nothing that can breach the bonds of love and commitment we've created. In fact, there never was.

# Chapter 36

# Errors and the ER

On December 29, neither of us sleeps all night. Michael is extremely restless, and I get up repeatedly to use the machine to suction the mucus out of his mouth and throat. In the hospital, specially trained staff put suction tubes way down into his throat. That's what he needs now, but I can't do it; I only have a "wand" to clean his mouth and the upper part of his throat. Toward morning, I'm groggy from lack of sleep and frustrated when, over and over, I must get out of bed, turn on the machine, and bend over him because he asks me to suction him. Sometimes he has no mucus in his mouth or throat.

"You have to cough. You have to cough!" I tell him.

"I have to cough, I have to cough, I have to cough," he repeats, as if reciting a litany. Tears start streaming down my face, and I long for someone to be here to help me.

The next day Zoie comes over, and Michael seems a little better. The nurse from home healthcare arrives, and I am so relieved, knowing she's trained to handle the situation. At last, I have some help.

I tell the nurse that Michael hasn't slept at all and is having trouble breathing, and he has a cut on his hand and a stage-one pressure sore on his right buttock. The nurse does her intake data-gathering, then listens to Michael's chest and says his upper respiratory sounds are so loud she can't tell whether or not he has congestion in his lower lungs. She then turns all her attention to his cut and pressure sore.

Zoie and I become increasingly concerned with his labored breathing and ask the nurse several times if she thinks Michael needs to go back to the hospital. She remains noncommittal and states she cannot make a full assessment of the situation with her stethoscope. She's sorry she does not have her "pulse ox" meter with her to check Michael's oxygen absorption. We find this lack of preparation to be odd, given the fact that both she and the doctor know Michael is still suffering from pneumonia, at high risk of aspiration, and on IV antibiotics. She reminds us that Dr. Clarence didn't order oxygen for home use.

Suddenly I begin to question the doctor's competence. *Why hadn't he ordered oxygen for Michael? Why hadn't I demanded that Dr. Granton take over Michael's case, instead of relying on his assurance that this new doctor was "very good"?*

After the nurse has been in our home for about an hour and a half, we're still worried about Michael's breathing and frustrated because the nurse is giving us no direction. Michael has been quiet but conscious, saying little. I ask him whether he wants to go back to the hospital, but he says he doesn't know. I ask the nurse whether we should call 911, but her reply is vague and noncommittal. Seeking another opinion, Zoie finds the number for our HMO hospice and calls to obtain information about their services. Perhaps we should look into this now, we think, since the home healthcare nurse seems neither prepared nor competent. The woman at hospice informs Zoie that they will not be able to make an assessment until after the New Year's holiday weekend. Tomorrow is New Year's Eve.

When Zoie mentions her father's labored breathing to the hospice nurse, she urges her to call 911. We decide to act on this advice. When we inform the home healthcare nurse of our decision, she says this is probably a good idea. My feeling of being adrift without a rudder is increasing. I'm becoming aware that instead of taking charge of the situation, the nurse is shirking her duties. She's anything but pro-active, having given us no clear direction on whether or not to call 911, and she didn't even offer to go back to the office to get her pulse oximeter so she could thoroughly assess Michael's condition.

After making our decision to call 911, I ask Zoie to wait while I rush upstairs to get Michael's list of medications; the paramedics always demand that. Foggy from lack of sleep, I'm suddenly focused on being prepared, getting everything in order. After a couple minutes' delay, I rush back downstairs and tell Zoie to call 911.

The nurse informs us there is no need for her to stay, since we've called 911. She goes, leaving her patient in crisis, before the paramedics arrive. Later, I file a grievance.

The response to the call takes only a few minutes. When the paramedics measure Michael's oxygen absorption level with their pulse oximeter, it registers 50 percent (normal range is in the 90s). Immediately, they give him oxygen. Because his reading is so low, they decide to rush him to the nearest hospital; there isn't time to take him to a hospital that's part of our HMO. In their hurry to get him into the ambulance, they knock over a table and small refrigerator and anything else in their way. There's no uncertainty; they know exactly what to do. Suddenly, the enormity of the situation breaks through my cloudy consciousness. Frightened, Zoie and I follow the ambulance to our local hospital, about a mile and a half away.

There, Michael remains on oxygen; his prolonged and unnecessary suffering due to oxygen deprivation is finally over. By the time he's settled in the ER, he actually seems to have revived. He begins talking and is quite alert.

# Chapter 37

# Finalities

Michael is moved from the emergency room to the intensive care unit. I'm not alone; my three stepdaughters are with me at the hospital. It's evening now, and Michael is much less responsive.

The doctor shows us into a small sitting room near the ICU. He tells us we must decide whether or not we want Michael to be intubated. This would mean placing a breathing tube through Michael's mouth and into his lungs and letting the machine breathe for him. The doctor explains that, for an indefinite time, Michael won't be able to breathe on his own. I know from past experience with my mother, during her last days in this same hospital, that intubation is a drastic and painful solution.

I feel removed, not completely present, as I listen to the doctor. I can't quite believe I'm sitting here facing this decision. I'm glad for his daughters' presence, glad I don't have to make this decision alone. I allow my rational mind to take over and guide me.

I explain that during a previous hospitalization, another doctor recommended against intubation for Michael if the issue ever came up. Michael's condition, he told us, makes it impossible for him to recover from such an invasive procedure. Michael had listened attentively and made the decision that he did not want to be placed on a ventilator.

Now, in that sitting room, face to face with the reality of the situation, I'm glad Michael's decision can help guide me now. We reach consensus fairly quickly: Michael will not be intubated. It's one of those rare occasions when all four of us are able to come together, united in our love for Michael. The choice appears inevitable. We choose not to put Michael through more suffering only to awaken—if, in fact, he does—to a life that, in his opinion, wouldn't be worth living. We've all heard him say, at one time or another, he would never want to be a vegetable, entirely dependent on others, and we know our decision is the best one we can make for him now.

Michael's nurse in the ICU is caring and compassionate. "I'll take good care of your father," he tells the girls as we leave Michael in his care for the night.

The next day I'm the first to arrive at the hospital, where I learn that Michael has been moved to a regular room. When I locate it, I'm relieved to find he has the room to himself.

The hospital has assigned a pulmonary specialist to Michael. When the girls and I meet him, he tells us Michael will not pull through this. I knew this, but now it's confirmed.

"Besides having aspiration pneumonia, Michael has an antibiotic-resistant urinary tract infection and a staph infection," the doctor says. He is kind and speaks gently to me. He even gives me a reassuring, sympathetic hug.

Michael is one of very few patients, and the hospital is quiet. As it turns out, it's being boycotted by most of the nurses, who are protesting substandard patient care. Ironically, due to the low volume of patients and the competence of the nurses who remain on duty, the hospital is serene and efficient, and Michael receives excellent care. Thankfully, I see no pickets; Michael would never cross a picket line.

When night falls, I'm alone again with Michael. He can't speak, and I'm not sure whether or not he can hear me. For a while he seems to be trying to let me know he wants something, and I ask him to blink his eyes once for yes and twice for no as I try to figure out what he wants me to do. He is able to do this, and I go through a series of things I think he might want, but he answers no to everything. In anguished frustration, unable to stop the tears, I tell him I just don't know what he wants. It can't be anything physical because I go over every possibility: repositioning in bed, more pillows, fewer pillows, light on or off, and such. I don't know why I don't think to explain once again where he is and why he is here. Maybe I just can't face saying it.

I tell him what a wonderful husband and father he is and how very much I love him. Shortly after we met, we made a plan to reunite in our next incarnation. We agreed to meet at our special place on the Stanislaus River on the date we met, June 22, but one hundred years later, in 2076. We would reincarnate and be together in our next lives. I tell him now that if that turns out not to be the best thing for him, I release him from that vow, but I will be there, waiting, nonetheless. As tears stream down my cheeks, I begin to apologize over and over for crying. I feel so helpless. All I want to do is hold on to him. At that point, he looks straight into my eyes and holds my gaze for a long time. His eyes are a shallow blue, as if the light behind them has faded. But his gaze is focused and unwavering. It's as if he's holding on to me with his eyes.

That night, I try to sleep in the hospital room. We've never spent a New Year's Eve apart, though we rarely celebrated. I lie down on his bed with him, but I have no room to sleep—even if I could—and I'm afraid I might pull out one of his tubes. I try lying on top of the other bed in the room, but the light is so bright sleep is impossible. I don't know whether or not it would be okay to turn the light off, because the nurse comes in frequently to check on him. I finally decide to go home, knowing I have to get some sleep if I'm going to be able to face tomorrow.

Yet once I'm home and in bed, I'm still unable to sleep. I toss and turn, trying to make some sense out of all that's happened. Underneath it all, my greatest fear is that I didn't do all that I could— that I made fatal errors—that I'm responsible for what is happening to Michael—that everything that's wrong is my fault.

I remind myself that I need to be there for Michael tomorrow, to act on his behalf as best I can. I wish with all my heart I could bring him home and arrange hospice care for him. Maybe, just maybe, I still can. I pray I'll be able to meet whatever challenges tomorrow will bring. I want Michael to know that I'm there with him and I love him. I hope he isn't afraid, and I hope he's as comfortable as he can be. I hope and pray all will be as it should, and finally, I surrender to sleep.

# Chapter 38

# New Year's Day

The next day is New Year's Day 2006, but that scarcely enters my mind. I arrive early at the hospital and am soon joined by Michael's daughters. I have brought his iPod and all his treasured music, some small speakers, a candle, and a picture of his beloved grandmother, who was his main source of love and nurturing during his youth.

When I enter his hospital room, I discover the doctor has ordered a morphine drip for Michael to make him comfortable and free from pain. Despite this indication of finality, a part of me is ever vigilant and on the lookout for mistakes or mishaps on the part of the medical staff. At one point, I notice the urine in his collection bag is unacceptably dark. I announce that I never let his urine get this dark and start to leave Michael's side to get a nurse. Zoie calls my name, bringing me back to reality. It no longer matters whether or not he is sufficiently hydrated. He is dying.

In midafternoon, Michael's daughters want to be alone with their father, and I allow this, knowing they need to connect with him, perhaps for the last time. I think it will be good for him, too, but for some reason, what is best for them is my foremost concern. I feel enshrouded by a dense haze, my heart breaking. At one point I find myself in the elevator with another woman, perhaps a nurse, and she tells me, "Things will get better." I realize I have just let escape a long—and probably mournful—sigh.

As I leave Michael with his daughters, I'm suddenly overcome with tears. I call Sally, a close friend, on my cell phone, but she doesn't answer. I leave a garbled, tearful message on her answering machine, telling her Michael is dying. Then I wander around the hospital, taking the elevator down to the basement cafeteria for a cup of tea and riding it back up to walk aimlessly around the lobby. I agonize over whether I'm doing the right thing by leaving Michael alone with his daughters, and I worry he might be wondering where I am or feeling I've abandoned him. They promise to call me on my cell phone if Michael's condition changes, but still, I'm uncomfortable not being right there by his side.

After about thirty minutes, I remember the hospital has a meditation room, and I decide to find it. When I reach the room, I notice a couple is already there, talking in loud voices to a third person. I'm miffed that they've taken over the room for their own purposes, and I don't go in. I decide, instead, to go back upstairs to Michael.

I'm forever grateful to that couple for ignoring the QUIET sign on the meditation room door. As soon as I enter Michael's room, I realize there's no time to spare. All three of the girls are standing quietly at the food of Michael's bed, and there's a stillness in the room that somehow lets me know Michael's time is near. I calmly pull up a chair and sit close to his bed. Holding his right hand in my right hand, I focus all my love and attention on him, saying, "I'm here, Michael; I'm here." As I relax into being with him, my breath and body become attuned with his. Gradually, each breath we take is spaced longer apart.

After one long exhale, I feel a slight movement behind me. "No,"

I say, not breaking my connection with Michael. "There's one more." And there is. Michael draws his last breath.

It's four in the afternoon on January 1—New Year's Day 2006.

Michael's is an easy, quiet transition. And then it's over, and I'm standing up. Suddenly, as if out of nowhere, Zoie hands me a Tibetan Buddhist *phowa* to read. It's a poem to guide the transfer of consciousness at the time of death. I read the following aloud:

> *Above the crown of your head, on a lotus with a moon and sun throne, sits Guru Buddha Amitabha in the Vajra pose. His holy body is radiant and ruby red, and he is wearing the saffron robes of a pure monk. He has one face, and his two hands resting in his lap hold a bowl filled with the elixir of immortality.*

I follow this with a lengthy Tibetan prayer for the time of death that ends:

> *Guru Buddha Amitabha, essence of the perfect truth of the Triple Gem, courageous one who liberates all sentient beings from the bondage of mundane existence and delivers them to the supremely blissful realm of Infinite Light, Victorious One, please release Michael and all others from the difficulties and fears of the death process and the intermediate state of the after-death plane. Easily guide Michael to your wisdom heart by inspiring him to thoroughly renounce the grasping at mundane existence and to achieve success in transferring*

*his consciousness. You are liberator of all beings. Please with*
*great compassion take Michael to your pristine realm.*

Softly, the girls leave the room, and I'm alone with my husband. I shut his eyes gently, surprised at how easily I can do so. There is no one there to protest, to be irritated at the intrusion. After a few moments, I go out to the hall where his daughters are standing, but soon I realize that I'm not ready to leave him. I go back in the room. He looks so much the same, as if he's sleeping. His body is warm.

The nurse comes in, takes his vital signs, and pronounces him dead. After a short while, the nurse asks me to leave; the law requires them to take Michael's body downstairs, where it will wait until taken to the crematorium. The nurse tells me he has to remove the tubes from Michael's body, and I tell him I don't want to be there for that.

There is nothing more I can do. I gather up the mementos I had placed on the windowsill, walk out of the room, take the elevator down to the main floor, and leave the hospital. I get in and drive home, alone.

With Michael's death, I feel as if I, too, have died. The light has gone out of my life. It's as if I'm a candle and Michael the flame, and his last breath has blown out the flame and left me alone in the dark.

As I enter our empty home, I feel like I'm in shock. As if in a daze, I fall into the living room chair that used to be Michael's. Suddenly, I'm struck with the power of his presence. Our souls seem to meet and intertwine with the passion our bodies once knew. As the connection builds, my breath becomes increasingly rapid. I surrender to this energy that is both inside and around me. After a timeless time, it reaches its peak and subsides. I'm left awestruck, my face wet with tears.

After a while I get up and walk over to the CD player. I put on a disk by Neil Young. As I listen to him sing "Harvest Moon," I begin to sway, holding my arms out and curved as if I'm dancing with Michael. With my eyes closed, I imagine him holding me and leading me across the floor. The lyric, "Because I'm still in love with you, I want to see you dance again, on this harvest moon," touches my heart, and I know it's a message from Michael. Tears and sobs mix with the lull of the music, and the song carries me off—carries me away to Michael. For just a bit, the pain lifts, and I feel loved and cared for once more.

# Chapter 39

# Synchronicities

The next morning, I'm struck by the physical intensity of my pain. In the center of my chest, my heart literally aches with such sharpness that I wonder if I'm having an actual heart attack. In a way, I am. The pain radiates down both my arms as they ache to hold him once more, and tears stream incessantly down my cheeks. I feel fragile, as if I might shatter at any moment. My only solace is to embrace Tibetan Buddhism through meditation and to build, in imagination and longing, a spiritual connection with Michael.

Two days after Michael's death, I visit my therapist for our weekly session. Sharing my grief and confusion with her gives me a sense of grounding and safety. As I emerge from her office, wearing a red fleece top that was Michael's—which still holds his comforting scent—I'm suddenly aware of his presence. He tells me to walk down the street to a shop we both knew. I hear his voice inside my head— *his* voice, not mine.

*"I want to buy you a gift,"* he says.

*"How will I know where it is?"* I ask.

*"You'll know."*

On entering the shop, I'm drawn to a red Buddha Board on my left, just a few steps from the entrance. It looks like a slim laptop computer, but, as the proprietor shows me, instead of opening to a screen, it opens to a blank surface on which one can write or draw with a soft brush dipped in water. As the red surface takes on the water, the images emerge in a darker shade of red and slowly fade away.

Immediately, I know this is Michael's gift; it's as if he has handed it to me. I purchase it, take it home, and place it on the coffee table in front of the couch. I sense that Michael has given me a beautiful symbol of impermanence.

I'm entranced as the first free-flowing lines I draw on the Buddha Board gradually fade, leaving just two drops of red. I watch in wonder as one disappears, then the other. I feel Michael sitting with me on the couch, and I thank him.

*"You have taken care of me for so long,"* he tells me. *"Now I will take care of you."*

The next night, a red ladybug appears on my bathroom mirror. Then, the following day, I look out an upstairs window and see a red-breasted robin sitting on my dormant nectarine tree—but it's the beginning of January, too early for robins.

The color red now fills my life: red leaves or flowers jump out at me when I take a walk, and another ladybug appears in the house; once, a ladybug even turns up in my car. The ladybug is the only insect I marveled at and didn't fear as a child. Each time, I know without question that this is a sign from Michael.

Several days after Michael's death, I'm sitting in my car in front of the supermarket at four in the afternoon, rereading the Tibetan Buddhist *phowa* I read in the hospital room when Michael died. Suddenly, I realize the significance of the color red. Red is the color of Amitabha Buddha: "His holy body is radiant and ruby red, and he is wearing the saffron robes of a pure monk." I have read and reread that *phowa*—and that line—every day, always around four o'clock, the time of Michael's death. Only now do I understand why the color red keeps appearing in my life.

In that first week, I spend most of my time in bed, unable or uninterested in getting dressed or even getting up. From bed, I phone the Tibetan Buddhist sangha in San Francisco and speak to a marvelously compassionate woman who listens to my story and gives me gentle comfort. She mentions an upcoming workshop in San Francisco that will focus on Amitabha Buddha. I'm amazed. I had never heard of this Buddha before Michael's death, and now I discover that an important Tibetan monk is offering a workshop focused entirely on Amitabha Buddha. I know I have to find the energy to get out of bed and attend this workshop, and I know it's a gift of special significance for me, offered at just the right time—auspicious timing, the Buddhists would say.

At the workshop, I reconnect with a wonderful woman both Michael and I knew at the Berkeley sangha before it closed. Her presence provides me with a connection between my life before Michael's death and my life now, and it gives me a sense of continuity.

Experiencing the benevolent presence of the monk is inspiring in itself. He's in tune with Western culture, speaks with an open and often amused style, and offers each of us a personal blessing. It's a warm and loving place to be at a time when I need these energies more than ever. He tells us that through Amitabha Buddha we can attain a kind of shortcut to enlightenment after death. Following him will be a good thing for Michael.

At noon we break for lunch. The San Francisco Museum of Modern Art is only a couple of blocks away, and I head for its familiar café where, so often, Michael and I had enjoyed lunch or a latte together.

On the way Michael seems to be speaking to me again, saying, *"I have something special for you in the museum gift shop."*

Heeding his directive instead of my hungry stomach, I go into the shop. It takes only a few moments for me to spot a pair of beautiful, light-catching red earrings in the glass display case. Amazingly, they're clip-on—the type I wear—and not pierced, as most are. The salesgirl takes the earrings from the case and hands them to me to try on. They're made of Lucite and cut so that, with movement, the two facets of their red, half-sphere surfaces alternate between translucent and opaque. They're unusual and beautiful, and I buy them and quickly put them on. I'm struck by the earrings' changing qualities; it's as if they're metaphors for the change from life to afterlife, holding both equally and allowing one to become the other as the light shifts—carrying both Michael and me within their orbs.

After the workshop, back at home, the connection with Amitabha Buddha and the red gifts continue to offer me hope. I read more about the Tibetan Buddhist view of death, wanting to learn about the different stages during and after death. Contemplating them gives me some sense of knowing and understanding, which helps me to feel less abandoned.

Every day I continue to read the *phowa* aloud to Michael. It's my way of continuing to take care of him. Even now—especially now—I can't give up my role as caregiver. I hope my voice will guide him through the different stages of his transition, toward enlightenment and away from delusion and fear. I have also put in a request for Tibetan monks to pray for Michael for forty-nine days, the length of time a person is thought to remain in the bardo states (the intermediate levels of consciousness after death and before rebirth).

During the days that follow, I'm immersed in a deep place of grief. At times I think I might disappear into it and never come back. It's overwhelming. There are times when I bury my face in one of Michael's sweaters and inhale his scent, imagining him close to me, in his physical form, and I weep. Sometimes I keen and wail, hearing myself as if from afar, wondering at the unfamiliar sounds that surge up from my heart to puncture the stillness of my empty house. At night, alone in bed, I toss and turn in his red flannel nightshirt, and in the day, I disappear into his warm, red fleece top, which falls halfway down my thighs. I long to hold him and to feel the comfort of his embrace.

I intend to experience grief consciously, not push it away or strive to overcome it. Now is not the time to abandon our love by hiding in the arms of oblivion. Yet, much of the time, I feel out of control, carried up and down on waves of grief, and often I sob uncontrollably. All the trite clichés I've ever heard take on new and real meaning for me: "waves of grief," "aching heart," "dark night of the soul," "tears welling up," "lump in my throat," "swallowing my tears," and on and on.

I have an illuminating dream on January 4, three days after Michael's death.

*I'm going on an amusement ride. It's a huge roller coaster, but it's inside, and it's going down into the interior of a place that has lots of twists and turns. It's supposed to be very severe and frightening, but I'm committed to riding it. At one point, I have to get out of the seat and climb up a thin metal ladder to another level. It's dark in here, ominous and dangerous. I'm not aware of other people; there seem to be some, but they are vague.*

In another dream I'm in an airplane cockpit, but even though I'm sitting in the pilot's seat, I'm not flying the plane. There's confusion as to where I should sit.

From these two dreams, I get a glimpse of another facet of my journey through grief: ascension. In the second dream, I'm flying—though confused and not in control. And even in the first dream, after my roller-coaster descent through grief into the depths of my psyche, a ladder appears, and I'm able to climb to the next level.

# Chapter 40

# Grief

I feel as if I'm in a pit, black and deep and full of longing. Still, there are patches of brightness when I feel connected to Michael, when I can recall his body, the feel of his skin against mine, his scent as I buried my head in his chest, his touch as he reached out for me. Yet the pain remains rooted in my heart. Each thought, each memory is accompanied by an intensely physical stab that radiates out from the center of my chest, down my arms and through my body. I have never felt such despair in all of my life, and I don't see how it will ever end. I can think of little but my memories of Michael; I can feel little more than my longing for him. A vast emptiness permeates every aspect of my life.

I scatter pictures of Michael throughout the house. There are photographs of him on his bike high up on the Flume Trail above Lake Tahoe, pictures I took of him at the ocean, snapshots of us in the Rose Garden where we were married, and others, from later, when he was in his wheelchair and we returned to celebrate our anniversary. Photo albums litter the floor in the living room and in my bedroom, always within arm's reach where I can grab them and take refuge in my memories.

Fourteen days after Michael's death, for a few moments, I discover an island of tranquility. It's evening, and I'm sitting in Michael's big armchair in the living room. A wonderful CD of Tibetan Buddhist chanting is playing softly. I glance at the clock and discover I've been immersed in praying and reading from *The Tibetan Book of the Dead* and reciting the *phowa* for almost two hours. Only because my voice has grown dry from reading aloud do I stop and notice the clock. I'm conscious that my heart is filled with love, my mind is at peace, and my body is relaxed. Michael seems close beside me. No longer do I yearn for his physical body, for it no longer exists. I vow to know Michael anew, in his spiritual form, and I feel joy and gratitude for the thirty years we were able to share. For these moments, the heaviness lifts, and I can feel my soul soar upward toward Michael's.

During this time, the support of friends comforts me, casting a lifeline into the sea of grief to which I inexorably return. On one occasion, not long after Michael's death, my friend Sophie comes over to take me out for lunch. As I leave the house, I feel as if I've endured a long illness. I'm weak and unsteady. As we sit down in the restaurant, I realize I can't be here; I have to leave. It's too much for me. She understands and takes me home. I feel fragile, as if at any minute I might break into a thousand pieces.

Family, too, brings me comfort. Zoie stays in touch by phone, and at the end of that first month my cousin Bo comes out from Reno to stay with me for a few days. I'm happy to see him, and his presence brings me solace. Later, Michael's brother, Steve, comes for a visit. We cry and reminisce together, drawing comfort from each other. He fixes things for me: light switches that no longer function, yard work that has been neglected, and a myriad of little things Michael could no longer do and I had ignored for so long. His repairs are a metaphorical healing for me, and his company gives me some relief from my loneliness.

Soon after he leaves, the grief wells up again. It is never far away. I sob and sob and sob, missing Michael now with what seems to be an even stronger intensity. Disbelief engulfs me. I cannot fathom how this has happened to us, how he can be gone.

Then sometimes I'm afraid I'm forgetting him, how he looked and felt. Other times, memories of him will overwhelm me—his touch, his vitality. Where is it? Where has it gone? I try to remember that I must learn to know and recognize him on another level, and yet I miss him so, his physicality, the *all-ness* of him.

On the last day of January—the month of Michael's death—I meditate with candles lit on either side of our statue of the Buddha. I place a picture of Michael against the Buddha and put a flower in front of it. I bring other things to the altar: a rock from the Stanislaus River, where we spent so many blissful summer days; Michael's picture of Green Tara, who represents compassion; a small carved eagle that Michael gave me as a remembrance of my vision in the clouds on our trip to Death Valley; a tiny, pewter dragonfly pin that Michael used to wear on his hat; and other tokens of our life together. With my eyes barely open, I see the light rays of the candles through my lashes like streaks of gold penetrating the darkness. When I open my eyes a bit more, I can see the rays above the candles coming toward me on either side of Michael's picture. I close my eyes and imagine Michael—a kiss—an embrace. I feel his presence in my heart, and I open up to it and send him my love. At this moment, I understand that I will always find Michael, not outside of me, but inside my own heart. I feel my love and his love as one. He tells me he is with me still, now and forever.

After this meditation, I continue to feel him in my heart, like an abiding river rock. As I let that feeling expand and surround me, I can feel that our love is everywhere. I exist in it, and it exists in me.

Later, while I'm writing in my journal, Boz Scaggs comes on the radio. I vividly recall how much Michael enjoyed his music and how it had become the background to much of our early love. My arms and thighs start to tingle as loss and sadness sweep over me and tears pour out of my eyes. Then I feel Michael around me and inside my heart. I go into the bedroom and lie down on the bed, burying my face in his sweater, again engulfed in his scent. I feel reassured, and then I feel his presence as a cooling sensation on my back and shoulders. I know he's comforting me, and I send love and gratitude to him in return. He seems to be using my own right hand to stroke my hair and face, and I remember how I held his right hand in mine as he slipped away.

I have so many unanswered questions I long to ask him: What was it like for you to die? Did I do enough to comfort you? Will we be together again? What did you want to tell me that last time you looked into my eyes and held my gaze?

I turn to mediums for answers and to books that describe the afterlife and near-death experiences. From mediums, I learn that Michael is okay—he's marveling at his newfound freedom and surprised to find himself no longer disabled. I'm told he misses me and feels my love, he loves me still, and we will never really be apart. I'm especially moved to hear that he appreciates all I did for him, as he often told me in that final year, and that from now on he will be the one to take care of me. I begin to read books on death and dying that Sally, my caring friend, has lent me. They cover near-death experiences and ways to communicate with those who have passed over. I find great solace and hope in these books. From writings by people such as Robert Monroe and John Edward, I learn that we are more than our physical bodies and that there is no death.

Yet, inevitably, day-to-day living brings me back to the mundane. Everything I do reminds me of Michael as he was. I pour the last of his prescription mouthwash down the drain to recycle the bottle, and I feel a pain and remember how I refilled that prescription many times, worried about his teeth, and checked to see whether he was using the rinse correctly. Now it's all irrelevant. I put in a load of wash and want to check to see whether he has put any clothes in his hamper. I regret that Una and I were so efficient in doing his wash that there are only a few items left that still carry his scent. I go to the grocery store and tear up when I pass the little containers of applesauce that he used for swallowing his pills when he could no longer take them with water; I used to spoon applesauce into his mouth several times each day, each spoonful containing just one pill. I remember vividly how carefully he swallowed and how intently I watched for signs of choking. I see someone on the sidewalk in a wheelchair and I look again, expecting to see Michael. I hang up a garment in my closet and see the lingerie he bought me and know I'll never wear it again because I can no longer wear it for him. I drive past the places where we went, I watch TV programs he loved, and I walk past books he started, still waiting to be finished. Everything has its charge and causes me pain.

# Chapter 41
# Life after Death

It takes me more than a year of pain and hope, fear and remembrance, to discover how to bring new motivation and meaning into my life. Sometimes the anguish of loss is so great that I see no point in struggling on without Michael. At other times, especially when I'm with a caring friend—engaged in watching a movie, taking a walk, or just talking—the pain recedes, and I get some respite from my grief. The pain of loss never really disappears, nor do I expect it to, but it does lessen in intensity and frequency.

I keep in mind the message my Wise Old Person gave me in the hospital when I was recovering from cancer surgery. He told me to look toward the North Star, clearly visible in the daytime sky during our imagined meeting. He told me to gauge every action I take by whether or not it furthers my progress to the North Star, for this star represents my soul's purpose. He told me to view my mother's diamond ring, which I always wear, as a symbol and reminder of that star. My guide on this path is my intuition, and its guidance is serving me well.

Dreams offer me a link to my subconscious and my intuition. One dream in particular brings my feelings of isolation and disconnection into stark relief. In this dream, I'm in a war zone:

*I'm high on the side of a mountain with other, younger women.*

*The scene is dark; there is little color. We see a huge aircraft being shot down. It looks as if it's going to crash on top of us. The terrain is too steep; we can't run away, and there is nowhere else to go. I tell the young woman next to me to pull the sleeping bag over her body to protect herself from the flying debris. I watch the pilot of the plane eject and fall downward and out of sight just before the plane crashes. The woman and I are now in a war-torn city. We are reuniting with others like ourselves. There are other people there who have not been in the war. They ignore us. We are survivors seeking our own company.*

As in the dream, often I feel trapped in a war zone of loss and emotion, unprotected and unrecognized, isolated from a world of people who don't see me, who don't share my grief. On the advice of my therapist, I join a support group. It feels like the right thing to do, and it turns out to be a wise decision. Being with people who really know and understand what I'm going through proves to be profoundly supportive. I learn that I'm not alone in my grief, and I discover that by sharing my own pain and experiencing my empathy for the pain of others, I begin to heal. As I watch others move through their grief and find ways to become active again, I gain hope.

During this time, I have another vivid dream that I share with the group:

*Michael and I are in San Francisco, and we have become separated. I have the van, and I have to pick him up to bring him home, but I don't know where he is. I ask someone where I can find Michael, and he tells me he is at the San Francisco*

*Museum of Modern Art.* "*You can find him in the memories gallery,*" *he says.*

With this dream in mind, I begin to leaf through the many journals I kept over the course of Michael's illness. Something inside me knows that, through my writings, I can begin to integrate all that has happened, that through honoring my memories, I can heal and bring meaning to my suffering. I bring my writings into therapy and read and discuss what I've written with my therapist. In its way, this is a life review.

One of Michael's dreams I recounted in my journal seems especially poignant right now. It's a dream he had after he began using the wheelchair. He's sitting along the wall in a dance hall. President Clinton comes over to him.

"Can you walk?" he asks Michael.

"I can walk," Michael replies, and stands up.

"Can you dance?" President Clinton asks.

"I can dance," Michael answers.

And they dance.

Once again, Michael's successful, vibrant, charismatic self is in the lead. Now, in my imagination, I add to this dream. I imagine President Clinton asking, "Can you fly?"

And I imagine Michael saying, "I can fly." And I see him taking off, in spirit, no longer bound to this earth. He is free.

From this time on, dragonflies no longer evoke the last time Michael could walk. Now, for me, dragonflies are a symbol of his strength and his soul in flight, and I have become the collector of dragonflies.

And I continue to write. With the encouragement of my therapist, I begin crafting my journal entries into chapters, and then into a book, in the hope that my experiences will inspire others who are caregivers to loved ones with a chronic illness.

The long process of writing this book gives me focus and a sense of purpose. At first, I must push myself, but gradually it draws me in, and finally it becomes a compelling and integral part of my life. It's something important for me to do—a reason to get up in the morning. By working to transform my uncharted journey into a story that might benefit others, I gain a clarifying overview of our life together during the last ten years of Michael's life. I can see how the lessons of love and compassion I learned were, in fact, my guides, and the gifts of caregiving were many. They included a soul-searching release of negative patterns, a plethora of challenging skills, and the assertiveness to deal with a medical system that sometimes saved my husband and at other times caused him to suffer. As my compassion for Michael increased, so did my compassion for myself. I even grew through my journey with cancer, developing an independent sense of self-worth

Neither of us had any idea what lay ahead when Michael was first diagnosed with MS, yet we were both determined to meet whatever challenges we might face. If we hadn't faced the unknown with determination, the only other option would have been to give up. I believe it was our love for each other and our commitment to our marriage that brought us through those difficult times and allowed our marriage to transform. Together, we learned to communicate openly and to empathize with and have compassion for each other, and, when necessary, to forgive. We did not do this perfectly, for humans aren't perfect, but we did the best we could. As time went on, our trust in each other grew. Many marriages don't survive the shock and realities of a chronic illness. I'm so grateful that ours was one of the lucky ones.

I know Michael, wherever he is, continues to learn and to grow. I know our love is the bridge that connects us still. I know I'm vastly more than my body, and spirit is greater than ego. My life's purpose now is to explore these spiritual realms and to discover and follow my soul's path anew. This is my new journey, one I will chart by following my North Star . . . and watching for dragonflies.

# Acknowledgments

My special thanks to go my psychotherapist, Dr. Kristina Holland, who encouraged me to turn my many journals into a book to inspire other caregivers. She gave me wonderful support during my years of caregiving and beyond. I am indebted to Linda Joy Meyers for her teachings and guidance during the early days of writing my memoir. The encouragement and attention to detail that I received from my developmental editor, Barbara Nordin, helped me craft my story into a coherent whole. My special thanks go to Diane Spechler, whose developmental editing helped me more fully realize my story. Her alacrity and encouraging direction were essential and greatly appreciated. My most recent psychotherapist, Dr. Bunny Stanfield, helped me uncover the dynamics of my marriage; with her compassionate insight and guidance my self-awareness and consciousness grew, inspiring my final revisions. My beta readers gave generously of their time and feedback to help me improve my writing. They include: Nora Gauger, Dr. Arthur Hastings, Susan Richey, Greg Kellegian, Mike Contino, and Krista Ericson.

My thanks go also to the women of She Writes Press: publisher Brooke Warner; my project manager Samantha Strom; Krissa Lagos, who assisted me with the forms needed for the publishing process; and others at She Writes Press who provided expert cover design, proofreading, and more. Special thanks go to my copyeditor, Jennifer Caven, who was meticulous and a joy to work with. My sister authors who formed our cohort group of writers publishing in June 2023 came together to share helpful information and provide inspirational support through our private Facebook group, and to them I am also indebted. All in all, She Writes Press is a wonderful group of women with whom to work, and the new friends I have made continue to enrich my life.

My years of study in transpersonal psychology at the Institute of Transpersonal Psychology (now Sophia University) in Palo Alto, California, empowered me to believe in myself and to access my higher guidance and wisdom. They laid the foundation that enabled me to persevere through the challenges of caregiving. I am indebted to the many excellent professors who were inspirational, caring, and exacting in guiding my learning and growth. They include Dr. Robert Frager, Dr. James Fadiman, Dr. Arthur Hastings, Dr. Charles Tart, and all the others who opened new doors of learning and awareness for me and inspired my creativity.

I want to extend my gratitude to the many medical personnel who helped my husband and me in times of need, including doctors, nurses, nursing assistants, physical and occupational therapists, EMTs, and a host of others. Special thanks go to my good friends who supported me during my many times of medical crisis and beyond: Sally Clark, Christine Hunt, Nora Gauger, and Sandy Cashmark, as well as Zoie and my other two stepdaughters, who dearly loved their father.

Thank you to my readers for reading my story. May it inspire you to claim your unique power and to believe in yourself as you persevere through the hardships of life while appreciating the gifts that life brings.

Most of all my love endures for Michael, my eternal partner and co-adventurer in life—this one, ones past, and ones yet to come.

# About the Author

photo credit: Ed Hensley

Suzanne Marriott is a memoirist and deep-travel writer who shares her transformative experiences with her readers. She was her husband's caregiver for the ten years he suffered from multiple sclerosis, and her writings on compassionate caregiving have been published in *The Union* newspaper's *Healthy You* magazine. Writer Advice awarded her the "Scintillating Start Prize" for the first chapter of her memoir, *Watching for Dragonflies: A Caregiver's Transformative Journey*. Her personal essay, *Indian Summer*, won the 2012 Fall Memoir Writing Contest for Women's Memoirs.com and was included in the eBook anthology *Seasons of Our Lives: Autumn*.

Suzanne's stories of deep travel have appeared in the award-winning online magazine *Your Life is a Trip* and in *Soul of Travel Magazine*.

Suzanne enjoys travel, both domestic and foreign. A native Californian, she has traveled up and down the coast of her state, exploring north into British Columbia and south into Mexico, where she fell in love with the colonial town of San Miguel de Allende and the Maya culture of the lower Yucatan Peninsula. She has been to Europe three times and hopes to continue exploring Europe's many cultures and natural wonders. When staying home, she enjoys reading in a variety of genres, including memoir, historical fiction, and books on spiritual growth. Her interests include transcendent experiences, afterlife communication, Jungian psychology, and Tibetan Buddhism. Suzanne finds healing and inspiration in nature and enjoys walking in the Sierra Nevada foothills and exploring the mountain beauty of Lake Tahoe.

Suzanne is a former teacher and grant proposal writer who holds a BA in English from the University of California, Berkeley; an MS in education from California State University, Hayward (now Cal State University, East Bay); and an MA in transpersonal psychology from The Institute of Transpersonal Psychology (now Sophia University). She is a member of The Institute of Noetic Sciences, Sierra Writers, and the National Association of Memoir Writers. Suzanne lives in an ecologically conscious cohousing community in the Sierra Nevada foothills. For more of her writings on compassionate caregiving, visit https://suzannemarriottauthor.com and www.facebook.com/suzannemarriottauthor.

# SELECTED TITLES FROM SHE WRITES PRESS

She Writes Press is an independent publishing company founded to serve women writers everywhere. Visit us at www.shewritespress.com.

*Bless the Birds: Living with Love in a Time of Dying* by Susan J. Tweit
$16.95, 978-1-64742-036-9
Writer Susan Tweit and her economist-turned-sculptor husband Richard Cabe had just settled into their version of a "good life" when Richard saw thousands of birds one day—harbingers of the brain cancer that would kill him two years later. This intimate memoir chronicles their journey into the end of his life, framed by their final trip together: a 4,000-mile, long-delayed honeymoon road trip.

*Dancing in the Narrows: A Mother-Daughter Odyssey Through Chronic Illness* by Anna Penenberg. $16.95, 978-1-63152-838-5
What happens when something unpredictable changes everything in your life? When her daughter is debilitated by chronic Lyme disease, single mother Penenberg descends into the underworld of Lyme treatment, entering into a desperate, years-long struggle to save her daughter's life.

*All of Us Warriors: Cancer Stories of Survival and Loss* by Rebecca Whitehead Munn. $16.95, 978-1-63152-795-1
Hearing of a loved one or friend's diagnosis with cancer invokes such fear that it is hard to know what to do next. This how-to guide—which includes heartfelt stories from twenty survivors and their loved ones, men and women, with seven types of cancers and all stages of the disease—is designed to demystify this terrifying experience for all involved.

*Here We Grow: Mindfulness through Cancer and Beyond* by Paige Davis.
$16.95, 978-1-63152-381-6
At thirty-eight years old, after receiving a breast cancer diagnosis, Paige Davis ventures into an unlikely love affair of a lifetime—and embraces cancer through a lens of love rather than as a battle to be fought.